D0983279

Claiming Reality

NEW FEMINIST PERSPECTIVES SERIES
Rosemarie Tong *General Editor*

UNEASY ACCESS
Privacy for Women in a Free Society,
Anita Allen

MANHOOD AND POLITICS
A Feminist Reading in Political Theory
Wendy Brown

Claiming Reality

Phenomenology and Women's Experience

Louise Levesque-Lopman

Rowman & Littlefield
Publishers

ROWMAN & LITTLEFIELD

Published in the United States of America in 1988
by Rowman & Littlefield, Publishers
(a division of Littlefield, Adams & Company)
81 Adams Drive, Totowa, New Jersey 07512

Library of Congress Cataloging-in-Publication Data

Levesque-Lopman, Louise.
  Claiming reality.

  Bibliography: p. 171
  Includes index.
  1. Phenomenological sociology. 2. Women—
Psychology. 3. Feminism—Philosophy. I. Title.
HM24.L455   1988   305.4'2'01   87-9827
ISBN 0-8476-7580-7
ISBN 0-8476-7581-5 (pbk.)

90 89 88
7 6 5 4 3 2 1

Printed in the United States of America

TO JOE AND LISA,
MY DEAREST FRIENDS FOR LIFE

CONTENTS

Contents

PREFACE

M Y INTEREST IN the phenomenological interpretation of experience originated in 1975 during a graduate seminar on "Some Pre-Theoretical Concepts of Sociology" (Phenomenology) led by Kurt H. Wolff at Brandeis University. One topic of concern was that of "meaningful lived experience" as presented in the theory of Alfred Schutz. Prior to 1975, although I was aware of Schutz's work in phenomenological sociology, I had read only isolated essays. The reading of his *Phenomenology and the Social World* (1967) and *Collected Papers I* (1973) was a revealing and moving experience, although also a frustrating one. As I thought about various experiences in my life—birthing having been the most powerful and most meaningful—I thought that there was a great deal of value to women's experience about which Schutz (and most of my male colleague-graduate students) seemed sublimely uninterested. Something, I felt, ought to be done to make the insights of phenomenology more accessible to women sociologists.

That same year, through independent study with Irving K. Zola, I became interested in the medical management—both bureaucratically and technologically—of childbirth, particularly within the hospital environment. I began to see how a redefinition and reinterpretation of childbirth from women's point of view could become a vehicle for women searching to "make sense" of our experiences, not through roles that are externally imposed but through our projects, our acts that are meaningful, purposive, and instrumental precisely as they stand.

It was not only what women experience as individuals during pregnancy and childbirth that I considered important to sociological investigation, but also the attitude that male culture had adopted toward female-body experiences. I began to see how objective (male) interpretations of the subjective meaning women bestow upon certain experiences of our own spontaneous life necessarily differ from the meaning the (male) observer attaches to them; and that what appears to men as the observers to be objectively the same behavior in several women is bound to have very different meanings or no meaning at all for women as the behaving subjects. In my writing in the years that followed, therefore, I addressed the task of working through Schutz's theoretical framework. Special attention was given to those aspects of his approach that seemed most relevant (or irrelevant) to sociological questions that I had been considering.

What I have been discussing so far is my experience as a student of phenomenological sociology whose orientation is part of a tradition in philosophy and sociology that reflects male supremacy. Thus it was necessary first to disentangle those aspects of Schutzian thought that might be ideological, and second to inquire into those realities of women's experience that have been represented in a way that, on occasion, turns reality completely "outside-in." This effort led me to a suspicion that some ideas of phenomenological sociology had applicability to particular substantive and methodological questions related to feminist research.

With the contemporary women's movement has come a great deal of questioning about the taken-for-granted cultural assumptions about women's realities. Also, the need to broaden the methodological base for more interpretive, reflexive, and subjective approaches to feminist research that can advance and transform feminist theory has become increasingly recognized in feminist sociology. At first glance, Schutz's work did not appear receptive to anything resembling a feminist perspective or feminist theory. In fact, as deeply informed about and dedicated to understanding the "human" situation as Schutz is, interest in and recognition of women as part of that situation is very obviously missing from his framework. This does not, of course, deny that many patterns, other than specifically feminine ones, are necessary for women's individuation.

This book attempts to provide a framework in which this kind of assertion can be made in a cogent way and in a way that differs from conventional methods by addressing two main questions: first, can phenomenological sociology provide feminist theory with conceptual tools for the description and interpretation of women's subjective experience; and, second, can a feminist perspective provide phenomenological sociology with empirical data on the social nature, construction, and transformation of women's consciousness? These questions are both logical and contradictory. Indeed, to a degree, any analysis that rethinks the most basic assumptions of the thinking that it examines is contradictory or at least contrary. Its aim is to question (more than to explain) and to learn to what essential points it can be reduced (not so much how a particular mode of thinking works). My specific analysis rethinks the use of some of the fundamental axioms of phenomenological sociology as they are confronted by a feminist perspective.

The analysis necessarily includes a brief review of: 1) the development of social theory according to male standards; 2) feminist scholars' efforts to understand women's subjective experience; 3) the origins and major features of phenomenological sociology (with the work of Alfred Schutz as its main source); and 4) the impact that these two approaches can have on research on women. These subject-areas create a background for the consideration of a traditional approach to the study of the social nature of women's experience.

The central focus of the book is, then, on the plausibility of phenomenological sociology as a methodological orientation for feminist research—that is, on how a phenomenological view of women's experience may be more consistent with feminist principles than conventional methods. In acknowledging the diversity of women's experience and the distinction of women's experience from men's knowledge-claims of men's experience as the universal, the book addresses the question of whether adoption of a phenomenological sociological approach attunes more to women's understanding of the meaning of our subjective experiences than other approaches. Because mind/body experiences specific to women have been ignored and unrecognized in sociological research, pregnancy, childbirth, menstruation and menopause constitute the main references to experience.

What is attempted in this book is not merely an adoption of the Schutzian model, but an imminent reformulation (reconstruction) of that model. Put in the simplest way, it is an attempt to consider the conceptual schemes of interpretation of Schutz's framework that may be of value to feminist research, while using Schutz's own framework to transcend his phenomenological sociology.

Lastly, the book acknowledges the differences between woman-defined social realities and others' (i.e. men's) definitions of women's social realities. Once the distinctive qualities of women's experience are identified, an effort is made to close that gap. This book is not offered as a final analysis, but rather, as a starting point in the development of a method that includes attention to women's intuitive and empirical knowledge of their own individual experience and also fits the current agenda of feminist research. To begin from the world as women actually experience it; to combine the analysis of substantive work with the theory that arises from this; and to consider approaches that share with feminism its interest in the personal and everyday life are topics to be checked against women's collective experiences.

ACKNOWLEDGMENTS

IT IS WITH PLEASURE that I express my appreciation to various people for their support and assistance in the publication of this book. I am particularly grateful to those reviewers who critiqued the manuscript and provided constructive comments: Richard Martin and Elizabeth May, with their emphasis on clarity, were especially helpful with their advice on style and organization; Barbara Rosenblum of Vermont College, Allie G. Funk of Appalachian State University, and Lynne M. Adrian of the University of Alabama provided valuable insights and support through their careful reading of the first draft of the manuscript; Sondra Farganis of Hamilton College and Ruth A. Wallace of George Washington University contributed conceptual and substantive comments and suggestions that were valuable in preparing the revision; anonymous reviewers contributed valuable time and constructive suggestions to both drafts of the manuscript.

I am also grateful to several people at Rowman & Littlefield: Arthur Hamparian, the publisher, for his enthusiastic commitment to the publication of my manuscript; Jerri McDermott, assistant to the publisher, for her competence in guiding the manuscript through the publication process; Mary D. Simmons for her editorial excellence and sensitivity in grasping the nuances of my work; and Rosemarie Tong of Williams College, editor of the New Feminist Perspectives series.

Kurt H. Wolff of the Department of Sociology at Brandeis University has earned my admiration and appreciation for the scholarly interest and perspective he has furnished so willingly over the years to my working through the essential themes of phenomenology. His detailed attention to my insights and interpretations continues as a source of intellectual encouragement and instruction. Irving Kenneth Zola, also of Brandeis, contributed generously and patiently to the enrichment of my thinking about medical and technological intervention during childbirth. Through many fruitful discussions and his own extensive writing, I was able to critically examine women's health issues. I am especially indebted to Jerome Boime whose untimely death several years ago still evokes in me a deep sense of grief. While at Brandeis, the influence of his teaching, his intensity of perspective, and his spontaneous intellectual humor drew my attention to philosophy.

I thank Sister Therese Higgins, president of Regis College, for the sabbatical that enabled me to pursue my writing; the Regis College library staff for never being too busy to meet my research needs; and Betty Tiberio for typing the final draft of the manuscript. I also thank my colleagues and friends on the Regis faculty for their intellectual support and personal encouragement. In particular, I want to thank Alex Liazos and Paula Schneider of the Department of Sociology and Social Work who, as good friends and wonderful colleagues, were the first readers of the first draft. Their insightful criticisms and common-sense understanding of the manuscript were presented as the first vote for publication.

Although, there is no way to personally thank the scholars in sociology and feminist studies who, collectively, have made it possible for me to formulate the questions raised in the book, I acknowledge their contribution. Without them, there would be no foundation for critique and investigation of other interpretations of women's experience. I hope that I have done justice to their ideas and perspectives.

Finally and more personally, my deepest appreciation is to my daughter, Lisa Levesque, and to my husband, Joseph Lopman, without whom my work and my life would be infinitely less meaningful. I treasure Joe's persistence for clarity in my writing that he combines so well with an intimate presence in my life. Also, it is in celebration of Lisa's birth and of what we experience together that my consciousness continues to emerge through the gift of her presence in my life and thought. This book is dedicated to them with my love and gratitude.

April 18, 1987
Newton Centre, Massachusetts

INTRODUCTION

THIS BOOK IS INTENDED for more than one audience. It is for readers who are familiar with phenomenological sociology but may not have considered its application to feminist issues; and it is for readers who are unfamiliar with phenomenological sociology and are seeking non-sexist approaches for their microsocietal analyses and research. For the latter group, an attempt is made to use straightforward language whenever possible. A glossary, following the main text provides additional clarification of phenomenological terms. What is not provided is a history of the relationship between phenomenology and sociology.

The task of this book is to explore the possibility of a feminist phenomenological sociology, using the work of Alfred Schutz as a main source of a theoretical framework; and to determine whether phenomenological sociology can make any great contributions to an alternative paradigm for feminist theory and feminist research in sociology at a time when there is a growing awareness of the tendency in feminist sociology to limit its methods and theories to those that stress the constraints and molding effects of social structures as the only source of reliable knowledge (Chodorow and Thorne, 1986). Phenomenology is a perspective that seeks to describe subjective experience and that can be applied to microsocietal research. As such, it promises to overcome the shortcomings of positivistic, objectivistic attempts to measure and count all aspects of human behavior. Feminists have been critical of such "scientific" approaches that reinforce patriarchal power to predict and control. Phenomenology is thus a correct place for feminists to look for a theoretical and methodological basis for research. *A priori* of these considerations is the presupposition that informs the whole book: that a feminist perspective within sociology carves out its own subject matter and provides new and illuminating reappraisals of traditional theory and methods; and that it also provides the possibility for transforming traditional Western thought by imbuing it with feminist principles, thereby tending in the direction of greater equality of perspective, methodology, and concept formulation.

Mention of a connection with phenomenological sociology may shock some feminists; it is a term that puts off a number of people who are motivated toward meaningful social change. Phenomenology can be and often is perceived as working within several abstractions that have no relation to the concrete lives we lead, and is of no help in analyzing the structures that are most important in our daily social life. This notion will be explored in relation to other sociological approaches so as to give greater clarification and possibly new insight for an application of phenomenological sociology to feminist research.

Phenomenological sociology is an approach related to symbolic interactionism that a few feminist scholars (Belenky et al., 1986; Kessler and McKenna, 1978; Levesque-Lopman, 1983; Reinharz, 1983; Smith, 1978; Zimmerman, 1977) have only recently begun to use. This is due, in part, to the recognition that to focus on the "self" is to focus on the individual—individual awareness, individual growth, individual action, and individual fulfillment—in contrast to stressing collective goals and macrosocietal processes. Thus, although in many parts of this book the importance of individual change and individual difference is emphasized, I also align myself with the feminist politics that stresses that women's liberation cannot be fully achieved without major alterations to the social structure of contemporary capitalist societies. A feminist analysis that grounds itself exclusively in individual consciousness is a limiting and naïve view. Indeed, consciousness strongly influences one's view of the world, but at the same time, one's social circumstances make significant contribution to the formation of one's consciousness. Thus:

> modern feminism reflects the composite nature of women's oppression with theorists taking consciousness as their starting point and moving towards a consideration of material reality, while others begin with the material reality and move towards an understanding of consciousness" (Spender, 1983:374).

Perhaps my discussion will narrow the gap between feminists who accord importance to macrosocietal and concrete analysis, and feminists whose focus is on the meaning, interpretation, and understanding of how individuals experience their social world, as well as furthering a critical dialogue among feminists from other disciplines.

In taking the point of view of women—to speak of women as subjects (we) rather than as objects (them)—I recognize that since I do not address variations in class, race, culture, and sexual preference among women, I am not speaking for all of "us." I try to caution myself against false universalism in my analysis and to be sensitive in not assuming that some (or one) women could speak for "all women"; for such an assumption obscures the actual differences experienced by women. Also, if women are to be more attuned to the diversity of their individual actions and interactions among social structures, they cannot define their subjective experiences—the transformation of individual consciousness, the changes over time of individual identity—through universal givens.

This book, then, is not so concerned with the universal features of women's experience as it is with why and how women's descriptions of individual lived experience differ profoundly from men's descriptions of women's experience. Women's experience in most cultures differs systematically from men's; yet it is nearly always men who describe women according to male categories, none of which tell women much about themselves. As a result, women learn to see themselves and experience their social world through the prevailing claims founded on only partial definitions of human experience—namely, masculine experience as understood by men. This book explores ways in which women correct the distortions, the oppositions and the differences between women's and men's descriptions of social reality and their consequences for gender-consciousness and gender-identity. Feminists' interest in women's socially constructed difference from men coincides with the recognition of racial, ethnic, and sexual diversity among women's experiences. Identification of distinctive aspects of women's actual situation of "being the same (in a species sense) as men; being different, with respect to reproductive biology and gender construction, from men" (Cott, 1986:49), might also provide a resource for the construction of a more representative human understanding of how women and men differ.

CHAPTER 1

Sociological Perspectives on Women's Experience

FEMINIST SCHOLARSHIP IN THE SOCIAL SCIENCES

THERE IS NO QUESTION that the women's liberation movement has, in recent years, stimulated a great deal of interest in analyzing women's lives. In response to an insistence that all aspects of female experience be recognized, considered, and redefined, feminist scholarship has shown that a feminist analysis is not simply a list of criticisms detailing the sexism of our social institutions. Rather, feminist thought transforms, in fundamentally profound ways, all the patriarchal ways of seeing, defining, thinking about, and understanding our experiences of the social world. This is not merely an academic exercise. What underlies these notions is not simply prejudice, but clues as to the actual experience that informs male consciousness. The process by which the experience of menopause, for example, is transformed into an ideology of male supremacy (Weideger, 1977) is crucial to our analysis of women's consciousness. The feminist critique of male thought in general must, however, proceed from something more dynamic than mere standpoint; it must have a theory and a method.

What follows is no more than a summary of a few of the origins, developments, and connections of some strands of feminist scholarship in order to show, that while feminist forms of analysis vary, they nonetheless share a commitment to the politics of exploring and validating women's experience and ending women's oppression.

Feminist scholars of the 1960s and 1970s demanded their right to conceptualize social reality and to judge ideas and intellectual products by their own standards and objectives. Scholars from different disciplines recognized that the patterns of differentiation and discrimination between males and females have been replicated throughout the social fabric. They argued that:

> the "person" has been considered to be *male*, and the *female*, the woman, has been defined in terms, not of what she *is*, but of what she is not. Woman has been defined as "not-a-man." And things female tended to be seen—in sociology, anthropology, history, as well as psychology—as anomalies, deviations from the male norm and ideal of the "person" (DuBois, 1983:107).

Feminist Kate Millet (1969) and Elizabeth Janeway (1974) took social psychologists to task for their pronouncements disguised as scientific description on what and how women ought to be. In their analysis, the meaning of "sex roles" became transformed. Their critique of what had been presented by male social scientists as "value-free" description challenged the concept of "sex role" that, in conventional sociological terms, was a social role dictated by the biological sex of the actor. According to their feminist analysis, "sex role" became a role assigned to the actor because of the gender-associated behavior linked by society with that biological sex. To such feminists, roles assigned on the basis of gender were a form of oppression, restricting and limiting women in their scope.

Dale Spender (1983) argued that the feminist perspective should be concerned with developing new criteria for what counts as "knowledge," rather than knowledge about females being "tagged on to" existing sexist knowledge. Part of this, she claimed, should be a rejection of conventional and sexist ways of construing social reality. Dorothy Smith discussed precisely this problem of appropriation by the existing and unchanged social sciences and, she argued in relation to sociology:

> It is not enough to supplement an established sociology by addressing ourselves to what has been left out, overlooked, or by making sociological issues of the relevances of the world of women. That merely extends the authority of existing sociological procedures and makes of a women's sociology an addendum (1974:7).

Smith challenged social science frameworks themselves and showed how their rational approaches come from the male experience of the social world. Her critique led to a recognition of the presence of women in the world but, for the most part, only as an addition to preexisting analytical frameworks. Although her critique was valuable for discovering women's experience and moving women from an invisible to a visible location in social science research, male-centered models continued to appear as the proper form of analysis with some consideration of how many women fit into these models.

Sheila Rowbotham (1973a) analyzed women's work as wage-laborers and as houseworkers. Her often political descriptions and her method broke through the boundaries of her theoretical framework. She revealed not only the theoretical dimensions of female labor but also its subtleties. Similarly, Jessie Bernard (1974) was as eager to see what women could do for sociology as she was to see what sociology could do for women. She argued that traditional research techniques were utilized in even what appeared as the most novel of the accounts discussed, and traditional concerns with the "basic standards" of research practice were adopted. Shulamith Firestone (1970) argued that biological motherhood lay at the heart of women's oppression. She held that it was only with the advent of a woman-controlled technology, which would free women from "the tyranny of their biology by any means available," that the ultimate revolution freeing women could take place.

Poet Adrienne Rich (1977) undertook a feminist analysis of motherhood. She divided the concept of motherhood into two halves, which she named "experience" and "institution"—subjective and objective, respectively. The point of this distinction was to enable her to discuss what had been done to women as mothers under patriarchy, as separate from what might be the experience of women in motherhood when it could be detached from, and freed of, the bondage of male domination. She also began to show us that our bodies have far more radical implications than we have yet to appreciate and that through the feminist approach, we will come to view our bodies as a resource, rather than a destiny; for as she describes, "the body has been made so problematic for women that it has often seemed easier to shrug it off and travel as a disembodied spirit" (Rich, 1977:21–22).

Also, from sociologist Ann Oakley (1979) we learned that it is difficult to feel neutral about childbirth, and that we still know little about women's subjective experience of giving birth. Oakley (1980) continued to remind us that it is still important that feminist theory create alternative methodologies for looking at experiences that appear most directly associated with our bodies, such as that of childbirth.

Within the discipline of sociology, then, since the resurgence of feminism in the 1960s, feminist scholars have begun to ground their work toward shifting the core of social theory as far as necessary in their efforts to create a woman-centered social theory. Some feminist sociologists (Spender, 1982, 1983; Roberts, 1981a; Westkott, 1979; Oakley, 1974a,b; Millman and Kanter, 1975) have begun to critique the propriety of a social science that remains several steps away from the "subjects" studied. In their challenge of the epistemological basis for "male-stream" sociology, these feminists also challenge the norm of objectivity that assumes that the subject and object of research can and must be separated from one another. The works of Evelyn Fox Keller (1980), Nancy Chodorow (1978), and Dorothy Dinnerstein (1977) give further testimony to the claim that only when women are brought in as subjects of knowledge does the separation between subject and object begin to narrow.

Carol Gilligan (1979, 1982) also points out that women have been missing as research subjects at the formative stages of psychological theories. This omission of women from scientific studies, she claims, is almost universally ignored when scientists draw conclusions from their findings and generalize what they have studied of men to lives of women. When woman's voice is included in the study of experience, however, women's lives and qualities are revealed, and we can observe these qualities in the lives of men as well. Feminists Gloria Bowles and Renate Duelli Klein (1983) argue that our theories must incorporate both facts and feelings in order to reveal the totality of women's experiences. Maria Mies (1983) furthers the argument with her claim that if women social scientists take their own subjective experience as a starting point and a guiding principle for their research, they become critically aware of a number of weaknesses of established research.

Millman and Kanter (1975) outline six major points that highlight the feminist critique of sociology. They are critical of frameworks that are derived solely from male experience or that merely recapitulate traditional perspectives on the social relations of the sexes. As feminist sociologists, they call for a revision of traditional work whereby a new sociology—one that better represents the experiences of women and men—is created. And as Barbara DuBois (1983) claims, to address women's lives and experiences in their own terms, and to create theory grounded in the actual experience and language of women is the central agenda for feminist social science and scholarship of the 1980s. Some feminists (Depner, 1981; Keller, 1980; Reinharz, 1979) suggest the increased use of qualitative research to better reflect the nature of human experience.

In sum, during the last two decades in particular, feminist scholars have applied their critique to various disciplines in an attempt to correct the misinterpretations of what was thought to be known and understood about our social life. Some recent feminist research has undertaken the problem of the "invisibility" of women in sociological inquiry. Such attempts have led to further realization that sociology's interest in women prior to 1960 was largely confined to women in male-related roles, such as dating, domestic relations, marriage, and divorce. Women were still invisible in the studies of economic, educational, political, and religious institutions (Snyder, 1979). During the 1970s, however, the exclusion of women continued to be acknowledged by feminists, and numerous studies emerged that have uncovered the importance of women's role in all the social institutions. Thus, a more fundamental project confronts feminist scholarship of the 1980s: the ellimination of discriminatory treatment accorded women in sociological theory and methods.

TRADITIONAL METHODS OF RESEARCH ON WOMEN

Heretofore, most current theoretical orientations in sociology—despite major controversies concerning the kinds of methods deemed relevant—have been united in presenting a general universalistic (and significantly masculine) account of human experience. Accounts of feminine deviations from universal principles have been equally ignored by nearly all male theorists. A genuinely adequate theory of experience, then, might lead to a critical appraisal of existing formulations in order to determine which problems and insights might provide a comprehensive view of women's experience. Although theory cannot itself be a vanguard for change, feminist researchers have also begun to question and explore theory construction, as they seek diversification of socially acknowledged experiences. Until recently, such experiences have been essentially defined and described by one legitimized form—a male-centered perspective in which the experiences specific to women are ignored, suppressed, or treated only in relation to the interests of men. Toward this end, further inquiry into all social theory and greater participation of feminist sociologists could be of immense value in changing the fundamental categories that define the discipline and that must be used as a base from which to criticize the concepts, categories and assumptions of thought.

Within traditional sociological perspectives, men have been the acknowledged theorists and researchers. Not only are the majority of sociologists male, but, more importantly, the concentration of efforts tends to be weighted largely toward content areas representing male interests and male values.

Both women and men have studied women from a male perspective; all theories about people, our nature and our behavior had been "man"-made. However long the areas and disciplines of study—history, philosophy, sociology, economics, or psychology—have been in existence, each evolved a relatively distinctive approach to knowledge. Many of the different disciplines do, however, share information. Sociology, for example, has underpinnings in philosophy as well as in history. Sociologists, in fact, frequently employ history to explain phenomena, and we see many overlapping premises and perspectives in the research and in the professional literature.

Social theory developed within a particular background that tended to ignore women or to place them in extremely inferior roles. Such predominantly male orientations are evident in the writings of almost all the classical theorists such as Auguste Comte, Emile Durkheim, Vilfredo Pareto, Ferdinand Tönniës, and Max Weber. In his early work, *Cours de Philosophie Positive* (1842), in which he coined the term "sociology," French philosopher Auguste Comte asserted that women are biologically inferior to men and will always be so. Biology, he claimed, was "already able to establish the hierarchy of the sexes, by demonstrating both anatomically and philosophically that, in almost the entire kingdom . . . the female sex is formed for a state of essential childhood" (Hunter College Women's Studies Collective, 1983:73). In his later work, *Le Système de Politique Positive*, published between 1851 and 1854, Comte proclaimed the importance of emotion over intellect and of feelings over ideas. In commenting on "The Influence of Positivism on Women" Comte refers to the importance of social feeling and the necessity for women's support of the modern movement. He wrote:

> Great as are the moral advantages which will result from the incorporation of the people in modern society, they are not enough by themselves to outweigh the force of self-interest aroused by the precarious nature of their position. Emotions of a greater and less transient kind must be called into play. . . Feeling, the most influential part of human nature, has not been adequately represented . . . On this, as well as on other grounds, it is indispensable that women be associated in the work of regeneration . . . Indispensable to positivism as the cooperation of women is, it involves one essential condition. Modern progress must rise above its present imperfect character, before women can thoroughly sympathize with it . . . Then and not till then, will the movement of social regeneration be fairly begun (1957: 227–29, 232).

Comte's claim of the primacy of emotion over intellect, of feeling over mind, and of the healing powers of feminity for a humanity too long dominated by the harshness of masculine intellect (Coser, 1977b) led to a decline in support from followers who could not concede to the idea that love was the answer to the problems of the time. Of that same emotion, however, Tönnies claimed:

> Women are usually led by feelings, men more by intellect. Men are more clever. They are capable of calculation, of calm (abstract) thinking, of consideration, combination and logic. As a rule, women follow these pursuits ineffectively. They lack the necessary requirement of rational will (Tönnies, 1877 in Snyder, 1979:49).

Emile Durkheim (1964) noted that marriage was better for men than it was for women; yet he also disclosed that such a circumstance (division of labor) was necessary for the effective operation of society.

Thus, there were few instances where women and the problems that they faced were acknowledged by social theorists. Georg Simmel is one of the few exceptions to the male-oriented pronouncements of sociology. His work concerning women was all but ignored until most recently. In 1911, Simmel (1984) recognized that cultural rather than physical conditions made it difficult for women to operate in human societies that, historically, have been so thoroughly dominated by males. He further argued that the division of labor had enabled men to compartmentalize their roles and personalities, making it possible for them never to have to commit their whole selves to a situation. On the other hand, women, brought up in a "man's world where a simple division of labor exists, must involve their total selves all of the time" (Coser, 1977a; Simmel, 1984).

In his description of the expansion of the dyad in regard to marriage forms, he speaks of the transition to a second wife as more consequential than it is to an even larger number:

> For it is precisely the duality of wives that can give rise to the sharpest conflicts and deepest disturbances in the *husband's life* (underlining mine) . . . The reason is that a larger number than two entails a de-classifying and de-individualizing of the wives . . . (Wolff, 1950:139).

With regard to love, in giving one's ego in its totality, he speaks of the artist and the form *his* art represents as one of very few to whom art offers possibility of revealing *his* whole inner life. However, he observes "especially often" that:

> Not only because they love do women unreservedly offer the total remainder of their being and having; but all of this, so to speak, is chemically dissolved in love, and overflows to the other being exclusively and entirely in the color, form, and temperament of love. Yet, where the feeling of love is not sufficiently expansive, and the remaining psychological contents of the relationship are not sufficiently malleable, the preponderance of the erotic bond may suppress . . . the other contracts (practical-moral, intellectual), as well as the opening-up of these reservoirs of the personality that lie outside the erotic sphere (Wolff, 1950; 325).

Lastly, in his essay "Prostitution," he speaks of the relationship between the nature of money and the nature of the prostitute (the indifference, infidelity, lack of ties, complete objectification, and detachment of both), and the relation of the sexes and the sensual act to money (the mutual reduction of two persons to the status of mere means, all personality and individual spirit extinguished). But when speaking of women specifically, he attributes universality to their "indisputably anomalous" sexual contribution, which he views as "supremely personal, as involving the innermost self." This, he claims "can be understood if one assumes that women in general are more deeply embedded in the species type than are men, who emerge from the species type more differentiated and individualized" (Levine, 1977:123). We see implied in Simmel's observations the assumption that women are closer to nature and that their characteristics are rooted in the "most natural, most universal, and most biologically important functions." Also, this "unity" of women's characteristics and functions in which there is less distinction than among men must be reflected in women's experience that seems to confirm that the "faculties, qualities, and impulses of a woman are more closely interwoven than those of a man" (Levine, 1977:123). We see this also implied in Simmel's discussion (exclusive of the sexist overtones) of the separation of sexuality from women's own sexual and "higher" sensibilities, his conception of the feminine role.

It is important to note not only the inferior position accorded women in society by most social theorists but also the fact that for years little attention was given to the prescriptive quality of such descriptions. Perhaps more important is the fact that during the long duration that such pronouncements about women were being made, changes were occurring in women's roles. Most social theorists, however, continued to assume either that women's activities had been unchanging or that they were simply not worthy of attention. Even as late as the 1950s and 1960s, Talcott Parsons, in his analysis of society, was claiming that social equality between women and men in society in general would create a competitive family atmosphere that might destroy family solidarity and ultimately destroy society itself (Snyder, 1979).

Sociologists have been especially concerned with "public" or group activities, as well as with questions of power, authority, and social order as they are created in groups. As Millman and Kanter (1975:x) documented in their work, sociology has focused on public, official, visible and/or dramatic role players, and definitions of the situation. The actors studied have primarily been men. Theories of the social world have been created by men, based on events and ideas as seen by men, and interpreted by way of associations and connections that match the experiences of men. The private events of women's lives, Janeway (1974) tells us, have been held merely private and, therefore, useful neither for understanding normal operations nor for having any consequence in the real world of action. Women have been visible when sociologists have dealt with the family, but even there sociologists have failed to look at the family's relation with society from the point of view of those whose roles have been confined to the family.

Such skewing of knowledge has had important consequences for all scholarship that draws upon the past to help to understand the present, or seeks theoretical constructions to explain how societies function. In the formulation of theories to explain social reality, the concentration of efforts has been weighted largely toward content areas representing male interests and male values, resulting in women finding themselves most discomforted by the gap between who they are and what they are supposed to be. In the continued search for self-knowledge, women find repeatedly that theory and method are essentially reasserting the same biases against women. Whatever women say or do can be dismissed as irrelevant to the rest of human experience and especially to the events of everyday public life. Because the tools of sociological analysis are developed from and are finely tuned to men's activities, they do not provide questions, concepts, images or even a vocabulary with which to conduct a thorough investigation of women's reality. It is the view of reality presented by these theories that feminist scholarship in sociology is unwilling to accept.

Phenomenological sociology is rooted in two disciplines, and because the portrayal of women in both is so similar, it will suffice to exemplify the position given women by noting a few philosophical ideas that reflect an overview of women. In writing about women, most male philosophers have also shared in the views characteristic of their times and places, and like social theories, philosophical theories are based on the findings of scientists who have, more often than not, been white upper- and middle-class men. Most of the "great" philosophers have produced passages or even whole treatises in which they explicitly explain the "natural" superiority of men and the inferiority of women (Harding and Hintikka, 1983:xi). Plato argued that, in general, women are less good at everything than men, but that some women are better than some men at particular activities and should be judged on the basis of individual capacities for ruling. Aristotle extended this idea by his numerous references to women as being inferior to men. Later philosophers, such as Augustine, Aquinas, Kant, and Spinoza, characterized women as lacking the rationality that men possess, thus limiting their contributions to society. Moreover,

in the work of the existentialists where one might hope to find concerns for the individual encompassing enough to include women, Kierkegaard's three stages of existence "disappointingly were for men only and not for women (Snyder, 1979:48).

John Stuart Mill (1970) was an exception to the tradition that excluded women from the political world. Mill, who was strongly influenced by Harriet Taylor Mills, wrote about the subjugation of women—that is, the underlying historical conditions of the subjugation of women, not their feelings of subjection—an argument that complemented that of Comte. They related women's oppression to a systematic critique of liberty and the relations between the sexes. Their work provides the "most comprehensive statement of the liberal perspective of feminist thought" (Andersen, 1983:247).

For the most part, men's experiences as members of a particular culture, social class, and gender inevitably shaped the way they viewed the world. Also, the male stance in philosophy became the official human stance from which men viewed themselves as subjects, the "we" of humankind. It is only recently that philosophers such as Pierce (1975), Moulton (1976), Daly (1973), Jaggar and Rothenberg, (1984), and others have begun to challenge these male orientations and reveal significant roles women play in society and significant concerns that women have about society and the way in which it functions.

Thus, in philosophy as in sociology, images of women, like other conceptualizations, have been formed from a male perspective. Under the general category of male philosophy, "we find a whole series of oppositions which haunt the male philosophical imagination: mind and body, subject and object, past and present, spirit and matter, individual and social, and so forth" (O'Brien, 1981:34).

REQUIREMENTS FOR A NEW PERSPECTIVE

From the perspective discussed so far we can begin to see how the knowledge—claims of the social sciences have been revealed by feminists to have been founded on distinctive masculine understandings from only masculine viewpoints. Descriptions and interpretations of women's experience have often reflected faulty theories that men have created about the "nature" of women. Distorted definitions resulted from men seeing women as something "other" than themselves and drawing unjustified inferences from this perspective. What are clearly missing are women's self-definitions.

As long as the images that women have of themselves are largely the product of men's perceptions and endeavors, they will continue to be perceived and to perceive themselves as objectified, simplified, and dehumanized. The first step, then, toward change has been to challenge the taken-for-granted, to become conscious of what women experience and of what significance and meaning women attribute to their own behavior. On knowing how women differ from men, "it is a subject on which nothing can be known, so long as those who alone can really know it, women themselves, have given but little testimony, and that little, mostly suborned" (Mill, 1970:24).

Feminist writers have found it important enough to address the manner in which women are portrayed in classical theory. Recently, such reassessments are being made through feminist scholarship (Bernard, 1972; Gilligan, 1979, 1982; Harding and Hintikka, 1983; Keller, 1980, 1985) that is contributing more to our understanding of women and society. Rather than appending their findings to the existing literature, they generate a new one altogether in which women are not just another focus but the center of an investigation whose categories and terms are derived from the world of female experience. Yet few investigations (Jean Baker Miller, 1977; Nancy Chodorow, 1978; Carol Gilligan, 1982) have concentrated on changing the theoretical cores of the various disciplines whose terms, categories, theories, and methods remain essentially unchanged. Thus, much of women's basic research lacks the continuity to force a fundamental reconsideration of women's research. Revisions must not be set apart or isolated from the dominant system, we mean to change.

A basic mandate of feminist scholarship of the past two decades was that social-scientific study not only be linked to social change but also to topics relevant to women's experience. What we had until then were frameworks and research topics that were derived solely from male experience. Even when it was women who were described, the perspective and the modes of definition remained embedded in perspectives and interests of men. What emerged as feminist scholarship, however, was not hostile to men, nor did it attempt to eliminate the achievements of male scholarship. Rather, it created a more elusive scholarship that encouraged inquiry about women in areas where very little was known and that attempted to correct the erroneous and questionable knowledge extent. The intent was to restore balance and use knowledge to reveal and eradicate the historical accumulation of the male stance as the official human stance, thereby creating a more egalitarian society in which both women and men would be freed from sexist perspectives. The feminist mandate challenged a scholarship that was unsysmpathetic to women, that denigrated women and projected a falsified image of women. Feminist scholarship put forth new paradigms based on the newly perceived reality, and by withdrawal of consent from the patriarchal construction of reality, changed the means by which women understand themselves and the world in which they live.

The inquiry of this book is based on a feminist orientation that will serve both to complement and to correct the established, narrow (male-oriented) perspective that presently exists in sociology in order to establish a more inclusive approach—an approach grounded in the experiences of women as valid subjects from which to extrapolate generalizations about the "human" condition. This approach will serve to broaden and interpretation, description, and definition of all human experience.

The inquiry begins with women's experience in its own terms and leads to a reassessment of knowledge; first, through reconceptualization, and then through new explanatory and descriptive systems. It acknowledges the study of women that places women's own experiences in the center of the process, and it examines the social world and women who inhabit it with new questions, analyses, and theories built directly on women's experience. As Mary Daly suggests, a feminist perspective requires of women scholars, at this point in history, a radical refusal to limit their perspectives, their questioning, their creativity, to any of the preconceived patterns of male-dominated culture (Roberts, 1981). Before one can proceed with analysis, it is necessary to elaborate the theoretical framework of concepts that either exclude or distort women; therefore, contemporary feminist scholars begin their analysis at the fundamental level of cultural and existential intrusions into the perceptions of female reality.

CHAPTER 2

Origins of Phenomenological Sociology

REPUDIATION OF POSITIVISM

FOR READERS UNFAMILIAR with phenomenological sociology, some background information will be provided to give an idea about the direction that phenomenological sociology has taken and, more importantly, about some of the direction that it might take. In a book of this limited scope, it would be impossible to do justice to a detailed history of the develement of this perspective. What follows is an overview of the foundations, ideas, central themes, methods, and theories of philosophical phenomenology and the ways in which the arguments in this approach were advanced and applied to sociological questions. Such an overview should provide sufficient background of the major areas that will pertain to discussions in later chapters.

Contemporary practitioners of phenomenological sociology trace their roots to the work of philosophers such as Edmund Husserl, Henri Bergson, Franz Brentano, and Maurice Merleau-Ponty; their closest source is the work of Alfred Schutz. And it is Schutz's work that is most representative of the transformation of the ideas of Husserl into sociology, and it is that orientation that is the basis for phenomenological sociology. Other traditional sociologists have been classified as phenomenologists in the sense that their ideas are influenced by Schutz's orientation to sociology. Early symbolic interactionists in particular may be defined as "phenomenological in a loose sense" because of their concern (similar to Schutz's desire to understand intersubjectivity) with the process of constructing shared meanings. This interpretation includes W.I. Thomas's "definition of

13

the situation," Charles Horton Cooley's "sympathetic understanding," Max Weber's *verstehen* (subjective understanding) and George
Herbert Mead's analysis of the self—"taking the role of the other,"
and possibly "the generalized other." It is misleading, however, to
label these approaches truly phenomenological for they are neither
derived from nor always compatible with the ideas of Husserl.

A good example of how phenomenological sociologists generally
work can be found in the writings of two of Schutz's students, Peter
Berger and Thomas Luckmann (1966). Their basic assumption is that
everyday reality is a socially constructed system in which people give
phenomena a certain order of reality; and this reality has both
subjective and objective elements. On the one hand, everyday life
presents itself as a reality interpreted by people and subjectively
meaningful to them as a coherent world. Thus society is actually
constructed by "activity that expresses subjective meaning." On the
other hand, although society is a human product, it is also an
objective reality; that is, society is external to the individual who is a
product of it. Maurice Natanson, also a philosopher, was influenced
by both Schutz and Mead in his use of the concepts of social role and
typification as a means of analyzing intersubjective consciousness.[1]

Of the current phenomenological approaches in sociology, ethno-
menthodology is considered the most prominent and the most unified in the United States. A subdiscipline of sociology, ethnomethodology derives, in large part, from the work of Schutz—the
"taken-for-granted world" being the cornerstone of ethnomethodology. Ethnomethodologists avoid the whole question of reality and
emphasize, instead, the study of the ways an image of social reality is
created. They stress understanding any situation from the point of
view of the participants. Rejecting the metaphysical assumptions of
empirical sociology—that there is a real social and cultural world
capable of being objectively studied by scientific methods—ethnomethodologists regard their approach as a radical break with all
branches of traditional sociology. Also, they attempt to develop more
"scientific" techniques to help sociologists get at the abdurate reality
of consciousness.[2]

It is commonly agreed that phenomenology has as a central task the
radical description and analysis of human consciousness, including the
general problem of how consciousness is constituted in its modes of
intentionality. In other words, a fundamental question of phenomenology is: How do we go about experiencing in our subjectivity that which
we do experience, and how do phenomenologists put into belief how
reality is structured and perceived in acts of consciousness (Tiryakian,
1973:190).

The theoretical underpinnings of phenomenological sociology are primarily derived from European phenomenological philosophy, the theme of which

> is concerned with the demonstration and explanation of the activities of consciousness of the transcendental subjectivity within which the life-world is constituted. It accepts nothing as self-evident, but undertakes to bring everything to self-evidence. It escapes all naïve positivism and may expect to be the true science of the mind in true rationality, in the proper meaning of this term (Schutz, 1973:120).

The term "phenomenology" was used as early as 1765, but it was only with Hegel that a technical meaning became attached to it. According to him,

> phenomenal knowing must be viewed in principle as the starting point from which the individual mind, through various stages and together with other individual minds, ascends to the Mind, who knows in full self-experience He [or She] is in Himself [or Herself] (Kockelmans, 1967:24–25).

Alfred Schutz is the major theorist associated with phenomenological sociology. Yet we must begin our discussion with the philosophical phenomenology of Edmund Husserl (1859–1938) who was the major influence on Schutz's theorizing. In fact, when people today speak of phenomenology, it is usually the work of Husserl that comes to mind. It remains outside the scope of this book to examine in detail his philosophical system. However, since his ideas have been selectively borrowed and used in the development of phenomenological sociology, in reviewing his contributions the focus will be on what was borrowed rather than on the details of his complete philosophical scheme.

In Western philosophy in the nineteenth and twentieth centuries, positivism had gradually replaced the classical intuitivism represented by the view that only intuition leads to apprehension of the ultimate reality. Husserl was disappointed by what he felt were degenerative tendencies in philosophy at the end of the nineteenth century, that favored the views of positivism or scientific objectivism as providers of the only possible kind of knowledge, thus reducing the significance of philosophy from its distinctive, autonomous, and deep inquiry. To a large degree his phenomenology was viewed as a repudiation of positivism.

> It challenged the underlying assumption of positivism that scientists through their five senses can simply and directly investigate the world about them, record their findings, and in time build up a body of

knowledge that accurately reflects the realities of the objective outside world (Timasheff and Theodorson, 1976:291–92).[3]

To Husserl, science did not mean empiricism and statistics but, rather, a philosophy that was rigorous, systematic, and critical. In utilizing science in this way, phenomenologists could ultimately arrive at absolutely valid knowledge of the basic structures of consciousness. In challenging the vision of science and the scientific method, which assumed that the factual world that exists out there is independent of and external to human senses and consciousness and can be directly known only through the scientific method, he questioned whether science was able to measure objectively an external world when the only world that individuals experience is the lifeworld of their consciousness. He advocated what he called the "radical abstraction" of the individual from interpersonal experience, claiming that investigators must suspend their natural attitude and seek to understand the fundamental process of consciousness *per se*. To do this, it is necessary to disregard the substance of their lifeworld.

He had intended that his own philosophy would radicalize René Descartes's search for certainty, a quest for those truths that would be self-evident and could not be doubted. Through a vigorously critical and systematic philosophical investigation, Husserl aimed to obtain absolute knowledge of things that we take for truths in our ordinary lives. But for both Husserl and Descartes these genuine truths that we attach to philosophical or scientific theories may be open to doubt. To Husserl, this is the general thesis of the "natural standpoint," or "natural attitude";

> In the natural attitude . . . [our] perception and thinking are wholly turned towards things, which are given to us as unquestionably obvious and depending on our standpoint, appear now in this way and now in that . . . Because of the success they [the various sciences] of the natural attitude have attained in the course of the centuries, those who assume the natural attitude feel no need to ask any question concerning their proper meaning (Kockelmans, 1967:28–29).

For Husserl, the phenomenological processes referred to his attempt to describe the ultimate foundations of human experience by inquiring in location outside the framework provided by established theories. That location is in the world of phenomena as given in immediate consciousness; it is in the world of our pretheoretical experience; it is in the world that we ordinarily experience before we begin to theorize about it. Thus,

> Husserl's call, "Back to the things themselves," means that we must return to the immediate original data of our consciousness. That which manifests itself there in "bodily presence" is apodictically evident. It

does not need any further foundation, but is true and certain (Kock-elmans, 1967:29).

Husserl's dictum "to the things themselves" was intended to counter-act the oversimplification that had distorted the relationship between the world we experience and the theories about it. Its main ambition was the exploration and description of phenomena that were devoid of reality attributed to them by actors in the real world and that had been neglected or completely overlooked. Thus for Husserl, 'phe-nomenology' meant that it is possible to describe the ultimate founda-tions of human experience by "seeing beyond" everyday experiences in order to describe the "essences" that underpin them (Cuff and Payne, 1984:152). No experiment or scientific observation could ever prove or disprove these essences, for they are the invariant properties of consciousness that do not exist in the real world; they are *a priori* to all experience and are found by observing them within the phenom-ena we perceive. We do this by setting aside, suspending or "bracket-ing" (a method Husserl called *epoché*) the natural attitude in order to be able to get to the most basic aspects of consciousness. This means that we have to detach ourselves from our usual ideas about the world and take experience not as experience but as a pure form of consciousness. This does not mean reduction *within* the empirical world but, rather, reduction *of* the empirical world, not only ideologi-cal factors but material factors as well. To bracket is to set aside the *idea* that the real world is naturally ordered. When we "put the world in brackets" we are able to get to the most basic aspects of conscious-ness to examine the stream of experiences—past, present, and antici-pated—that constitute our existence and our knowledge. The "phe-nomenological *epoché*" does not leave us confronting nothing. On the contrary,

> I apprehend myself purely: as Ego, and with my own pure conscious life, in and by which the entire Objective world exists for me and is precisely as it is for me. Anything belonging to the world . . . exists for me—that is to say, is accepted by me—in that I experience it, perceive it, remember it, think of it somehow, judge about it, value it, desire it, or the like (Husserl, 1969:21).

Under the phenomenological reduction, acts of consciousness are considered solely as experiences of objects, as experiences in and through which objects appear. But the phenomenological reduction reveals itself as the medium of access to whatever exists and is valid. It permits us not only to make but also to exploit this disclosure, i.e., to render it fruitful for concrete analyses and investigations.

The phenomenology that Husserl proposed is not one that brackets existence, but one that brackets everything originating in scientific theories and philosophic conceptualizations. We are, therefore, able to see why, according to Husserl, the natural attitude is a source of bias and distortion for the phenomenologist and an obstacle to the discovery of phenomenological processes.

Husserl is acknowledged as having established phenomenology as a method that examines phenomena as they are apprehended in their immediacy by us as social actors; that begins with individuals and their own conscious experience; and that tries to disregard the substance of their lifeworld—prior assumptions, prejudices, and philosophical dogmas. For if all that they know is presented through consciousness, only when separated from the substance of their lifeworld can the fundamental and abstract properties of consciousness that govern all people be examined. Husserl also proposed that in perceiving phenomena in the world as objects or events of some kind or another, we necessarily assume these objects and events can be seen, heard, and touched by others. In short, we assume they are, in essential respects, the "same" object or event *for others* that they are for ourselves. Thus the foundations of experience do not reside within the mind of an individual in isolation, but rather, are part of what Husserl called the "world of lived experience." This world is a *social* world known in common with others.

In asking us not to take the notions we have learned for granted, but rather to question our way of looking at our being in the world, Husserl accommodated the disillusionment at the turn of the century with the impersonality of science and positivism—and the calculating practicality of the social life that they encouraged and supported— and the new interest with the predicament of individuals in their everyday concerns.

DEVELOPMENT OF PHENOMENOLOGICAL SOCIOLOGY

The most important influence in the development of phenomenological sociology in the United States has been the advancement of Husserl's arguments by Alfred Schutz (1899–1959). Born in Vienna, Schutz left Germany to go to the United States as World War II was approaching. A social philosopher, Schutz sought to adapt Husserl's philosophical phenomenology to the study of the problems of the social sciences through an extension and modification of the approach of Max Weber. He wanted to produce a phenomenology of social life which, for him, meant producing the basis for a better sociology (Cuff and Payne, 1984:152). To develop a subjective sociology in the tradition of Weber while also meeting, like Husserl, the demands of a rigorous conception of science put Schutz in a paradoxical situation. Much of his work was devoted to the questions of how it is possible to grasp subjective meaning structures by a system of objective knowledge; how social actors create a common subjective world; and how social order is maintained within this creation.[4]

As a philosophical sociologist, Schutz examined how mundane understanding of social life is constituted and organized. Mundane understanding includes our individual awareness of the world in general, our knowledge of other people, and our interpretation of "subjective" and "objective" meanings. It also includes our grasp of comunication and the "sense" we "make" of social action and social relationships, both in face-to-face interaction and in more remote contacts.[5]

Schutz, like Husserl, was absolutely intent upon avoiding the dehumanizing irrelevances that tended to be imposed by positivism. For Schutz, the social world is a reality constituted by people in the course of their practical actions. He considered it a more philosophical than scientific task to look beneath human action at the ways in which it is formulated, expressed, and interpreted in everyday life. What Schutz proposed in both his conception of the social world and sociology was a methodological application of phenomenological *epoché*—that is, he intended to suspend or withdraw, or "bracket all natural or conventional beliefs about the 'real' nature of the social world and the 'real' status of social scientific constructs" (Schutz, 1967). By bracketing our biographical situation in everyday life together with its system of relevances, we adopt in their place the interests, systems of relevance, and values of the "scientist qua scientist," the disinterested observer par excellence. Within these constructions lies the possibility of abandoning the intellectual inauthenticity that gives priority to *what* we see rather than *how* we see.

This does not imply denying or even doubting the existence of the world. Bracketing merely changes our attitude toward the world, allowing us to see more clearly. We set aside preconceptions and presuppositions—what we already "know" about the social world; we refrain intentionally from all judgments related directly or indirectly to the experience of the social world.

> What we have to put into brackets is not only the existence of the outer world, along with all the things in it, inanimate and animate, including [other people], cultural objects, society and its institutions . . . but also the propositions of all the sciences (Schutz, 1973:105).

What is left after the reduction is the intended objects and the intentional acts, our consciousness of the social world, ready for examination and description as it is experienced.

DEPARTURE FROM HUSSERL

This is one of the points on which Schutz and Husserl differ. For Husserl, one must be able to bracket the natural attitude in order to reach the most basic aspects of consciousness. To Husserl, the natural attitude presents itself as an obstacle, a source of bias and distortion for the phenomenologist because, in the natural attitude, perception and thinking are wholly turned toward things that are given as unquestionably obvious with no need to question their proper meaning. Schutz departs from a strategy of holding the individual in radical abstraction and of searching for a pure form of consciousness. Indeed, Schutz is interested in consciousness, but as it is constrained by the larger culture with its language, typifications, and recipes. His objective was to develop a sociology based on the interpretations of the social world by the actors being studied. He wanted to investigate what essences could be found in a particular type of experience, people's experience of the social world. Thus for Schutz, the natural attitude is not a barrier, but rather a basic subject in itself of phenomenological investigation. By examining the natural attitude, one can uncover the basic structure of people's commonsense (everyday) experiences. Schutz's concerns with the natural attitude itself represent an inversion of Husserl's *epoché*—that is, we in the natural attitude do not suspend our belief in material and social reality, but the very opposite. We suspend doubt that it is anything other than how it appears. This is the *epoché* of the natural attitude.

As we shall see in Schutz's further application of phenomenology to the study of the social world, he does accept Husserl's notion that social actors hold a natural attitude and lifeworld that is taken for granted and that shapes who they are and what they do. For example, although Schutz recognizes that social actors are creative and they construct the social world through their conscious activity, he provides us with a dialectical image of social reality in which, on the one hand, people are constrained by social forces and, on the other, people are able and are sometimes forced to overcome these constraints. He also accepts Husserl's notion that people perceive that they share the same lifeworld and act *as if* they live in a common world of experiences and sensations. Husserl initially made reference to the lifeworld as a concept that emphasizes that humans operate in a taken-for-granted world, a world composed of objects, people, places, ideas and other things that people perceive as "out there" in the external world and as setting the parameter of their existence for their activities and for their pursuits; a world that permeates their mental life. This lifeworld, according to Husserl, is rarely the topic for reflective thought, even though it structures the way people act and think. It is presumed to be a world experienced collectively—that is, people act "as if" they experience a common world. However, since they experience only their own consciousness, they have little capacity to determine scientifically if this assumption is correct.

WEBER'S SUBJECTIVE MEANING

In his attempt to adapt Husserl's philosophy to sociology, Schutz incorporated Max Weber's concept of *verstehen*, a German word for understanding. Weber felt that sociologists had an advantage over natural scientists that was revealed in the sociologist's ability to *understand* social phenomena. Weber's special use of the term *verstehen* in his historical research refers to the meanings that people themselves attach to their own actions. In order to make sociological sense of the world, Weber claimed, sociologists must, in the final analysis, rely upon the sense that the actors make in the course of their own ongoing relationships. Weber's emphasis on the subjective meanings of social actors forms the very basis of his interpretive method of *verstehen*, a concept that coincides with Schutz's notion of the meaning that the individual imparts to relations of everyday life. In other words, he places the focus on the individual's own definition of the situation.

Weber's "method" of *verstehen* is essentially one in which he takes into consideration the behavior of others. The subjective enters Weber's sociology when he argues that the meanings that actors themselves attach to events should be understood in any sociological investigation. Also, Weber's entire theoretical and methodological efforts are devoted to understanding individual actors as if they are isolated individuals, each forming subjective understandings of the actions of himself or herself and of others. He does not, however, indicate how these understandings come together to sufficiently produce the sort of orderly and common social world in which we live. Thus *verstehen* is not intersubjective; it is private and personal to each individual's own consciousness.

Schutz emphasizes this aspect of Weber's approach in his analysis of the structure of meaning to the individual and the relationship of that meaning to the conceptions of others. In other words, he places the focus on the individual's own definition of the situation. He believes that the meaning one imports to the interaction situation may be shared by the person with whom one is interacting. He calls this the "reciprocity of perspective," a concept that makes explicit the notion that common-sense (everyday) individuals assume (and assume that others do also) that if we were to exchange positions (both in space and perspective), each would see the world as the others had. The issue is not whether a reciprocity exists, but whether it is believed to exist. And if such belief is present, it must by definition be evident in consciousness, the basic field of phenomenological investigation (Freeman, 1980:123).[6]

For example, because the musicians in an orchestra share their meanings of the situation with the conductor, the musicians could exchange positions with the conductor and experience the situation in the way the conductor did (Schutz, 1971: 158–78). According to Schutz, in these situations people are acting on the basis of the taken-for-granted assumptions about reality. They suspend doubts that things might be otherwise, and interaction proceeds on the assumption of the reciprocity of perspectives.

Schutz does not see the mind amenable to scientific study, and he admits that in his work he is going to "abandon the strictly phenomenological method" that has historically focused on mental processes (Schutz, 1967:97).[7] Yet he offers many insights into microsubjectivity. A phenomenological sociology must start, he says, "with the way meaning is constituted in the individual experience of the solitary Ego. In doing so we are able to track meaning to its very point of origin in the inner-time consciousness in the duration of the ego as it lives through its experience" (Schutz, 1967:13). In this regard we can understand Schutz's agreement with Weber that action is defined through meaning. We can also understand Schutz's attraction to Weber's work on social action in his attempt to formulate a concept of subjective meaning. Schutz's analysis of *verstehen* emphasizes his main points as to how sociologists can obtain objective results about subjective activities. He notes that

> both defenders and critics of the process of *Verstehen* maintain, and with good reason, that *Verstehen* is "subjective." Unfortunately, however, this term is used by each party in a different sense. The critics of understanding call it subjective, because they hold that understanding the motives of another . . . [person's] action depends upon the private, uncontrollable, and verifiable intuition of the observer or refers to his [or her] private value system. The social scientists, such as Max Weber, however, call *Verstehen* subjective because its goal is to find out what the actor 'means' in his [or her] action, in contrast to the meaning which this action has for the actor's partner or a neutral observer (Schutz, 1973:56–57).

Schutz also noted that *verstehen* is an experiential form whereby commonsense individuals know their world and carry out their daily affairs.

We have merely a *chance* to understand the Other's action sufficiently for our purposes at hand; . . . to increase this chance we have to search for the meaning the action has for the actor. Thus, the postulate of the "subjective interpretation of meaning," as the unfortunate term goes, is not a particularity of Max Weber's sociology or of the methodology of the social sciences in general but a principle of constructing course-of-action types in commonsense experience (Schutz, 1973:24–25).

To both Schutz and Weber, *verstehen* is "subjective" in the sense that it determines what meaning the action has for the actor. For Weber, social action (behavior to which the individual attaches subjective meaning, as compared to mere reactive behavior) and social action (subjectively meaningful behavior that is influenced or oriented toward the behavior of others) are open to interpretive understanding by the sociologist. Schutz thought that Weber tended to confuse the meaning of the subjective experience of the person to be studied with that of the scientific observer. Schutz, in fact, is critical of Weber for failing to differentiate between the two types of meaning and for failing to make it clear that only objective meaning contexts can be the subject of scientific sociological study.[8]

Having acknowledged Husserl's argument that social scientists cannot know about an external social world out there independently of their own lifeworld. Schutz advocates Weber's strategy of introspection into people's consciousness. Only by observing people in interaction rather than in radical abstraction can the process whereby actors come to share the same world be discovered. This notion represents abandonment of Husserl's phenomenological project, thereby liberating phenomenology from philosophy and allowing sociologists to study empirically what Schutz considered the most important social reality: the creation and maintenance of intersubjectivity—that is, a common subjective world among pluralities of interacting individuals.

Schutz outlines three crucial differences between common-sense attitudes and scientific attitudes of actors toward the social world. First, the actor is pragmatically oriented to the social world; the scientist, in contrast, is disinterested. Second, the stock of knowledge of the scientist is scientifically derived.[9] Finally, the scientist must become detached from his or her biographical situation during the investigative process. Typifications within the common-sense world, in contrast, receive a unique biographical articulation.[10] Schutz cautions sociologists, as observers of social reality, to distinguish between their own experiences and interpretations of their subjects' lived experience. Although common-sense assumptions pervade sociological practice, we can curtail our role, according to Schutz, through methodological attention to terms and in distinguishing acts with and without communicative intent; for example, Schutz discloses various meanings of the "understanding of the human act" (Schutz, 1967:110–12). He concludes that some interpretations of another individual are interpretations of the observer's own experiences. Specifically,

> there is, first, the interpretation that the observed person is really a human being and not an image of some kind. The observer establishes this solely by interpretation of his [or her] own perceptions of the other's body. Second, there is the interpretation of all the external phases of action, that is, of all bodily movements and their effects. Here, as well, the observer is engaging in interpretation of his [or her] own perceptions . . . In order to understand what is occurring, he [or she] is appealing solely to his or her own past experience, not to what is going on in the mind of the observed person. Finally, the same things may be said of the perception of all the other person's expressive movements and all the signs which he [or she] used, provided that one is here referring to the general and objective meaning of such manifestations and not their occasional and subjective meaning (Schutz, 1967:112–13).

Understanding the other person, then, implies more than interpreting one's own experience of the other's body movements, and use of signs. It involves

> grasping those things of which the external manifestations are mere indications. To be sure, interpretation of such external indications and signs in terms of interpretation of one's own experiences must come first. But the interpreter will not be satisfied with this. He [or she] knows perfectly well from the total context of his [or her] experience that . . . there is this other, inner, subjective meaning (Schutz, 1967:113).

Thus, disinterested observation and the interpretation of subjective meaning by means of typical constructs is by no means the exclusive province of social science. On the contrary, all of us find ourselves in situations in everyday life where we act as disinterested observers to some degree in trying to infer the subjective meanings of others by means of common-sense typical constructs. In such cases we are not directly interested in the interaction or its outcome. In this sense we are detached and disinterested. This permits us to see more and less than the actors themselves. Since we are observing them from the outside and, therefore do not really know their motives and meanings, if we wish to gain an understanding of their transaction, we can only relate it to similar ones in "typically" similar situations, and thereby construct the participants' motives from the limited and fragmentary sector of their actions that we observed. Schutz acknowledges, however, that there is no guarantee, but only a likelihood that the everyday person as a disinterested observer will truly understand the participants' acts. The more typical, standardized, and institutionalized that pattern, of course, the greater is the likelihood of understanding.

Nevertheless, important differences remain between the nonscientific constructs of common sense and those of science. According to Schutz, these differences may be summed up as the deliberateness, self-consciousness, and methodicalness with which social scientists assume their disinterested posture.

REFLEXIVITY AND THE SUBJECT/OBJECT POLARITY

Phenomenologically, to understand how we understand demands rigorous reflexivity.[11] We must make our words, definitions, idealizations, and perspective objects of investigation along with whatever type of social action concerns us in our studies. When it is phenomenologically based, reflexivity promotes attention to constitution.

> Phenomenologically, reflexivity involves reflectively grasping the genesis of understanding in reflective and prereflective acts of consciousness. Sociologically, reflexivity necessitates attention not only to terms, definitions and idealizations but also to the intentional activities that objectivate them as meaningful tools for studying social reality (Rogers, 1983:145).

Reflexivity also elicits attention to the subject/object polarity, a presupposition that underlies theoretical debates among social scientists. The questions: how can we treat subjective data in objective terms; or, alternatively, how is it possible to establish objectively verifiable theories of subjective meaning-structures? In phenomenological terms, these questions are concerned with the constituting objective results about subjective activities and their consequences without distorting the social "things themselves."[12]

In confronting and delineating the dimensions of the subject/objective polarity in the social sciences, Schutz established some principles toward its solution. He held that the subject matter of social sciences demands a kind of understanding distinct from that of natural sciences. The problem of understanding in the social sciences, he claims, involves determining what constitutes "adequate understanding for the purposes at hand"—that is, for objectively treating subjectively meaningful phenomena. Only the actor

> knows the span of his [or her] plans and projects. He [or she] alone knows their horizons and, therefore, the elements constituting the unity of his [or her] acts. He [or she] alone, therefore, is qualified to "break down" his [or her] own action system into genuine "unit acts" (Schutz, 1978:52).

The solution to the methodological problem described by Schutz does not involve specific methods, but rather, his acceptance of Weber's position that "all scientific explanations of the social world *can,* and for certain purposes *must,* refer to the subjective meaning of the actions of human beings from which social reality originates" (Schutz, 1973:62). We *can*—for certain purposes—*must* refer to the subjects' activities and their interpretations of those activities by considering projects, life plans, available means, relevances, situations, and knowledge on hand, among other things (Schutz, 1973:35). Schutz is consistent in his implication that even when our purposes do not necessitate such considerations, we must nonetheless maintain the reflexive awareness described earlier. In addition, he insists that adequate understanding of social reality necessitates attention to subjects' activities and motives (Schutz, 1978:10, 44, 52).

ATTACHMENT OF MEANING TO EXPERIENCE

Schutz observed that much of experience is apprehended as a stream of duration, the *durée,* within which nothing is discrete or well defined. Moments of the *durée,* or inner time, are part of a constant and unbroken transition. This transition is interrupted only in the reflective glance of consciousness, which in focusing on aspects of the stream, produces segments (intentional unities) that are regarded as discrete. Schutz emphasized that the reflective glance of consciousness can only focus on a past (and thus already completed) experience, since experience in its immediate present is part of an unbroken flow of duration. For example, if we live immersed in the flow of duration, we encounter undifferentiated experience, each phase of experience melting into the next without any sharp boundaries. Each phase, of course, is distinct in its quality from the next insofar as it is held in the gaze of attention. Yet when we turn our attention to our lived experiences, they are marked out from one another; that is, an experience, constituted as a phase or as one experience that in its "running-off" is undifferentiated and shades into another, now stands out as a "full-blown experience," already past and elapsed, apprehended not by living through it but by an act of attention. Discrete experiences exist only from the reflective glance. Only the already experienced is meaningful, not that which is being experienced (Schutz, 1967:51–53). Within this context Schutz shows that meaning must always refer to the intentional activities of the human subject; that meaning resides in intentionality, which transforms a past experience into something distinct and discrete, in short, into a subjectively "meaningful lived experience." It now becomes clear that, according to Schutz, we formulate the meaning of our experience as that which we "connect" with our experience as a result of our interpretation looked at from the present now with a reflective attitude. As he explains,

> the "meaning" of a lived experience can be reduced to a turning of the attention to an already elapsed experience, in the course of which the latter is lifted out of the stream of consciousness and identified as an experience constituted in such a way and in no other (Schutz, 1973:215).

Also, action is conduct based on a preconceived project, and it is the project that makes action phenomenologically meaningful from the point of view of the social actor. Without the project, action becomes mere unconscious doing. Moreover, if the project takes into account another actor, then the action becomes "social action." Since, for Schutz, all action necessarily involves the choice among projects, if there were no alternatives among which to choose, action would require no project and would be reduced to mere unconscious doing. Action that involves projecting and choosing between alternative projects becomes necessary only when the application of recipes to typically defined situations is no longer adequate for the accomplishment of practical purposes—that is, when situations become problematic.

When situations become problematic, typical knowledge and routine patterns of conduct are no longer sufficient for the mastery of situations. Action, as previously indicated, necessarily involves choosing among projects. Therefore, the behavioral response to situational problematics necessarily involves choosing among alternative lines of conduct. In the enactment of the chosen project of action, new experiences are constituted; and addition has been made to the existing stock of knowledge. Action, as Schutz has formulated the concept, represents the manifestation of voluntarism at the microlevel. In choosing among projects of action, the actor is a "free agent." Choosing, however, is limited by the actor's stock of knowledge on hand, the set of types that underlies the actor's conception of and behavior within the social world, the parameter within which choice takes place (Schutz, 1973:67–96).

The above discussion of meaningful experience and action is significant for understanding Schutz's claim that Weber is mistaken in holding that in action, as contrasted to reflexive "behavior," the actor attaches a meaning to what he or she does; that we understand by "direct observation" the meaning of what a person is doing when carrying out an act such as giving birth—for to call this activity "giving birth" is already to have interpreted it. And this is "objective meaning," which refers to placing observed behavior within a broad context of interpretation. Moreover, Weber's discussion of meaning-

ful action does not take account of the fact that action is episodic, and
from the subjective point of view of the actor, has, in Bergson's sense,
a duration—it is a "lived-through" experience. Because Weber fails to
give attention to this, he does not see an ambiguity in the notion of
action, which can refer either to the subjective experience itself, or to
the completed act. It is mistaken to suppose that we "attach" meaning to action that is being lived through, since we are immersed in the
action itself. The "attaching" of meaning to experience, which implies
a reflexive look at the act by the actor or by others, is something that
can only be applied retrospectively, to elapsed acts. Thus, it is even
misleading to say that experiences are intrinsically meaningful: "Only
the already experienced is meaningful, not that which is being
experienced" (Schutz, 1967:52).

INTERPRETATION OF SOCIAL ACTION

Weber's conception of social action also leaves a question unanswered
for Schutz: How does the actor experience others as persons separate
from himself or herself, but with their own subjective experiences?
The reflexive categorization of acts depends upon identifying the
purpose or project that the actor was seeking to obtain—a project,
once attained, turns the transitory flow of experience into a completed episode. In this respect, Schutz criticizes Weber for not distinguishing the project of an action—its orientation to a future attainment—from its "because" motive. Projects, or "in-order-to" motives,
have no explanatory significance in themselves. Schutz explains this,
referring to the action of putting up an umbrella when the weather is
wet: The project of opening the umbrella is not the cause of that
action but only a fancied anticipation. Conversely, the action either
"fulfills" or "fails to fulfill" the project. In contrast to this situation,
the perception of the rain is itself no project of any kind. It does not
have any "connection" with the judgment. "If I expose myself to the
rain, my clothes will get wet; that is not desirable; therefore I must do
something to prevent it. The connection or linkage is brought into
being through an intentional act of mine whereby I turn to the total
complex of my past experience" (Schutz, 1967:91–94).

Thus, in further advancing his analysis of social action, Schutz
separates motives from meanings and differentiates between two
types of motives—"in-order-to" and "because." Both involve the
causes or meaningful reasons for an individual's action but only
"because" motives are accessible to the sociologist. "In-order-to"
motives are the reasons an actor undertakes certain actions in order to
bring about some future occurrence. These motives are only apparent
when the action is taking place. They are part of deep consciousness,

the ongoing stream of consciousness, and as such are inaccessible to the sociologist. His comment to science leads him to see these as idiosyncratic processes that are not amenable to scientific study. Both "because" motives and "in-order-to" motives are too subjective, too individualistic for his orientation to the study of shared-meaning systems. What is of concern to him, to sociology, is the objective meaning context—the sets of meanings that exist in the social world that are shared by a collectivity of actors. And since they are shared rather than idiosyncratic, they are accessible to sociologists as they are to everyone within the collectivity.

Schutz builds his analysis of social action upon the same basic ideas concerning our knowledge of other selves generally. Thus, for Schutz "any conscious experiences arising from activity directed toward another self is . . . social behavior. If this social behavior is antecedently projected, it is social action" (Schutz, 1967:146). Schutz sees all social action as directly interlocking, reciprocally motivated, mutual involvement.[13]

> In the living intentionality of the direct social relationship, the two partners are face to face, their streams of consciousness are synchronized and geared into each other, each immediately affects the other, and the in-order-to motives of the one become the because motive of the other, the two motives complementing and validating each other as objects of reciprocal attention (Schutz, 1967:162).[14]

TYPIFICATION, PARAMOUNT REALITY, AND PROVINCE OF MEANING

Also central to the understanding of the conduct of others, according to Schutz, is the process of typification (or ideal type), whereby the actors apply interpretive schemes to grasp the meanings of what they do.[15] Typifications function both as a scheme of interpretation and of orientation for each member of the group. The chance of success in human interaction is enhanced when the scheme of typification is standardized. And it is against this background of a discussion of the natural attitude toward the life-world that Schutz follows Weber's lead on the problem of social action. Schutz argues that if we retain the natural attitude of people among people, the existence of others is no more questionable to us than the existence of the outer world. The essence of the social-world is for him its commonness, the fact that it is a world shared by the multiplicity of individuals living and acting within it, in mutually interlocking activities. However, the mere fact that we are all actors engaged in a variety of intersubjective relations does not guarantee that we grasp the significance and structures of these relationships.

In any face-to-face encounter, the actors being to the relationship a stock of "knowledge in hand," or "common-sense understandings"— that is, social recipes or conceptions of appropriate behavior—in terms of which they typify the Other, are able to calculate the probable response of the Other to their actions and to sustain comunication with them. An actor's stock of knowledge is taken for granted as "adequate until further notice"; it is a totality of "self-evidences changing from situation to situation" (Schutz, 1973:74). The major part of the actors' stock of knowledge has been passed on to them (in what Schutz calls tradition) by their social group—parents, teachers, friends, and the anonymous world in general.

Schutz contrasts the wide-awakeness of ordinary life with dreams, the theatre, fiction, and fantasy. In each of these, the reality of the experience is constituted differently. The reality of the stage is not the reality of daily life. In our ordinary day-to-day affairs time is a continuous flow. In dreams we go back and forth, as we do in novels and the cinema. We regain within the paramount reality the common-sense world of our preflective, everyday lives for as long as we choose to cognitively perceive the world in this way. The lifeworld we share (the perspectives that we hold) is seen as the many discrete modes of acting and being that Schutz calls "finite provinces of meaning" within which we make distinctive understandings and interpretations.

> The stocks of knowledge that are applied to make sense of the conduct of others, according to Schutz, constitute and operate within different "finite provinces of meaning" or "multiple realities." It is part of the normal competence of a social actor to shift between such provinces of meaning: to be able to transfer, for example, from the utilitarian world of labour into the real of the sacred, or into the play-sphere (Giddens, 1976:29–30).

Thus periodically we submit ourselves to a radical modification by which we escape the paramount reality and enter a new province of meaning. The passing of one to the other can only be performed by a "leap," as Kierkegaard calls it, which manifests itself in the subjective experience of a shock (Schutz: 1973:232). By altering the cognitive style of our consciousness we not only perceive the world differently, but also unquestioningly accept a new reality removed from the common-sense world we formerly experienced. Schutz cites various examples of shocking experiences that shift the accent of reality from the common-sense world to other finite provinces of meaning: the shock of falling asleep removes us from the paramount reality into the reality of dreams; the impact of a mental illness can remove us to the world of insanity. Each of these new, finite provinces of meaning, as well as any other we might experience, has its own particular cognitive style that organizes and coordinates all possible experiences. Cognitive styles are situated somewhere within the polar extremes of the paramount reality (where consciousness is fully alert and tense) and the reality of dreams (where consciousness is totally passive and relaxed).

Since what passes for a paramount reality is simply a practical agreement that everyone will act "as if" they had the same understanding and perspective as the others, the idea of a paramount reality is always a social construction; but there is no single objective reality.

> The assumption that there really is a paramount reality is the natural attitude of Every [person], who does not doubt that the world exists or the form it takes. The phenomenologist must overcome this natural stance by suspending the faith Every [person] has in reality (McNall and Johnson, 1975:53).

INTERSUBJECTIVITY

Schutz's phenomenological sociology begins, as we have seen, with an analysis of the natural attitude of the world of daily life or the life-world. From the outset, the world of daily life into which we are born is intersubjective in a number of ways. It is where we encounter the other; it is where we perform all our acts directed toward objects, tasks, and others in the world; and our actions open up a world that is "ours" just as it is "mine." In this shared world, a stock of knowledge, which supplies schemes of interpretation of past and present, is at hand and determines anticipations of things to come. Schutz points out that this taken-for-granted world consists in shared ideas, a common system of typifications and relevances. Only a small part of one's knowledge of the world originates in personal experience; most is derived from vocabulary and syntax of everyday language as a scheme of interpretation and expression.

> As used in everyday life, language is a treasure house of preconstituted types, each bearing an open horizon of unexplored typical contents. All forms of recognition and identification, even of real objects of the outer world, are based on a generalized knowledge of the type of these objects or of the typical style in which they manifest themselves (Martindale, 1981:583).

Schutz's particular concern with intersubjectivity, then, is primarily "intramundane"—that is, the concrete understanding by us of the Other whose existence is taken-for-granted in the world of daily life. Also, by means of the automatic synthesis that Husserl calls "associa-

tive transfer of sense," the other's organism is automatically constituted for me as an organism similar to mine, and, more particularly,
as a body organism such as I would experience were we over there
where that physical body now is. According to Schutz, we encounter
and experience the other's organism, and experience our self as
experienced by the Other only within the face-to-face relationship.
And when certain events occur on, or are produced by, the other's
body, it is the complex time structure of this occurrence, and its
interpretation by the actors, that reveals the sharedness of the occurrence. That is to say, when, as Schutz explains it, in simultaneity we
experience the working action as a series of events in outer (standard)
time and inner *(durée)* time, unifying both dimensions into a single
flux called the living present, we and the other simultaneously live
through a pluri-dimensionality of time. And this "living through a
living present in common" constitutes the mutual tuning-in relationship, the experience of the "We," which is at the foundation of
intersubjectivity (Schutz, 1973:219–21).

In one sense I know the experience of the other more immediately
than I know my own, because I must reflect upon my own experience
in order to know it; whereas the experience of the other is available to
me in what Schutz calls the "vivid present" (Schutz, 1967:102). My
own present action becomes an object of consciousness for me only in
reflection, because, while I am expressing myself through language
and gesture, I am focused upon the response of the other rather than
my own expression. Because I live in my own "vivid present," the
immediacy of my own speaking and acting is not accessible to me as
an object.

However, I can never totally experience, in the same completeness
of the Other, the richness and particularly the other's consciousness,
because the other's emergent self, located in a particular biographical
context, is a unique perspective on the world that cannot be dupli-
cated. "My lived experience of you, as well as the environment I
ascribe to you, bears the mark of my own subjective Here and Now
and not the marks of yours" (Schutz, 1967:105).

Thus the world of one intentional self is never fully accessible to the
world of another. The most that can be expected is that, through the
utilization of common cultural understandings, open interpersonal
communications, the reciprocity of perspectives that can emerge from
imaginative efforts to "take the role of the other," the self can
approximate the perspective of the other.

Since the social sciences, phenomenologically considered, do not
deal with the question of the reality of the world, but rather, with
human relationships within this world, Schutz's theory of intersubjectivity and the question of knowledge of the other person are of

primary importance. But not only is the lived-world open to the past in the way just mentioned, it is also open to the future that is partially "ours" but, to a greater extent, is also "theirs"—those who belong to future generations. The intersubjective world thus constitutes a temporal context of human actions open in both directions and contains systems of meaning for us within which we understand ourself, things, and other persons. The intersubjective lived-world is the basic context of human action, and Schutz contributes to elucidating the meaning of actions within this context.

In Schutz's view, Weber fails to reveal the intersubjective nature of the social world—that is, as it is experienced by the actors as *common* and *shared*. By this he means:

> Events in the everyday social world are not experienced as entirely personal, as having a meaning for "me" which may or may not happen to be the same meaning they have for "you." If this were so, then communication between individuals would be a matter of chance (Cuff and Payne, 1984:153).

Through the use of the phenomenological reduction, Husserl held that it is possible for the social scientist to understand and describe the intentional acts of our subjects. By extension, it would seem that the meaningful action of others can be grasped by this method. But Schutz shows how Husserl's idea of intersubjectivity fails. He argues that intersubjectivity "is not a problem of constitution within the transcendental sphere, but is rather a *datum* in the life-world (Schutz, 1966:82). True to its method, Schutz's phenomenology views social actors as comprising free persons making choices within the context of the value system of a particular society. The phenomenological basis for understanding permits the interpretation of human life in terms of goals, purposes, and meaning orientations. It sees the structures and institutions of society not as the product of material conditions or deterministic forces, but the outcome of value considerations. This means that social institutions are objects of consciousness, not determinants of consciousness itself.[16]

Rather than seeking essence of social phenomena (e.g., of corporations, of the state or society), Schutz examines the structures of the lifeworld that those phenomena presuppose. For Schutz, these structures included a mundane intersubjectivity as an ontological given. The life-world, intersubjectivity, and the natural attitude were examined by him through the eidetic science which he called the "constitutive phenomenology of the natural attitude." All social sciences, he claimed, take the intersubjectivity of thought and action for granted, and they have their specific meaning and way of existence. Questions of mutual understanding and communication, the structure of consciousness (meanings, motives, ends, acts), the interpretation of the observer of the Other's meaning, the interpretation of the social relationship cannot be answered by the methods of the social sciences alone. They require a phenomenological analysis (Schutz, 1966:116–17).

CHAPTER 3

Critique of Phenomenological Sociology

GENERAL CRITIQUE: MILLS AND GOULDNER

ONE THEME THAT is being developed so far in this book is the role of women in traditional models of sociological inquiry. The approach to this theme is by way of a consideration of phenomenological sociology as a possible framework for woman-centered research. Having reviewed a broad feminist view of some methodological problems in social sciences that arise in connection with scholarship and research on women, and having been introduced to (or become re-acquainted with) the origins and development of phenomenological sociology, the task now is to consider a brief account of the current conception of the relationship between phenomenological sociology and other sociological perspectives. A primary concern is to broaden the base from which to later challenge, from a feminist perspective (that might also converge with demands from other perspectives), the presuppositions of classical scholarship, traditional methods of inquiry, and meaning attributed to objects of sociological investigation.

C. Wright Mills is credited with providing one of the most comprehensive expositions of the shortcomings of contemporary sociology. He challenges sociologists "to understand from the inner life and external career of a variety of individuals" (Mills, 1959:5). Stressing the cultural responsibilities of the social sciences, Mills emphasizes the importance of the "sociological imagination" in people's everyday lives:

> What they need, and what they feel they need, is a quality of mind that will help them to use information and to develop reason in order to achieve lucid summations of what is going on in the world and what may be happening within themselves . . . By such means the personal

35

uneasiness of individuals is focused upon explicit troubles and the indifference of publics is transformed into involvement with public issues (1959:5).

His view was that, before one can grasp the significance of large-scale social developments (bureaucracy, capitalism, technology), one must have explored them in terms of the individuals involved in their social situations. One's personal experience with domination, for example, only becomes intelligible when it is seen as part of a larger pattern of social interaction (Ferguson, 1980:111). The sociological imagination thus connects "personal troubles of milieu" with "public issues of social structures" (Mills, 1959:8). It helps individuals to understand their own experience by locating it within its historical context. This aspect of defining one's own situation reveals, in fact, the dialectical unity between the two conditions of liberation. That is, in order to analyze our own situation, we must become aware of other individuals who share the same situation and locate ourselves in relation to them. We must take the perspective of the other, for "the sociological imagination . . . in considerable part consists of the capacity to shift from one perspective to another and, in the process, to build up an adequate view of the total society and of its components" (Mills, 1959:211). Part of defining one's own situation, then, is to locate the link between personal troubles and public issues. In fact, as Mills points out, one of the disguised aspects of domination is that we believe our problems to be the result of some personal inadequacy rather than social or structural abuses. And the "promise" of sociology, according to Mills, lies in honoring the "human variety" through interdisciplinary, historical, and comparative studies.

Finally, Mills addresses the status of reason and freedom:

> Great and rational organizations—in brief, bureaucracies—have indeed increased, but the substantive reason of the individual has not. Caught in the limited milieux of their everyday lives, ordinary men [and women] often cannot reason about the great structures—rational and irrational—of which their milieux are subordinate parts. Accordingly, they often carry out series of apparently rational actions without any idea of the ends they serve, and there is increasing suspicion that those at the top as well only pretend to know. The growth of such organizations, within an increasing division of labor, sets up more and more spheres of life, work, and leisure in which reasoning is difficult or impossible . . . (1959: 168–69).

Mills implies a crisis of common sense and a crisis of reason: people feel the inadequacy of their knowledge as well as the need for a "quality of mind" capable of clarifying their worlds and their selves. In response to this dissatisfaction with sociology's rationality and its thwarting of the sociological imagination, Mills calls for a sociology that is aware of its responsibilities and whose language is clear and vibrant; whose assumptions are explicit and rooted in historical, philosophical, and psychosocial knowledge; and whose preoccupation is with problems relevant to understanding the "human condition."

Further criticism is presented by Alvin Gouldner (1962, 1970) who writes of a "coming crisis" in sociology. Although he discusses matters that also preoccupy Mills—such as the social organization of sociology and its misguided values—his plea is for a "reflexive sociology," i.e., one that preserves in it the presence, concerns, and the experience of the sociologist as knower and discoverer.

It has been claimed with some irony that Gouldner's critique lends itself to acceptance of a phenomenological sociology.

> In inveighing against buried presuppositions ("domain assumptions"); in assuming a connection between knowledge of self and knowledge of the world, and asserting the primacy of the former; and in rejecting the independence of science from common sense, Gouldner leaned toward a phenomenological sociology (Rogers, 1983:11).

Gouldner's reflexive sociology is sometimes referred to as phenomenological because it rejects the notion of strictly objective observers and emphasizes understanding the life situations and underlying assumptions of sociologists and their perspectives. This approach, however, is not truly phenomenological, for central to it is an analysis of the empirical world—that is, Gouldner relates types of sociological theory to the social and economic conditions of various historical periods and the class and other life circumstances of the theorist.

Another factor leading to a tendency to refer to Gouldner's sociology as phenomenological is his attack on the "myth" of value-free sociology as part of the ideology of sociologists. He criticizes functionalists and symbolic interactionists for what he says is their belief that the sociologist, as a scientist, does not and should not make value judgments about human affairs. According to Gouldner, Weber's distinction between value judgments and statements of fact, which he claimed were necessary to social science, has been clearly distorted by most contemporary sociologists.

> The "value-free" rule of science has become the excuse for sociologists not to become actively, forthrightly involved in the issues of their societies. Hiding behind claims of "objectivity," sociologists veil the fact that their work does serve the interests of the status quo, or of the social elite that funds and directs the research they do (Gouldner, 1970).

Gouldner calls this doctrine an ideology because it is not only a falsehood and a distortion, but it also serves the material interests of those sociologists who profess it. By contrast, he offers a different ethic for sociology: that the sociologists state and acknowledge the value preferences inherent in all research and in their own work in particular, and admit to readers that only a person with subjective biases, moral leanings, and complete social involvement can do sociology.

Finally, Gouldner advocates an integration of the social sciences based on philosophy, history, linguistics, and hermeneutics. Such integration will, presumably, advance the understanding of social life on the level of practical reason—again, the suggestion of a leaning toward phenomenological sociology.

The critiques by Gouldner and Mills have provoked considerable debate among sociologists. Gouldner's proposals, for example, do not alleviate the axiological and epistemological dilemmas that preoccupy other sociologists. Lewis Coser notes:

> Present developments in American sociology . . . seem to foster the growth of both narrow, routine activities and of sect-like esoteric rumination . . . Together they are an expression of crisis and fatigue within the discipline and its theoretical underpinnings (1975:691).

Also among the persistent criticisms of sociology is the doubt that the neopositivist methods alone can elucidate social life. Meshed with the concern about the epistemological grounds of sociology are demands for clear philosophical foundations that extend beyond a logic of inquiry. Another claim is that sociologists need to reflect more about their work, particularly its epistemological bases and its cultural consequences. Finally, some critics advocate skepticism toward the contrasts between science and folk knowledge. They consider crucial the knowledge people have to society, and they argue that sociology should focus on how people reconstruct their knowledge of social reality, not only in the historical production of the world, but also in the continuing creation of that world on a day-to-day basis (Ritzer, 1983:339). The call for sociology to be more reflexive, more aware of the common-sense assumptions undergirding the discipline, and more attentive to the subjective dimension of social life and the meaning of the world for its actors has met with some response. The personal and the everyday are important and interesting and must be included in the subject of inquiry, i.e., what people spend their life doing must be the subject of research. All three concerns are related to the link between sociology and philosophy. Each alludes to the necessity of disclosing and clarifying that link—in short, desegregating sociology and philosophy—so that sociologists might resolve the specific issues that are included in those concerns. Thus "a properly phenomenological sociology must focus on a neglected sociological practice. It consists in examining the everyday world in terms of scientific relevances instead of indigenous actors" (Rogers, 1983).

These concerns imply the possible benefit of a philosophical framework that address both epistemology and human experience; that also address the relationship between experience and knowledge, between the practical and the theoretical attitudes and between common sense and reason; and that provides methods for determining and controlling presuppositions and for becoming more rigorously reflective. In sum, as sociology has demanded a philosophy that responds to the question of how human experience discloses realities, phenomenological sociology has been considered a possible framework suited to these tasks. In general, the phenomenological approach has been regarded as "helpful" to sociology, but only when used in combination with other methods. The extravagant claim that it was the only genuinely philosophical method led to a strong reaction against it, with the unfortunate results that its specific merits have been forgotten or ignored" (Farber, 1966:14).

The main charge leveled against phenomenology in the social sciences is the supposed unreliability of its method of inquiry, especially the "hopeless subjectivism deriving from its reliance on understanding *(verstehen)*" (Dallmayr, 1981:116). In locating his position between Husserl and Schutz, much of Weber's work has been grossly misunderstood (McNall and Johnson, 1975:52). It is one thing to argue against the positivist approach in all of its variations; it is another to defend the relevance and the importance of the subjective in an effort to understand our actions and especially our interactions with each other.[17] For example, "subjective" enters Weber's sociology when he argues that the meanings that actors themselves attach to events should be understood.

> Weber emphasizes that, under no circumstances, should the concept "intersubjectivity" be taken to mean that the relationships among people have no objective consequences for them. For these relationships do, of course, affect the quality of their being, their "life-chances," even whether they shall live or die. The intersubjective world assumes, in certain historical circumstances, an "objective" quality so that people act and follow patterns "as if" the patterns were totally independent of people's will, "as if" the patterns were iron inexorable laws. To understand this phenomenon one must study history, economics, social stratification, relations of power and domination, etc., as in fact Weber did (Zeitlin, 1973:170).

RESPONSE: SCHUTZ

Indeed, the response of phenomenological sociology to contemporary criticisms of sociology is not an indulgence in psychic idiosyncracies, but the elucidation of social action in a meaning context from the actor's perspective. Schutz, in fact, points out:

> Understanding is not only a methodological device, but a common-sense experience involved in intersubjective encounters of everyday life; viewed in this sense, an interpretive endeavor precedes and is at the basis of the most rigorous scientific pursuits (Dallymar, 1981:116).

Implied in Schutz's conception of the reciprocity of perspectives is the assertion that concentrated care and imagination is often required to assume an unaccustomed role, particularly a negative one. Taking an incongruous role, then, might involve imagining oneself within radically different life experiences with radically different systems of relevances and typifications—and apprehending them from the perspective of participant rather than observer. For example, a male physician trying to understand childbirth as perceived by the woman having the experience might try a variety of methods to gain a perspective that is incongruous with his own experience, his biographical situation, and his stock of knowledge. He might try to imagine what contractions are like based on his medical knowledge; he might engage in a fictional account of what he imagines the experience to be like (based on media portrayals perhaps); or he might establish a We-relation with a woman who might share her birth experience with him. However, reciprocity, like defining one's situation, characterizes relations between equals, each of whom has recognized the subjectivity of the other; it does not characterize relations in which attitudes and roles are in opposition. Nevertheless, that the physician might not be attuned (as is most often the case of male physicians) to the experience from the perspective of the woman, does not invalidate his experience. Rather, it is understood merely from a different perspective and different criteria, namely those of the scientific method. In just this way, we may distinguish between the work of sociology that is objective knowledge and the work in sociology that is relevant to assessing sociological descriptions from the standpoint of subjectivity. The latter, however, according to Schutz, does not rule out the former on the ground that sociology *must* characterize social life as it is experienced through a reciprocity of perspectives. Thus the observation:

> If instead of defining the everyday reality as Schutz does, we were to define it in a way that would allow institutional arrangements, we would begin to see how problematic everyday realities are and how inappropriate the suspension of doubt may be. In Schutz's scheme, however, we are basically uncritical. We live and work in an unproblematic world whose meaning and validity we grasp readily and unerringly. Scientists, if they follow Schutz's methodological injunction, need only

grasp the meaning of one's acts as one understands that meaning. The unavoidable result of following this injunction would be description in the most superficial sense (Zeitlin, 1973:182).

There are also substantive problems that are considered by critics as those which emerge from the center of the phenomenological paradigm and its preeminent concerns with the underlying structures of subjectivity. The social world that Schutz presents is a relatively self-contained world ("worlds within one's actual reach" or zones in which face-to-face interaction can take place) so narrowly defined so as not to permit the penetration of social forces that would allow us to see how problematic the social world is. There is, then, a "sense in which Schutz not only abstracts the everyday world but idealizes it as well; throughout his work is the implication that everyone's common sense, taken-for-granted assumptions about our everyday world are always tried, tested, and valid. The determination of our life-world by the socioeconomic institutional realities is left largely unexplored by Schutz, and, indeed within the phenomenological tradition more broadly. As one critic has remarked: "The impression overall is one of an analysis of subjectivity without articulation of structural imperatives" (Derber, 1979).

Schutz does recognize that it is possible to do useful social scientific work that does not treat the social world from the standpoint of subjectivity. Also, the phenomenological *epoché* of the natural attitude is only a temporary suspension of doubt for clarifying the structure of such a lifeworld. Later such doubts may be systematically studied. He says:

> Doubtless *on a certain level* real scientific work may be performed and has been performed without entering into the problems of subjectivity. We can go far ahead in the study of social phenomena, like social institutions of all kinds, social relations, and even social groups, without leaving the basic frame of reference, which can be formulated as follows: "What does all this mean to us, the scientific observer?" But this, he adds, "does not alter the fact that this type of science does not deal directly and immediately with the social life-world, common to us all, but with skillfully and expediently chosen idealizations and formulizations of the social world which are not repugnant to its facts (Martindale, 1960:205).

Schutz's view is that no matter how well it does work, social science would be defective and inferior if it fails to deal directly with the common social word as it presents itself to those who experience it. He also holds that it is always possible to go back to the subjective standpoint and that we must go back to it if our interest is at all in the social world.

Another area of criticism, according to Schutz, is the failure of phenomenological sociology to account for social conflict. He centers on self-other interactions that take place between "equals" (intersubjectivity), thus omitting other types of interactions that might be referred to as political—those that do not take place between equals, such as those between the birthing woman and her physician. To assert and defend one's own defintiion of one's situation is also to demand a realm of freedom within which to make and carry out choices and actions. To protect one's own definition of the situation from invasions of those attempting to dominate it, one must be able to control the relevant social objects.

I think that from what follows we might conclude that there is a sense in which this criticism is justified. Yet I think, too, that there are problems that confront social science research that can be resolved not only along social-structural lines. Our problem, then, is not to arrange the approaches to the study of the social world in a hierarchical or antagonistic arrangement, but, rather, to sketch the purposes and domains of each and to pay some attention to their possible points of contact. This is the point at which a Marxist critique becomes relevant.[18]

MARXIST CRITIQUE: CONCURRENCE AND DISTINCTION

The Marxists maintain that, within capitalist economic systems, the capitalists can enforce their definition of the situation and maintain their economic dominance over the workers precisely because they control the relevant social objects—the mode of production and the norms and rules that govern its operation (the relations of production). In order for the workers to assert their own definition of their situation, they must be able to seize control of these social objects and direct them in such a way as to redefine the economic situation according to their own standards (Ferguson, 1980:112).

Similarly, for a birthing woman who is dominated by her physician (and the medical establishment) to be able to assert and defend her definition of the situation, she must have control over the relevant social objects (norms and rules governing the patient-physician roles and the relations between patient and staff (the "rules of the game"). Lacking the necessary control over the relevant social objects, including the values and rules that govern conduct, women are not in a position to define their own situation, and so they have been forced to accept the definitions imposed by men.[19] Thus, the ability to define one's own situation, from a Marxist perspective, includes both freedom from outside interference and freedom to pursue one's own projects and choices.

There is modern interplay between Marxian and Schutzian thought, which has been the focus of recent discussion (Westkott, 1979; Bartky, 1977; Gorman, 1977; Sallach, 1973; Zeitlin, 1973; Psathas, 1972). Psathas points out that one reason that accounts for the mutual attractiveness of Marxist and phenomenological thought during the early decades of this century is that both attempted:

> To overcome the despair and relativistic confusion characteristic of the *fin-de-siècle* epoch and of a disintegrating liberalism. Reacting against positivist reductionism and compartmentalization of knowledge as well as against neo-Kantian antinomies, both perspectives sought to recover the unifying source of all knowledge and experience behind the dichotomies of nature and history, subject and object, external and internal, contingent and transcendental domains (Psathas, 1972:308).

One point of fundamental concurrence between Marx and Schutz is that the everyday-life activity of people is subjective and intersubjective. For Schutz, the foundation of all socially derived knowledge is the assumption of intersubjectivity. Similarly, Marx's major criticism of mechanical materialism is that it fails to conceive of reality subjectively—and, therefore, fails to comprehend the significance of practical human activity (Marx, 1947:197 in Sallach, 1973:28).

The most fundamental methodological similarity between Marx and Schutz is their interest in dialectics.

> The effort to get behind the empirically given in search of the concrete levels of social mediations that define, and in turn are influenced by, the original phenomenon, is characteristic of both approaches to methodology. Yet even this hypothesized similarity must be understood dialectically: theoretical mediations defining the dialectical quality of Marxism are entirely different from those within each system. The foundation of dialectical phenomenology is the free, reflective selfconsciousness of beings who are essentially open to their spatial and temporal worlds; the Marxian dialectic is based on the totalizing materialism that includes subjectivity as one moment within a determining objective historical movement (Gorman, 1977:162).

There are other significant distinctions of the two theorists, particularly in their points of departure and their treatment of the member/actor of the social world. Schutz begins his analysis from the standpoint of the individual member in the everyday world. He describes how we see the world, although he emphasizes that our perceptions are molded intrinsically by our concepts. He also examines the ways we come to have similar perceptions to those of others—how we put together the phenomena we experience in such a way that we all construct a similar or shared everyday world. Schutz postulates the existence of an abstract, isolated individual whose special relations are problematic and who assumes the facticity and "givenness" of the modern social world (Schutz, 1973:306–11). Throughout his analysis of the social world, intersubjectivity, and society, Schutz assumes free individuals voluntarily accept the social recipes that are part of society and appear in their stocks of knowledge at hand. People in the common-sense world, as Schutz sees it, unquestioningly accept and obey rational-action patterns characterizing the surrounding social environment, but, at the same time, do so freely, always determining for themselves what they accept and obey. Yet if, in fact, our behavior is determined by socially derived typifications existing independent of us, then the converse appears more plausible: social behavior is apparently caused by factors independent of the subject. As Gorman concludes in his critique:

> Our abilities to freely choose a project in the common-sense world are illusions, for, as Schutz himself implies, we could not do otherwise than what is expected of us. This is certainly a strange notion of freedom not only limiting what we are socially able to do but actually prescribing the one course of behavior we must voluntarily choose. Freedom, when defined in this manner, cannot be distinguished from its opposite, and surfaces as a meaningless concept of little practical importance. If individuals are free and action is subjectively meaningful, then social institutions and culture—analytically distinct phenomena into which conscious actors are thrown—cannot shape or mold them in some vaguely objective sense (1977:73–74).

The everyday world is "from the outset a pre-interpreted one" with a system of relevances "founded upon the basis experience, of the fundamental anxiety, of each of us: I know that I shall die and I fear to die" (Schutz, 1973: xxxvii,xliv).

Marx's starting point is quite different. He begins with the "social" individual, claiming that every member is created by social processes and continues to be defined by social processes. Thus the intrinsic and imposed relevances that are defined abstractly in Schutz's framework are defined by Marx in concrete and historical terms. Also, all of Marx's concepts are rational; social objects are not seen as things, but rather, as clusters of relations. Individuals for Marx do not exist apart from the complex and intertwined set of social relationships that create and sustain them. The concept of "member," therefore, would be regarded by Marx as ahistorical and abstract.

Another major distinction between Schutz and Marx is Schutz's recognition that structural constraints go far to define the everyday world. These constraints, however, exist external to the individual in the form of "imposed relevances," those interests that are not freely chosen by the individual. Schutz does acknowledge that whether an interest is freely chosen (intrinsic relevance) or not freely chosen (imposed relevances) is a complex and fluid process in the everyday world (Schutz, 1973:74–76). Although the system of relevances refers to a wide range of phenomena, there is frequently an objective or structural component of the imposed relevance, albeit concealed within Schutz's theoretical orientation that apprehends it only from the subjective standpoint. In other words, "an abstract and atomized 'member' is buffeted by powerful 'imposed relevances' which (although the members subjectively construct their meaning) have no subjectivity of their own" (Sallach, 1973:28–29).

The empirical members with whom Marx is concerned are the "species beings," those who differentiate themselves from animals. He then traces the ways in which human actions accumulate, become institutionalized, and create the everyday world of individuals.

> In contrast, Marx retains the fundamental characteristics of a context (e.g., historical epoch, conjecture) while allowing superficial characteristics to drop out. When moving from a high level of generalization to the concrete, Marx removes simplifying assumptions and undertakes to analyze the historical situation in its full complexity. Thus, rather than employ general categories to house a changing content (e.g., imposed relevances), the Marxist method rquires that generalizations must always have specific historical elements. The result is an analysis of a specific situation which takes into account the personal and subjective aspects of social structure (Sallach, 1973:29).

Finally, Schutz argues that science be included in the "world of life," which includes subjectively established and maintained structures that are both historical and concrete and serve as an important component of the intrinsic and imposed relevances of the individual actor (Schutz, 1973:259). In phenomenological terms, to fully reintegrate the everyday world and the world of scientific theory, it is necessary for the researchers to consider the way in which they, as subjectively active members of the life-world, are located within the larger social structure and, by extension, the way in which they effect the relevance systems of others. In doing so, sociologists would be recognizing themselves as social actors as well as theorists, objects as well as subjects. As long as researchers confine their attention to investigations of the social world that they share with the social actors they study, it is easy to take for granted the meanings that are involved. For when they concentrate attention upon the behavior of individuals, they also ignore the fact that they are involved with more than mere observation.

Of value to Marxists, however, is Schutz's portrayal of the way in which the modern common-sense person who accepts the unquestioned facticity of the world of the Here and Now—an inviduated, as opposed to rational, self-definition, a subject/object separation wherein actions and events are interpreted subjectively or objectively in proportion to their immediacy—views his or her everyday world. Interpreted in this manner, "the work of Schutz is rich in insight into the dynamic of ideological hegemony and false consciousness as well as insight into the dynamic of rapid and far-reaching shifts in consciousness" (Sallach, 1973:32).

And so we may come to recognize that far from confronting each other as incompatible ways of studying the same phenomena of experience, the phenomenological sociological perspective and the Marxist perspective on the social world are simply different undertakings for the purpose of acquiring different kinds of knowledge.

In view of the above summary of criticism and responses, the reader may have begun (or continues) to question exactly what Schutz's phenomenological sociology can contribute to a feminist perspective and, in particular to a description of women's experience. Indeed, as participants in the lifeworld, women's perspectives must be taken into account in any adequate description that follows Schutz's framework. Therefore, now that some of the background of Schutz's work has been located and, to some degree confronted, according to male critique, his work will next be examined from a feminist perspective, particularly at the points where their methodologies reflect plausible or inplausible contributions to understanding and describing women's experiences of pregnancy, childbirth, menstruation, and menopause.

CHAPTER 4

Structures of Knowledge from a Feminist Perspective

POLITICS OF RESEARCH

THE CONTEMPORARY FEMINIST MOVEMENT has made the need to uncover every aspect of women's experience an immediate political issue, and in so doing has begun to redefine what is personal and what is political, questioning the present scope of what is defined as "politics" (Rowbotham, 1973a; Roberts, 1981a; Eisenstein, 1983). Feminist understanding of feminist theory is that "the personal" is truly the political. For feminists, the point of sharing information about personal life and personal experience is to connect these to something that can transcend the personal. What women may think is an individual problem may be a social predicament and hence a political problem. What were thought to be personal, ideosyncratic problems, once shared with other women, appear to fall into a pattern that, with variations, characterizes other women's lives.[20] The "commonality underlying the diversity" is revealed (Mitchell, 1973): thus, the insistence on the deeply political nature of everyday life and on seeing political change as personal change that continues into the 1980s. Interest in "the personal" and our discussion of women's "subjective" experience is in harmony with a feminist exploration of the relationships between various forms of knowledge and representations of women's experience based on traditional sociological inquiry. What follows is a consideration of the various preemptive arguments about the "structure of knowledge" and the contexts within which such knowledge is generated, and of whether the established theoretical frameworks can be changed in order to more accurately represent women's point of view.

Feminist writers of the 1970s produced great interest and enthusiasm for theoretical critique. Within this critique are the assumptions

47

that feminist theory will be done by women and be about women
(Bernikow, 1980; Hochschild, 1975; Hubbard, 1983; Smith, 1974, 1977,
1978; Stimpson, 1984; Westkott, 1979). There is among these and
other feminists the strong sense that women might know more about
women than men; that male sociologists doing research on women
are frequently unable to "take the role of the Other" when their
subjects are female. Louise Bernikow (1980) notes Virginia Woolf's
claim of the "purity" of the "disintered" quality between women. She
asserts that women are "natural" with each other; that when a man
walks into the room, women mask ourselves. This is her reference to
the political—that women's feeling for a man does not exist apart
from the ways of being in the world, from the necessity that women
please men to survive. Her example of a man observing women
talking with one another but not offering a report on what they say
because he is not "part of the conversation," refers to the absence of a
female point of view in literature. In sociology, as in literature,
philosophy, anthropology, psychology, and other areas where
knowledge-claims are formulated, "many of our stories are told by
narrators who have no part in the conversation" (Woolf in Bernikow,
1980:5).

Certain methodologies (frequently quantitative) and certain research situations (such as having male sociologists study women's
realities) may systematically prevent the elicitation of certain kinds of
information that may be the most important for explaining the
phenomenon being studied (Millman and Kanter, 1975: xv–xvi).
Women talk about the world from the standpoint of our priorities and
our experiences; it looks different from the world picture of men,
particularly when we talk about our bodies. There is little sociological
account of the relative importance attached to these areas in the
totality of women's experience. What does exist are distortions derived from a narrow scientific conception imposed on the descriptions
of women's experiences—pregnancy, childbirth, menstruation, and
menopause, for example—by male observers. They have produced
many descriptions of what is *not* the way we conceive or perceive
these experiences. Although we do not question the importance of a
male perspective in studying society, we do question this perspective
when it serves to exclude women's perspective as equally important
and valid. Until both are included in the study of our social world, we
will continue to receive distorted images, as we have from past study.
Of immediate and fundamental interest to many feminists, therefore,
is the interrelationship of being in the world and the resultant
theories that are formulated. This implies that women cannot see
themselves through conventional methods; that women's lives and
experiences must be defined in their own terms; and that established

beliefs and theories require extensive "debunking" from a feminist perspective.

Closely associated with the interpretation of feminist research as research "on" women and "by" women is the notion that it also ought to be research "for" women. To some feminist scholars (Eisenstein, 1983; Roberts, H., 1981a; Rowbotham, 1973a, 1973b), certain aspects of these assumptions are disconcerting and restrict the radical implications of a feminist approach when they are presented as unchanging principles.

> The criticism of a male theorist who does not inform his theory by an understanding of the questions raised by the women's movement would be the same as the insistence that theorists who are middle-class must learn from the action of workers if they are to interpret the history of the working class . . . In saying that a woman should be employed to study theory we also have to question the mode of study, not try to create a female equivalent to a professional elite whose academic knowledge has no relation to the social needs of most people . . . Similarly, in saying that we choose to study a woman's theory we should not perpetuate a notion of "Woman" as an isolated, frozen category, an unchanging entity (Rowbotham, 1973a:xxi–xxii).

Hester Eisenstein (1983:x) also cautions that the woman-centered perspective, as it promotes retreat from a male-tainted world, has its own dangers. Retreat to a woman-identified culture she claims, could reestablish the barriers between the personal and the political. For example, in the mid 1980s feminism is increasingly understood by feminists as a way of thinking created by, for, and on behalf of women, as "gender-specific." Women are its subjects, its enunciators, the creators of its theory, of its practice and of its language. When this intensification of emphasis on women as the subject of feminism coincides with an emphasis on women as feminism's object and focus of attention (women's experience, literature, history), there are risks. "The doubling-up of women as subject and object can produce a circular, self-confirming rhetoric and a hermetic closure of thought" (Mitchell and Oakley, 1986:27).

Also, to discard the entire apparatus of a masculine perspective could result in greater distortion of social reality than already exists. If, in our research, we begin to polarize lifestyles, activities, and experiences, we limit the possibility for change rather than recognize overlapping areas. We fall into the trap of masculine ideology that exaggerates gender differences by its incomplete and prejudicial view. A consciously shaped woman-centered perspective, then, could evolve from an association of feminism with the liberation of traditional theories. This means not merely changing theories but redefining them; not merely equalizing them but humanizing them—

so that women research men's topics and men research women's topics.

Making such a perspective available, however, is not a problem-free enterprise. As feminists develop theories and attempt to make them available in a male-dominated discipline, we must acknowledge that we can only "make sense" with what we know.

> And yet so much that we know is suspect because it has been encoded by men and may work against our own interests. It means that our ideas in the main are still monitored through male agencies and we run the risk of having our representations distorted, of our words being used to divide us, or of disappearing. This is particularly the case when we provide information on our own processes, on the controversial issues among us; because of the way society is structured, rather than being perceived as diversity, our points of debate over class, ethnicity and sexual preference, for example, can be used to discredit us and devalue our movement. But this is part of the pattern of our oppression (Spender, 1983a:379).

We can, however, begin to transform our perspective by acknowledging that the social relations of women, just like those of most men, have altered over time, and that most women's experiences have been looked at through the specific claims of men. We first need to focus on women's experience, and we can do this if we go outside the scope of what description we have. Second, if our understanding of women's and men's experiences is to gain a new perspective, we need the conscious commitment to share our commonality and to acknowledge and respect our diversity.

Much of the feminist theory in the United States during the 1970s analyzed questions raised by the women's movement mainly in psychological terms. Nancy Chodorow's (1978) analysis provided a plausible psychological basis for the male experience of woman as "Other," and the fact that men learn to define themselves as "not-Other," not woman. Carol Gilligan (1979) pointed out that women have been missing even as research subjects at the formative stages of psychological theories. She and Jean Baker Miller (1977) showed how the "responsibility orientation is more central to those whose conceptions of self are rooted in a sense of connection and relatedness to others, whereas the rights orientation is more common to those who define themselves in terms of their relationships and connections to others." Like Chodorow, Evelyn Fox Keller (1980) and Dorothy Dinnerstein (1977) questioned the apotheosis of scientific inquiry. Keller revealed the fundamental congruence between maleness as culturally defined and the scientific world view that dominated Western thought. She argued that modern Western thought is "genderized"—that is, it is associated in a cultural sense with "maleness" and "masculinity." Nature is viewed as female, and the "knower of nature" as male; "male" is equivalent to "human" while "female" is both deviant and inferior. The ideology of women's nature that has evolved would have us believe:

> Menstruation and menopause are a dirty deal; . . . There is no special value, no advantage or superiority to be gained from the process of cyclicity, or any benefit to be derived from the discrete changes that mark the transition from puberty to cyclicity and from cyclicity to post-menopause. It has led us to believe that we would, in fact, be better off without a hormone system that differs from men's as though the functioning of male sex hormones were the superior model from which to make judgments (Weideger, 1977:229).

One might argue that male perspectives are not only distorting because they are partial; they are inherently distorting because they are taken to be the norm. And when the male perspective of experience is taken to be the description of the human experience, the resulting theories, concepts, methodologies, inquiry goals, and knowledge-claims distort human social life and human thought. The consequence, according to Keller, is a form of self-selection of a certain "male" personality type that is reinforced by the profession among its practitioners. This self-selecting process also leads to the assumption that where the behavior of women is different from men's definitions, it can be classified as "deviant." As Dale Spender notes:

> When one group in society possesses the power to decree its own experience as the only meaningful, ordered and normal experience, it also has the power to define that which is *outside* its experience as meaningless, chaotic—and abnormal (Spender, 1983b:369).

By the late 1970s, Gerda Lerner (1977), Ann Oakley (1979), Adrienne Rich (1977), Dorothy Smith (1978), and other feminists referred to a woman-centered analysis of perspective—that is, the view that female experience ought to be the major focus of study. I place my work in the tradition of these and other theorists and researchers who believe that conceptions of knowledge and truth that are accepted and articulated today have been shaped throughout history by "male" cultures in which women's experience has been treated as secondary or invisible. Drawing on their own perspectives, visions, and experiences, men have constructed prevailing Western thought, written history, and set values that have become the guiding principles for men and women alike. Rich, for example, argues that women see the world differently from men. The dualism that characterizes Western philosophy, she explains, is a product of a male objectification of women. Also, the dualism of "inner and outer," or "me-not-me"—impacted by male culture, subjects women to the alienation from our consciousness of our bodily experience. Rich questions whether women can "think through the body" to connect with what has been so inaccurately misrepresented—our great mental capacities, our highly developed tactile sense, our genius for close observation, our complicated, pain-enduring, multi-pleasure physicality (Rich, 1977:284). In response to Shulamith Firestone's (1970) view that it is not the fact of women's capacity to reproduce that is the basis of women's oppression, but the mode by which that fact has become integrated into the system of male political and economic power over women. Rich argues that once that system is dismantled, then motherhood itself will become a transformed and a transforming experience for women rather than a victimizing experience. Thus, a woman-centered consciousness, a "revolution" of consciousness newly linked to bodily experience could provide women researchers with sufficient interest in and respect for themselves to encourage exploration of our own experience, thereby creating new categories of thinking, describing, and knowing.

Oakley identifies sexism in sociology as the counterpart of discrimination against women in society. She notes that the dominant value system of modern industrialized societies assigns greater importance and prestige to masculine than to feminine activities. Similarly, in sociology, women as a social group are invisible or inadequately represented; they take the insubstantial forms of ghosts, shadows, or stereotyped characters (Oakley, 1974b). In her terms, the conventional theoretical orientation of sociology is sexist. It has treated women's experience merely as inclusive of man's experience, not as a separate, individual, or different one. The neglect of research on women's experience and the wider issue of the bias against women in sociology as a whole are two obviously connected themes. She sees this reflected particularly within sociology's tendency to adopt the values of the wider society. Because our society, which sociologists study, is one in which the position of women and their points of view have been overlooked, underrated, and historically distorted, sociology, both as a male-dominated profession and as a male-oriented discipline to some extent reflects the sexism of the society if studies (Snyder, 1979:40).

Rowbotham's analysis centers on an emergent female consciousness as part of the specific sexual and social conjuncture, which it seeks to control and transform. But its very formation serves to change its own material situation. Rowbotham describes women's reflection as reflection from outside ourselves, the structuring of ourselves not as subjects but as Other. As members of an intelligentsia, women have learned to work inside a discourse that we did not have a part in making. The discourse expresses, describes, and provides the working concepts and vocabulary for a realm in which women are strangers. Also, the ideologies of our society have provided us with forms of thought, images, modes of expression, in which we have been constrained to treat ourselves as observed from outside, as other. The issue, then, is not only that men perceive women from masculine perspectives, but that given the nature of socialization, all members of society, including women, perceive the female from the prevailing masculine perspective. "From our first breath . . . we inhale the environment that teaches us a vision of feminity so pervasive and complete that it appears to be our own . . . that to reject it has almost the force of rejecting ourselves" (Ruth, 1980:85). Rowbotham argues that women have to understand themselves from their own descriptions of Here and Now, rather than as a projected abstract ideal. But there are obstacles to this activity. Until recently, all theory, all connecting language, and all ideas that allowed us to see ourselves in relation to a continuum or as part of a whole were external to us, and we had no part in their making.

> As women, we inhabit our world with a "double consciousness." We are in our society but in important ways also not "of" it. We see and think in the terms of our culture; we have been trained in these terms, shaped to them; they have determined not only the ways in which we have been able to perceive and understand large events, but even the ways in which we have been able to perceive, structure, and understand our most intimate experiencing. Yet we have always another consciousness, another potential language within us, available to us. We are aware, however inchoately, of the reality of our own perceptions and experience; we are aware that this reality has often been not only unnamed but unnameable; we understand that our invisibility and silence hold the germs of both madness and power, of both dissolution and creation . . . We are observer and observed, subject and object, knower and known. When we take away the lenses of androcentrism and patriarchy, what we have left is our own eyes, ourselves, and each other. *We* are the instruments of observation and understanding; *we* are the namers, the interpreters of our lives (Rowbotham 1973b).

ALIEN DISCOURSE

The exclusion of women from existing language, from theory, results in our alienation from generalizations. In particular, "according to all reflections, we are not really there . . . We are oppressed by an overwhelming sense of not being there" (Rowbotham, 1973b:35). The langauge and therefore the theories that we have to work with still lack the very concepts by which the experience and reality of women's lives can be identified, described, and understood. Also, as a result of language, there are great gaps in the knowledge about women because of the lack of adequate methodological tools to study what we do know ourselves: "the words aren't there and the concepts are shadows" (Spender, 1983c:30). The power of the dominant ideology to define our experience may leave women without even the language with which to begin to shape such an alternative ideology. Even when we speak with one another, we may find it difficult at first to describe our views. When we learn to do so, we may still find ourselves unable to articulate clearly to men what seems clear when we express our views to other women. To develop a vocabulary for expressing our own reality and goals, women have begun to talk and work together toward the establishment of new conceptual frameworks for understanding our experience. Thus, in order to generate words and concepts that refer to and clearly reflect women's experience, we will need methods of inquiry that open up our seeing and our thinking to a new approach that actually derives from women's experience.

Changing language or occupying existing words is only one imperative of a feminist perspective. Women have to change the meanings of words in the process of taking them over. As Rowbotham also argues, there is a long inchoate period during which the struggle between the language of experience and the language of culture becomes a kind of agony, a sort of "mixed blessing." The struggle is happening now every time a feminist has to justify her position amidst the alien structures of the large work organiztion, or every time a feminist encounters a situation of sexism, or every time a feminist writer looks at theory from a new perspective. Sometimes feminist critique results in our either borrowing from or rejectng totally the theory of the dominant class; other times it leads to reconstructions of theories that direct knowledge construction and include new methodologies.

VALUATIVE ASSUMPTIONS

This approach corresponds with the feminist critiques (Greer, 1984; Levesque, 1981; Oakley, 1979, 1980; Rich, 1977; Shaw, 1974; Arms, 1973) of medical institutions in both their failure to take up and treat as legitimate women's experience of their bodies, and their success in excluding women from its practice as they appropriated control over Western medicine during the last two hundred years. One major consequence of this mystification has been the failure to represent the meaning of childbirth and menopause to women (as actors) themselves. Thus, I agree with Sandra Langer that the feminist perspective on women's experience appears to be at the cutting edge not only of revisionist practice but of revolutionary social consciousness as well; and as feminists,

> what we are forced to recognize is that ours is a shared complementary experience . . . and there are compelling reasons to give that "other" experience, the women's experience, the same respect and representation that "male modes" of seeing have always received in our society (Langer, 1984:96).

Feminists in sociology have just begun to confront social theories and methods of research that have been formulated from a sociological perspective that is representative of a male-dominated ruling class that originates and is organized in terms of the relevances of the institutional power structures that constitute those positions (Bernard, 1972). A basic critique of sociology from the feminist perspective, then, implies that its origin stems from a false or limited premise—namely, that the male point of view is a correct and adequate vantage point from which to view and explain the world of human experience.

Another problem that results from a male-biased view of women's experience is that of omission. As Thelma McCormack notes about research:

> When researchers go out into the field, women are "there," of course, and their presence is noted. But since the initial focus so frequently is on male[s] . . . women are unlikely to emerge in the final write-up as anything more than "there" (McCormack, 1975:158).

She also raises the question that if male researchers can "take the role of the acting unit" when the "unit" is male, can they not also do so when the unit is female? She concluded that they cannot, as long as socially defined categories create structurally separated "persons"— males and females defining each other "as Other." Also, to the degree to which the definition results in physical and psychological segregation, male researchers are limited in their access to women's places and women's minds (and vice versa).

Within this context, certain aspects of social reality are systematically ignored. These have to do with the everyday life experience, the importance of which becomes more obvious within a feminist perspective. Dorothy Smith (1974) underscores the basic limitations of a sociology where women's place is subordinate, ignored, or invisible. She says:

> Women appear only as they are relevant to a world governed by male principles and interests. To the extent that women sociologists accept that perspective, they are alienated from their own personal experience . . . The exclusion of women from the "real" or "important" world of sociological investigation arises because of the more general belief that

what women do is trivial and not worthy of scientific enterprise. Those experiences that make women different from men and that might provide them with unique or unusual approaches to problems presented within this enterprise are excluded from attention (in Daniels, 1975:346).

Research, then, from the conceptualization of questions to the interpretations of results is not a neutral, value-free enterprise. Quite the contrary, "historians of science are making us aware that . . . the individuals who make observations and create theories are people who live in a particular country during a certain time in a definable socioeconomic condition, and that their situations and mentalities inevitably impinge on their discoveries" (Rosser and Hogsette, 1984:42).

That theory and research assume male behavior as standard or normal is certainly not a new discovery. Yet the issue is sufficiently important to our discussion of a feminist perspective in sociology that it merits repeated attention. The male standard so thoroughly pervades research in sociology that gauging its impact on theory has been difficult. Consider the concept of meaning. Male-defined (Weber, Mead, Schutz) criteria guide the conceptualization and implementation of studies of social interaction. Further assessments of social interaction are based (often implicitly) on the reciprocity of perspectives that are derived from studies of male social behavior. Women generally meet these criteria, but unthinking and automatic reliance on male definitions seriously limits access to that information. Potentially there is a wealth of information not typically enacted by male experience. Thus feminists aim to broaden analyses by including the widest possible range of meaningful experience not all of which, although, is routinely experienced by men. This kind of expansion promises to enhance our understanding of the options open to individuals attempting to exert influence.

BEYOND THE SOCIOLOGICAL IMAGINATION

There is a common, often criticized notion that contemporary sociologists, symbolic interactionists in particular, have moved beyond the concept of what Eisenstein (1983:100) refers to as the "radical separation of the observer from the observed." Although this perception relates more to our later discussion, it will suffice here to clarify that this "shift" in perspective is not a consequence of men's awareness of their assuming that their experience could speak for that of all people, or of their notice of the unconscious sexism in their language and assumptions. Rather, it is more a response to male critiques of male sociology—such as those of Gouldner and Mills mentioned earlier—

calling for a more reflexive sociology and a sociology that connects personal troubles with public issues, respectively. However, Gouldner's and Mill's ideas do coincide with feminist principles. Gouldner's premise is abasic to feminist perspectives on research of social institutions and women's and men's experience within them. Feminist writers who stress the need for a reflexive sociology advocate that the sociologist take her own experiences seriously and incorporate them into her work. One result has been an attempt to integrate conventional theoretical orientations of sociology with a feminist perspective, feminist theory, and methodology and practice, thereby avoiding the type of academic discourse that models itself after and focuses upon traditionally masculine concerns and settings. Indeed, by taking their own subjective experience as a starting point and guiding principle of research, women discover the theoretical and methodological shortcomings of an androcentric concept of scientific investigation.

Mills's claim that the central task of sociology is to understand personal biography and social structure and the relations between the two also parallels the feminist perspective that comprehends women's private experience as it is related to social conditions. His idea that the relationship between personal troubles and public issues also corresponds to the premise of feminist perspectives on sociology: that a woman's personal experience is situated in specific social and historical environments, and that these environments influence not only what her experience is but also how she thinks about it and comprehends it through her discovery of shared experiences with other women. An objective of feminist research, then, is to replace "value-free research" with what Marie Mies (1983) refers to as "conscious partiality," partial identification with the research objects. Conscious partiality, as she defines it, differs from mere subjectivity or simple empathy. It enables the corrections of distortions of perceptions on the part of research "objects" and the researchers themselves (Mies, 1983:122–23). A correction of the distorted male-oriented perspective involves "returning to women themselves" for the description, meaning, personal significance, social importance, and understanding that women attribute to their own concrete, everyday life. Pregnancy, childbirth, menstruation, and menopause, for instance, are rarely recorded reflectively. These concealed dimensions of women's everyday life have not only an obvious bearing on women's identity, but also on aspects of human experience that have been regarded as too trivial and too mundane to be topics of sociological research. Although these experiences may have been important to the women who experienced them, their insignificance and triviality existed within a male-dominated context.

Within a feminist perspective, women define and interpret our own experiences, and women redefine, and rename, and give greater credence to what other people (i.e. male experts) have previously defined and named for us; and women become the experts, the authorities, and the sources of knowledge about ourselves. This approach also supports the notion that a woman knows something to be true because she lived through it and has her own feelings and reactions, not merely the feelings and reactions that she is supposed to have, that she herself expects to have.

To some extent women have been barred from experiencing their own consciousness.

> We encounter ourselves in men's culture as "by the way" and periph-
> eral. According to all the reflections we are not really there. This puzzles
> us and means it is harder for us to begin to experience our own identity
> as a group. This gives female consciousness an elusive and disintegrat-
> ing feeling. We are the negative to the positive. We are oppressed by an
> overwhelming sense of not being there (Rowbotham, 1973b:35).

It takes an enormous effort even to be able to feel our own feelings and think our own thoughts (DuBois, 1983). In the process, however, the naïve, sexist generalizations about the commonalities of all human beings are superseded by women's own categories that incorporate both fact and feelings revealing a totality of women's experiences. This task has been no easier in sociology than in philosophy, history, psychology, or anthropology. In regard to these experiences, we find a bias we cannot ignore. In sociology there is no attention given to menstruation, for example, that is not a reference to an unpleasant aspect of feminity; to menopause as a crisis—a medical and social problem. Within the women's movement itself, analysis of the life cycles of women's bodies and the ways in which one stage of life leads to the next is just beginning to evolve. It is, in fact, difficult to get theories to "expand" their vision to admit the new perspective of women's experience. Our findings do not fit the established paradigms. We rank priorities differently; we study different literature; we put family and reproductive relationship near the top of our list; and we want to know aspects of women's culture previously buried. We need, therefore, to re-organize theory solely around our own priorities (Coyner, 1983:67–68) that incorporate both facts and feelings revealing the totality of women's experience. Feminist sociologists recognize the need to go further than Mills's sociological imagination. The relationship between biography and history is not easy to discern when considering women, since so many of history's generalizations have denied and distorted the experiences and roles of women. Women's biography, then, also requires an ability to reinterpret this history in light of what we have learned from doing feminist scholarship. Perhaps our most demanding challenge in overthrowing these images will come from within each of us as we begin to believe what our bodies and feelings tell us.

Some feminist sociologists have come to regard theories, methods, and conceptual schemes as inherently constricting and have attempted, therefore, to be as eclectic as possible. But we might be in error to blame the conventional methods when the real problem might be how and by whom they were used. Because the forms of thought and images that express our experiences of our spontaneous life have not been ours, but rather, the products of specialists occupying positions in the ideological apparatus, our descriptions, definitions, and opinions have had to conform to approved standards that, in the last analysis, have been men's. This means that, as we have begun to formulate our own categories, we have had to validate them against the collective experiences of other women rather than accept them merely as our individual experiences. Also, by collectivizing our experiences we have begun to appropriate our biography. Women have different life experiences (and women experience life differently), and that gives rise to different interpretations that are equally valid for those experiences. The most ordinary of lives in its uniqueness and in typicality can reveal a whole culture. No experience is dismissed as unworthy of our interest. The personal testimony of any woman is a source that can enlarge the scope of research. Thus to address women's lives and experiences in our terms, to create theory grounded in actual experience and language of women is the central agenda for feminist social science scholarship.

Millet (1969) located the disjuncture or rupture that exists between experience and traditional Western thought—the symbols images, vocabularies, concepts, frames of reference, and institutionalized structures of relevance—in a relation of power in which men dominate women. That is, in relation to men (the ruling class), women's consciousness does not appear as an autonomous source of knowledge, experience, relevance and imagination. Nor does women's experience appear as the source of an authoritative general expression of the world. She reexamined theories and revealed how sociology, among other academic disciplines, had been formulated and directed by males holding male views of the "natural" order—males superior. She concluded that we had learned to practice, in Rowbotham's terms, a "nihilistic relation" to our own consciousness. Thus, the idea of women's dissociation of consciousness from male experience suggests not only a freeing of consciousness, but also a tension between consciousness and experience. For the meaning that women ascribe to our own experience is reducible neither to the experience

itself nor to the dominant ideology. Although women's consciousness is influenced by the ideas and values of "male" culture, it is
nonetheless uniquely situated and reflective of women's concrete
position. Moreover, women's unique interpretation of our own conforming behavior affects that behavior in ways that are revealed only
through reference to women's consciousness itself. Thus, another
challenge and hope that a feminist perspective brings to sociology is
the reinterpretation and profound illumination from the perspective
of women's consciousness.

GENDER AND EXPERIENCE

Most women currently engaged in sociological research do not need
to be told the significance of gender; their own experience confirms
this. Much of the work of feminists, which has appeared up to now,
has been concerned with making women "visible" in sociology,
arguing that much of conventional sociology either ignores women's
presence or views it and presents it in sexist or distorted ways.

Traditional perspectives in sociology mirror society in not looking at
social interaction from the viewpoint of women. This is accounted for
in part by the discipline's attempt to be recognized as a "real science"
and the consequent need to focus on the most objective and measurable features of social life. Such approaches coincide with the academic values of the traditional male culture, reflected in the criteria
used to determine what is suitable for research and what is not. Thus,
one of the contributions of the personal experiences of women in
research is that we are beginning to recognize some features of this
male culture. For example, we know that they are part of a dominant
belief system that does not offer an accurate description of women's
lives or explain the difference in the social and economic status of
women and men (Hubbard, 1983:1). This means that women's experience has not been represented in the making of "our" culture. It also
means that the concerns, interests, and experiences that form "our"
culture are those of men in positions of dominance. Finally, it means
that the forms of thought women make use of to think about
themselves and their society originate in special positions of dominance occupied by men. A feminist reflecting on her own experience,
is, then by definition, both "inside" the culture participating in that
which she is observing (reflecting upon) and "outside" the culture
using thoughts and images not arising directly or spontaneously out
of her consciousness.

Stanley and Wise (1983b) present one theory that is useful in
determining how we can know and understand women's realities.
They begin with the premise that women's experiences constitute a

separate ontology or way of "making sense" of the world. Their notion of a female world of meaning, contextually grounded in women's experiences, is one that recognizes similarity in form but wide variation in both content and expression of women's experience (Cook, 1984:194). Such an understanding incorporates the experiences and consciousness of the researcher into the research process. Also, central to the inclusion of the researcher is a notion of feminist consciousness-raising viewed not as an endpoint but as a process more or less continual throughout life. A feminist consciousness, then, can lead to a type of creative insight stemming from the experience of contradiction and transformation. Within this formulation, the "reality disjunctures that women encounter create ruptures or 'click' moments which help reveal the hidden, taken-for-granted aspects of sexual assymetry" (Cook, 1984:194). Such a moment might be woman's discovery of coming to have a feminist consciousness.

> This experience, the acquiring of a "raised" consciousness, is an immeasurable advance over that false consciousness which it replaces. We begin to see why it is that our images of ourselves are so depreciated and why so many of us are lacking any genuine conviction of personal worth. Understanding things makes it possible to change them. Coming to see things differently, we are able to make out possibilities for liberating collective action as well as unprecedented personal growth— possibilities that a deceptive sexist social reality has heretofore concealed (Vetterling-Braggin, 1977:33).

Other feminists also suggest that the researcher's own experiences are an integral part of the research and should, therefore, be described. What this might look like could be expressed in Husserl's phrase, "To the things themselves"—thereby seeing research as a process that occurs through the medium of the presence of the person in the research. As sociologists, women learn to examine the ways in which our experimental methods can bias our answers, but we are not taught to be equally wary of the biases introduced by our implicit unstated and often unconscious beliefs about the nature of reality. To become conscious of these is rather difficult. One first difficulty results from how sociology is taught—its methods, conceptual schemes and theories based on and built up within the male social universe. Thus, at the start, there is a disjunction between how women experience the world and the concepts and schemes available to think about it. As Smith points out in her discussion of learning to become a sociologist, from the sociological literature she learned:

> To think sociology as it is thought and to practice sociology as it is practiced; I learned that some topics are relevant and some are not; and I learned to discard my experienced world as a source of reliable informa-

tion or suggestions about the character of the world. When we write a thesis or a paper we learn that the first thing to do is to latch it on to the discipline at some point—usually by showing how it is a problem within an existing theoretical and conceptual framework and working within the vocabularies and conceptual boundaries of what we have come to know as the sociological perspective (Smith, 1974:8).

We learn a way of thinking about the world that is recognizable to its practitioners as the sociological way of thinking.

For the most part male sociologists have distanced their research from personal experience, perhaps "bracketing" it with "common sense" and other more subjective forms of knowledge. By doing so, two distinctions arise: first, that traditional male research does not address personal experience (men's or women's) as a topic of research; and second, they do not incorporate autobiographical or literary material into sociological accounts of men's (or women's) reality. Here we see that the rational merges with the masculine, that the practice of sociological inquiry blends with the male culture. Thus we are not dealing only with male dominance within the larger culture, but also with the dominance of men in the field of sociology. This is not to say that the feminist emphasis on "the personal" and the masculine emphasis on the impersonal (rational) are necessarily irreconcilable. And, as we have indicated, feminists have begun to explore the relationships between various forms of social knowledge.

QUALITATIVE AND QUANTITATIVE

Most empirical research on women gives very little information about women's true consciousness or women's individual and social history. When focusing on the "official" actors and actions, sociology has set aside the equally important locations of private, supportive, informal social structures in which women participate most frequently. In childbirth studies, for example, sociologists have focused upon the relationship between persons officially labeled "patient" (birthing women) and the official agents of medical care (physicians). Only those having a place in the formal structure defined by this relationship are included, thereby excluding the relationship of a birthing woman to herself, the fetus, other women, family, and other individuals involved but having no place in the formal structure. The virtual exclusion of women, of their lives, experiences, work, and struggles from most sociological research has further contributed to feminist criticism of the dominant quantitative social science research and methodology—that it is used as a tool for promoting sexist ideology and ignores issues of concern to women. As a result, some feminists have suggested the increased use of qualitative research in order to better reflect personal experience. That is not to say that traditional or contemporary qualitative methods do not contain sexist biases. But in looking to those approaches that start with people's experience of and within everyday life, qualitative methods appear to have more in common with feminism than rational and positivist approaches do (Reinharz, 1983:201). Some aspects of qualitative approaches that support feminist research goals are:

1. Questions resulting in qualitative data do not have the constraint of allowing only a limited number of answers.

2. Qualitative data is analyzed using the language of the respondent. Distinction between qualitative and quantitative research is not always a function of the kind of data collected, but generally responses remain "as is" and are not quantified for analysis.

3. Qualitative data convey a deeper feeling for a more emotional closeness to the persons studied (Jayaratne, 1983:144).

Qualitative data is rarely seen in traditional male research and, in most social science disciplines, the more qualitative aspects of data are rejected as being too "female." However, among the major arguments the feminist criticism directs at traditional approaches to knowledge is that they concentrate on the distortion and misinterpretation of women's experience by describing and measuring them in objective "male" terms, such as controlled experimentation, specific quantitative and statistical techniques. The historically pervasive association between masculine and objective (scientific) is a topic that Keller (1983:188) addresses in her discussion of a "genderization" of science:

> When we dub the objective sciences "hard" as opposed to the softer, i.e., more subjective, branches of knowledge, we implicitly invoke a sexual metaphor, in which "hard" is of course masculine and "soft," feminine. Quite generally, facts are "hard," feelings "soft." "Feminization" has become synonymous with sentimentalization. A woman thinking scientifically or objectively is thinking "like a man"; conversely, a man pursuing a nonrational, nonscientific argument is arguing "like a woman."

It is not that qualitative and quantitative research are not conducive to feminist research. On the contrary, feminist researchers advocate uses of both to develop, support and, explicate theory.

SUBJECTIVE AND OBJECTIVE

Keller and Grontkowsky (1983) identify two features of the scientific conception of objectifiability. The first is the separation of subject from object, i.e., the distinction between the individual who perceives and the object that is perceived—or as Smith (1974:8) describes it, the separation of the knower from what he or she knows and in particular the separation of what is known from any interest or biases that he or, she may have that are not the interests and concerns authorized by the discipline. This relationship parallels that of expert to that of nonexpert; it parallels the privileged relationship of the producer of knowledge, the subject, to the object of knowledge the object (Fee, 1983:19). It also characterizes the individual existing in an atomized state of contemporary capitalist society. Our own socially constituted being is represented in such notions as the disinterested human observer and a value-free social science. Westkott explores the subject/object dichotomy in relation to the distinction between the person conducting the research and the person about whom knowledge is developed. She explains that the ideal of objectivity was advocated by nineteenth-century positivists who argued that the subject who conducts research should always guard against allowing feelings to contaminate the research.

The second feature of the scientific conception of objectifiability identified by Keller and Grontkowski (1983) is the move away from the conditions of perception, i.e., the separation of knowledge from the unreliability of the senses, or, so to speak, the dematerialization of knowledge. Values, like feelings, political commitments, or aesthetic preferences belong to the domain of subjectivity and of individual "bias." Indeed, subjectivity is regarded with suspicion, as a possible contaminant of the process of knowledge production, and one that must be governed by stringent controls. Arlie Russel Hochschild suggests that perhaps the main reason sociologists have neglected to study feeling and emotion is that sociologists, as members of the same society as the actors they study, share their same feelings and values. She explains:

> Our society defines being cognitive, intellectual or rational dimensions of experience as superior to being emotional or sentimental. (Significantly the terms "emotional" and "sentimental" have come to connote excessive or degenerate forms of feeling) (Hochschild, 1975:281).

Also, in defining social science's two images of the social actor—the first, the conscious, cognitive actor who portrays people as consciously wanting something (e.g., money or status) and consciously calculating the merit of various means toward an end; the second, the unconscious emotional actor who is guided by unconscious motivations, and does or thinks things whose meanings are better understood by the social scientist than by the actor—Hochschild concludes that both omit or neglect conscious feeling. She suggests that the first approach to the sociology of emotion is to study what and how people think about emotion and feeling, which might be accomplished by a third approach, that of the sentient actor, in which sociologists attend to the actor's own definition of his or her feelings. Associated with this image is a line of inquiry that seeks to relate feelings to the labeling. She recommends that research start with the latter and elaborate it in a depth-psychology direction (drawing from Dollard) and in a cognitive direction (drawing from Blum and McHugh). Feeling, thus conceptualized, can be elaborated in a sociological direction.

This view seems reasonable and noncontroversial. There are, however, the insistent and recurrent problems of the feminist researcher-as-actor involved in the construction of gender differences where rationality is in opposition to nature, and the public realm is in opposition to the private realm. What is needed, therefore, is more of a re-organization of knowledge that changes the relation of the sociologist to the object of her knowledge. This involves placing the sociologist where she is actually situated, namely at the beginning of those acts by which she knows or will come to know; and making her direct experience of the everyday world the primary ground of her research.

Also, as long as women sociologists stand at the center of a contradiction in the relation of our discipline to our experience of the world, transcending that distinction means setting up a different relation than that which we discover in the routine practice of our research.

> The radical feminist critique of science and objectivity, therefore, needs to be developed in ways that will allow us to identify those aspects of scientific activity and ideology which need to be questioned and rejected, without at the same time abandoning the ideal that we can come to an even more complete understanding of the natural world through a collective and disciplined process of investigation and discovery (Fee, 1983:16).

What then becomes possible is less a shift, an opposition or a contrast in approaches to research than a different conception of how they are or might become relevant as a means of understanding our experience and the conditions of our (both women's and men's) experience.

WOMEN AS SUBJECTS

The value and significance of women's experience, traditions, and perceptions in and of themselves should be affirmed by research. In order for research to affirm women's experience, such as of childbirth and menopause, there must be clear deviations from conventional research and perceptions of these experiences. An initial difference in women's research on childbirth, for example, is the identification of strengths, values, and positive functions of being pregnant and birthing, a difficult objective within the assumptive framework of past investigations. Such an affirmative approach represents a long-missing and needed complement to the volumes of work on the objective, scientific, and medical aspects of childbirth. As Rowbotham (1973b) has noted, the exploration of our own sexuality is a crucial factor in the creation of a revolutionary female consciousness. We have to discover our whole selves, not simply the selves that fit into the existing male world. Any continued acceptance of male standards and values can only perpetuate the very social structure that legitimizes oppression, competition, divorce of emotion and reason, and other features of male ideology in need of revision.

The main recent version of the notion of objectivity in research has emphasized the importance of universal application of social science methods as the best guarantee against the bias of subjectivity. In its application to feminist research, the criticism of objectivity continues:

> The aura of objectivity can be maintained so long as the object of knowledge, the "known," can be an "other," an alien object that does not reflect back on the knower. Considering women only as *objects* of social knowledge fails to challenge this disassociation. Moreover, it is consistent with the wider cultural objectification of women, in which our basic humanness is denied, but our externally determined characteristics can be categorized and related to one another like other phenomena (Westkott, 1979:425).

As Smith, Westkott, and other feminists agree, when women study women the complexity of women as objects of knowledge reflecting back upon women as subjects of knowledge is revealed. "By insisting that women be entered into sociology as its subjects . . . we ourselves can 'look back' as subjects constituted as objects, and in doing so, we disclose its essential contradiction" (Smith, 1977:139). In this respect, women are not identified with the abstract "human being" or the general and impersonal terms "men," "he," and "his"; nor are they merely inserted within the category of "people." When women study women we present ourselves as members of a specific social category who occupy specific positions in society where everyday-life experiences are specific to the individual. The emphasis upon the idea that subject and object are experiential further reflects the commitment of feminist researchers to grounding sociological inquiry in the concrete everyday life experience of women rather than in abstract categories to which they had previously been assigned (Reinharz, 1979). Smith argues that this aura of objectivity can be maintained so long as the object of knowledge, the "known," can be an "other," an alien object that does not reflect back on the knower. It is only where women are also brought in as the subjects of knowledge that the separation between subject and object breaks down. The issue for feminists of course is not merely that of objective versus subjective approaches, but rather one of liberation from constraints of research paradigms that are simply incapable of meeting the new requirements of feminist scholarship. Thus by achieving liberation from the constraints of traditional "malestream" modes of inquiry, and by developing thoughtfully the communal aspects of content and method, women may succeed in creating those new research paradigms needed for the scientific revolution.

The feminist perspective, as presented in this book, discredits sociology's claim to constitute an objective knowledge independent of the sociologist's situation. For those of us who are seeking knowledge of women's experience, the ideas of freedom from patriarchal domination within the theories, concepts, and methods of our discipline—particularly within both subject and object, knower and known—leads us back to our own original but unspoken knowledge of sociology's claim to be about the world in which we live and its failure to account for or even describe its factual features as women find them in living them. Rowbotham points to the separation of research topics into male interests that have been explored and female interests that have not as the first step in filling in the gaps.

The task of feminist research of the 1980s, then, is not only to make women "visible," but also to raise questions about theories and methods, to define problems of gender divisions among researchers and the research process, and to challenge the language and application of research findings. Implicit assumptions about how women do and should experience everyday life penetrate all subject areas as a method of discovering our experience and seeing it from our perspective. Also, the previous assumption that women's experience is best understood in comparison to or in relation to men's experience limits and distorts knowledge about women's social life. Although I am not fostering the idea that, as sociologists, the purpose of studying women's experience is justified solely in terms of our past exclusion as the subjects of knowledge, I do agree that in correcting the male-oriented perspective, feminist analysis must involve direct inspection of women's immediate bodily experience.

In the effort to distinguish between women's and men's experiences, traditional research has neglected or excluded the variety within women's experience, or they have assumed that generalizations can be applied to everyone in a particular setting, irrespective of location and position. It is possible that women are not as homogeneous a group as they often appear in traditional research. Indeed, it seems likely that there is tremendous diversity in how women experience their everyday life. If so, we need to recognize it. Meaningful experience, for instance, may be manifested in countless ways, not all of which are evident from male-defined perspectives. A closer examination from a feminist perspective of women's experience—its versatility and range—should prove useful in informing us of possibilities as well as probabilities. What must, in particular, be focused upon are the ways in which a woman who has gone through specific experiences sees herself and the meaning that she attaches to those experiences. For, from the feminist viewpoint, one of the most important dimensions of variability is that which occurs among individuals of the same sex and within the same individual at different times. It is this dimension that has been most neglected, and it is traditional research that most directly challenges previous assumptions and explanations grounded in earlier male-dominated theory. Women, above all, want to say what their own lives have been, are, and will be, not permitting male ideology to define and explain what woman's experience is or is not or should be. Feminist researchers can then use diverse research to formulate more questions on the consequences of beginning from the experience of women that may yield new concepts, new theories—or new meanings to existing categories—and new methods of "making sense." It is therefore to an examination of phenomenological sociology as a plausible approach to feminist research that we shall now turn our attention.

CHAPTER 5

Phenomenological Approach to Women's Experience

IDEALIZED MYTH

IN LIGHT OF THE FEMINIST ARGUMENT that conventional descriptions of experience are fundamentally at odds with the viewpoints of women as social actors, Alfred Schutz's phenomenological sociology may be relevant to the study of the subjective nature of women's experience. Before this framework can be applied to a study of women, however, it must be determined whether the framework itself has the potential for taking account of conceptions of knowledge, of ways of learning, knowing, and valuing that are specific to, or at least common to, women. By maintaining that the sexist bias is primarily in the perspective and visions of Schutz's work, in his mode of reasoning, and, only secondarily, in the substantive theories of his phenomenological sociology, we must be on guard that "in the interests of immediate justice we may jettison one of the most powerful tools of modern thought, and throw out the baby with the bath water" (McCormack, 1975:4). Thus in, reexamining Schutz's basic assumptions from a feminist perspective, we might also raise, in a preliminary way, new conclusions and new directions for phenomenological sociology that have implications for research on both women and men.

Phenomenological sociology brings together, as we have mentioned, two well established disciplines, philosophy and sociology, each carrying within its own tradition an assortment of theoretical dispositions and a division of labor. From time to time, both have included aspects of other disciplines such as history and economics into theirs, and even now there is overlap between them. Phenomenology provides the tools for describing and understanding a variety of social phenomena. Much of the work done in it has no direct bearing on women's experience. The biases are fairly standard: the neglect of sociological research by women and for women, the masculine bias embedded in the structure of social theory, the invisibility or distortion of women as subjects of knowledge, and the conventional modes of establishing knowledge. It is unlikely that the commonly accepted stereotype of women's thinking as emotional, intuitive, and personalized and, therefore, less valuable than rational and objective ways of knowing has not penetrated Schutz's work.

Feminist researchers interested in pursuing a phenomenological sociological orientation are presented with an asymmetric set of material. Within it there is the major bias of judgment of the experience of women according to male norms, either by ignoring or by not recognizing that woman's experiences differ from men's. This assumption rests on a further assumption that women and men share the same social reality. One immediate response to this assumption might be to reject all sociological study, because everything that has been created in culture—all universal values, all notions of who we are—have been made in a society in which men have been dominant. But the problem created by simply rejecting everything, and inverting existing male values to make a female sociology out of everything not male is that the distortions of gender differences are still perpetuated.

A review of both the classic (Descartes, Bergson, Husserl) and more recent (Schutz, Luckman, Natanson, Berger, Psathas) studies with a phenomenological orientation confirmed a suspicion: women are virtually invisible. Welcome exceptions have been Maxine Sheets' (1966) writings on the phenomenology of dance, Mary Zimmerman's (1977) study on abortion, Pamela Fishman's (1978) analysis of the hierarchical interaction between women and men, Mary O'Brien's (1980) contribution to our understanding of reproductive consciousness and the numerous writings of Dorothy Smith whose tremendous insights influenced some of the ideas in this chapter. Also, Stephanie Demetrakopoulis (1983) supports feminist sociologists' development of a feminist methodology that consciously locates social experience in a set of social relations; Liz Stanley and Sue Wise (1983b) focus on women's experience as a way of making sense of the world; and Iris Young (1984) describes alienation of the pregnant body. These scholars have begun to decipher the realities of the cultural stereotypes (or ideal types) of women's lives as well as to study the impact of the cultural myths on women's conception of their lived experience. Other feminist writers, Kitzinger, Oakley, Reitz, Rowbotham, and Weideger, although not all phenomenologists, have questioned specifically why sociologists have not recognized the obvious contradictions between women's real-life experience of pregnancy, childbirth, menstruation, and menopause, and the idealized myth of these experiences. Thus we must caution ourselves to not allow our recognition of existing male categories of meaning to influence and shape our observations. Rather, we must remain cognizant of the wide range of individual gender differences and of the possibility for creating new ideal types and for reconsidering those in existence. Ultimately, in order to be applicable to feminist theory, any methodological orientation must be an approach that celebrates differences rather than denies them, that encourages expressions of the fullness of individuality.

At first glance, the subject areas in Schutz's work appear to be non-gender-biased. The phenomenological *epoché*, meaningful lived experience, typification, reflection, intersubjectivity, and multiple realities are presented as the context for description of human consciousness and meaning construction. To examine whether or not this is so, we must question to what extent the experiences of women are actually represented in the discussion of these phenomena; to what extent representations of women are inclusive of our social location and position; and to what extent women's consciousness and meaning construction can be revealed through Schutz's phenomenological sociology.

SUBJECTIVE MEANING

To the degree that Schutz has taken seriously the Husserlian injunction "To the things themselves" in Schutz's essays, we see the world through male actors as they define, cope, interact. For example, Schutz takes us into the world of intersubjectivity where "the stranger," "the homecomer," and "the citizen" are understood, described, and acted upon according to a reciprocity of (male) perspectives. While Schutz shows us how much more we "understand" of the Other than we thought, he neglects how much more we *feel* in socially arranged ways than we thought. We are not shown, for example, how socially induced feelings lead us to rely on false assumptions of a reciprocity of perspectives. Such reciprocity is probably not a constant feature of all social actors. For example, those who experience themselves in accustomed social settings where different hierarchies prevail may be more concerned about the subjective aspects of their experience—feelings, emotions, coping strategies, bodily sensations—than those higher up, those who are objective onlookers and are more concerned with the smooth running of schedules and routine practices and procedures.

Although we will discuss later and in greater detail the differences in perception between the experience as perceived by the individual having the experience and the experience as perceived by the objective onlooker, it suffices to say here that neither image is wrong; but that the latter is only partly useful to women by what is highlighted. It is assumed that both participants know what each other wants or does not want, needs or does not need, feels or does not feel. In positing a model of a "rational" actor, Schutz does not deny that actors feel; but however, he does imply that little is lost when feelings are ignored or categorically included under the terms of sharing in a face-to-face relation.

A Schutzian concept that also implies rationality is that of meaningful lived experience. Like Weber's model of social action, Schutz's model of meaningful action is rational; it is conduct based on a preconceived project, made meaningful through the reflective glance of consciousness of the social actor. The meaning one attaches to an experience resides in the intentionality of the actor—the purpose or project the actor was seeking to obtain—which lifts the experience out of the *durée* (the stream of duration of consciousness, the actually ongoing life itself) and transforms it into something discrete (segments or intentional unities), a completed episode. Also, the orientation of action to future attainment is significant to Schutz's analysis of social action as it pertains to meaning and motive. For instance, in refering to the action of the various levels of breathing that a woman can perform during the muscular contractions during labor, Schutz would argue that the project of the breathing is not the cause of the action, but the action that either fulfills or fails to fulfill the project of counteracting the pain from the bodily contractions.

He would also argue that the perception of the labor itself is no project of any kind since it does not connect with the judgment: "If I leave myself unguarded, I will feel the pain of the contraction." The connection emerges only through the intentional act of the birthing woman whereby she turns to the totality of her past experience—the intentionality of her project (to become pregnant) brought to fulfillment by her action (intentional bodily movements) leading to her completed project (childbirth). Although one is able to accept the logic of this analysis, it is clear that the emphasis is on the "because" motives (her "expectations") that are accessible to the sociologists as a disinterested observer. Schutz distinguishes between "because" and "in-order-to" motives. "Because" motives explain the project in terms of the actor's past experience, such as in the following example: when a person puts up an umbrella because she follows the principle "If I expose myself unprotected to the rain I will get wet and soon it will become unpleasant. The way to stop this is to open my umbrella, and this is just what I will do." "Because" motives explain the project in terms of the actor's past experience: "I open my umbrella because it is raining." First, I see that it is raining, and I remember that I could get wet in the rain and that would be unpleasant. The way to stop this is to open my umbrella, and this is exactly what I will do." Once a because-relation, an experience prior to the project (opening the umbrella) is the motivating factor, this is done, the in-order-to motive motivates the action and is the reason it is performed.

"In-order-to" motives refer to the future, to the state of affairs to be brought about by future action: "If I open my umbrella I shall avoid the displeasure of getting my clothes wet. Putting up my umbrella keeps me dry when it is raining and I now take it for granted in performing the action" (Schutz, 1967:88–92). The "in-order-to" motives, the reasons that an individual undertakes certain actions in order to bring about some future occurrence, according to Schutz, are part of the ongoing stream of consciousness *(durée)* not accessible to the sociologist or the actor. We have to question this assumption. Through retrospective glance, it appears quite likely that I can know or identify the factors that caused me (when I am also the researcher) to behave in one way and not in another at a particular time and place. And in my desire to understand the everyday-life of women as it differs among women and from that of men, I require access to the motives of both; for the motives for the same action may differ at particular times and particular places and among particular individuals. That Schutz's commitment to objective science led him to regard motives as too subjective, too individualistic, and too idiosyncratic for his orientation to the study of shared meaning systems is understandable. It gives further testimony to his acceptance of objective meaning contexts that are shared by a collectivity, the (male) culture as a whole. We have already indicated the sexist bias in generalizing from the experience of only one segment of society to create an explanation of the meaning of experience of both women and men. Such an ideology denies both the experience and the objective situation of women, as well as ignores and conceals a sexual division.

The significance of Schutz's acceptance of objective meaning contexts and their accessibility to sociologists and to everyone in the collectivity is that they can be studied scientifically. Again, we need not argue the logic of Schutz's position. We do, however, need to argue three points. The first is the notion of the collectivity and its male representation of meaning contexts. Detailing collective experience becomes the main criteria by which meaningful conceptual categories emerge. That Schutz deals only with male experience does not preclude the investigation of female life. As a scientific method, Schutz's phenomenological sociology exemplifies the communal frame thought by feminists to be better able to identify the sexist biases sociologists inevitably bring to their work and to correct the bias. The second point appears more relevant to feminist examination: it is the claim that motives for actions are too subjective for sociological study. Feminists have become increasingly aware of the role played by the subjective in the construction of knowledge and the tendency of traditional sociology to treat the subjective as "merely" subjective or as so idiosyncratic that scientific investigation, concenred with patterns and generalities, cannot seriously study it. Schutz overlooks the possibility of finding patterns in the subjective experience of individuals, and denies the researchers access to other's experience unless they can, in advance of their study, be assured that order and structure will be found.

The second point appears more relevant to feminist examination: this is the claim that motives for actions are too subjective for sociological study. The criteria used by Schutz to distinguish between what is and what is not suitable for study reflect his attempts to recognize sociology as "real science" with objectivity as a legitimate goal of scientific research. As noted elsewhere in this book, objectivity is also associated with value-free sociology that feminist and other critiques of sociology have deemed a myth. Feminists have become increasingly aware of the role played by the subjective in the construction of knowledge. They challenge the notion that individual experience is too subjective, variable, and inaccessible to be studied. Also, their claim is that "pseudo objectivity" is practiced when subjective factors are not explicitly taken into account.

The third point of argument within Schutz's concept of meaningful action is his focus on the rational calculations through which deliberation emerges into conscious activity, nearly bypassing the actor's consciousness of emotional states altogether. This image, like that of meaningful lived experience, does not deny affective consciousness. Rather, the focus on conscious, purposive action, and the emphasis on unconscious promptings and motivations force conscious feelings into an unrecognized category. We need a synthesis of meaningful experience, one in which the actor is both conscious and feeling, purposive and emotional. In this manner, experience will be seen as more than deliberations or unintentional activities or blind expressions of uncontrolled emotions. As conscious beings, women and men consciously respond to their feelings and to the cultural expectations concerning them. They are often aware of their emotional states, which stand out against a taken-for-granted background stream of experience. With a change in attention, the taken-for-granted becomes problematic (noticed by them), and these emotions stand out and they are conscious of them. Also, they as actors select and apply a variety of labels to these states from among the emotion vocabularies available at their time and place in the social world. They apply a meaning context to them.

INTENDED MEANING

In general, when sociologists study emotion they distinguish between the data received from the subject and their inferences from them. But because emotions are not always quantitatively measurable or even perhaps accurately recorded, described, or defined by the subjects, what often becomes sociological data is not the experience as experienced by the subject. As subjects of our own research, however, women might be able to attend to our own definitions of our emotions and to the intended meaning of those emotions. Also, we might discover what our inner experiences refer to (e.g., reflection on past experience, anticipations of future experience), and what social relations (e.g., between birth women and their husbands), social situations (e.g., the hospital environment or the home), or rules (e.g., staff regulations) reveal or inhibit their appearance.

The possibility of our not understanding the meaning that we attach to our world and to our own actions appears to contradict Weber's interpretive method of *verstehen,* which places emphasis on sociologists' understanding the sense that the actors make of our relations and events of everyday life. And this, Weber claimed, was subject to study through scientific processes. Feminist critique challenges the Weberian definition of rationality for its inability to account for the emotional and psychological complexity of social life. It also suggests that the concept, *verstehen,* is deficient because in a sexist society one must ask who is doing the interpreting. When women are interpreting women, the possibility exists that those concepts will take on new meaning.

Although Weber mentions that taking into consideration the feelings of others was essential, he focused on their meaning to the individual, as understood by the researcher. As a special method for the social sciences in general, Schutz regarded *verstehen* as absolutely essential "both in everyday life as we interpret the action of one another and in social science where our goal is to arrive at a meaningful comprehension of social reality that, at the same time, has some significance in common-sense terms" (Thomason, 1982:48). This advocates a sociology in line with Schutz's recommendation and the norm of objectivity. Unable to derive emotions from empirical formulations, Schutz encourages only the rational conduct. To this extent, Schutz separates the emotional and the personal from the rational and the instrumental. Yet as feminists have been asserting, an emotional reaction or personal experience is often the foundation for critical self-reflection.

Similarly, Schutz argues that the meaning one imparts to the interaction situation may be shared with the person with whom one is interacting by means of a reciprocity of perspectives. Unlike Weber, however, he admits that we can never experience the consciousness of others in the same completeness as they experience it, thereby rendering our understanding of their existence only as it is given to us. Some interpretations of the Other—bodily movements and other expressive movements and the use of signs—are derived from interpretations of the observer's own experiences. Yet Schutz cautions us as observers of social reality about distinguishing between our own experiences and interpretations of our subjects' lived experience, which he maintains necessitates self-disciplined self-consciousness through methodological attention to terms, definitions and the idealizations that underlie them. Such understanding results from the existing vocabulary of the interpreter who, feminists note, is most often part of the male culture but certainly need not be.

Differentials of power, a subject-area constantly emphasized by Weber, does not appear as a major concern in Schutz's work. Weber claimed that social analysis must encompass much more than the "clarification of what is thought about the social world by those living in it"—with attention to both unacknowledged effects of action and with respect to determining conditions not mediated by the conscious actor (Giddens, 1976). How, then, can phenomenological sociology explain and properly understand the meaning of experience between "the women of aristocracy and the peasant woman; between the middle-class college student and the waitress who serves her?" (Hamilton, 1978:13). Would these women be able to find the correlates of the theory in their experience? In each instance, the two social locations and bases of knowledge and experience are in one sense, in equal relation. The male culture, however, as it is constituted by male values stands in authority over that of women. In working as sociologists with established modes of thinking and inquiring, many female sociologists have learned to discard our experienced world as a source of concern, information, and understanding, and to confine and focus our insights within the conceptual malestream frameworks and relevances of the discipline.

We need not judge phenomenological sociology deficient for largely ignoring the power relations between researcher and subject and the political relation between theories and methods. On the contrary, the phenomenological method provides a technique for the treatment of "universal" experience, i.e., for all types of experience. Thus, although Schutz's definition of meaning in the interaction situation is, in terms of its recognition of intersubjectivity, a significant departure from Weber's, it nonetheless assumes a congeniality and equality among perspectives. By not acknowledging perspectives within an unequally constructed social order, Schutz allows the views of the powerful to become equated with the definitions of universal, scientific truths. Feminists could strengthen Schutz's position on intersubjectivity by injecting the notion of structured inequality and the imposition of truths by powerful forces.

In acknowledging that only the actor knows the span of his or her plans and projects, available means, relevances, and knowledge on hand among other things, and that researchers must refer to the subjective meaning of the actions of others and to the subjects' activities and their interpretations of them, there is also the assumption that all participants come to understand the motives and intentions of others. This implies an attention to terms, definitions, and idealizations as tools for scientific study of social reality and also reflects a narrowness of the concept of "human being" by its limited ways of understanding human behavior. For Schutz, it is more important that we treat subjective data in objective terms; that we produce objective results about subjective activities. Yet by focusing only on the rational rather than including the emotional aspects of intersubjectivity, Schutz further limits an understanding of the behavior of women and men.

The actors' grasp of the meanings of what they do is derived from their application of interpretive schemes—the process of typification. Given that women and men inhabit distinct social worlds, the numerous recipes for responding to others have been imposed on women so that we respond in what we know to be situationally appropriate ways, rather than acknowledging or expressing different views. Although claiming that analyses of We-relations will illuminate the significance of the realms of contemporaries and predecessors from whom their stock of knowledge has been handed down, the sources of influence (mostly male) are not distinguished by Schutz according to their varying power or domination over women or men.

Thus, face-to-face encounter described by Schutz represents typification in its universality insofar as it embodies socially shared understanding. Within the embodiment of typification, stocks of knowledge are applied to make sense of the conduct of others and to allow individuals to calculate and gauge their actions and the probable responses of others to their actions. There is relatively no concern with the nature of power or its distribution in society. Schutz's

scheme recommends that behavioral responses to problematic situations involve choosing among alternative lines of conduct, implying a
response to situations rather than to people. This also adheres to the
scientific method that is premised on the exercise of rationality.

Schutz's recommendation for sociology is that it acknowledge the
subjective activities that create its subject matter. This position is
congruous with one aspect of the feminist perspective—that of com-
bining objective (quantitative) methods with subjective (qualitative)
methods. Feminist scholars emphasize the idea that subject and
object are humanly linked. They reject the dichotomy between observation and experience. Also, in common with the phenomenological
tradition, the feminist perspective dissents from malestream emphasis upon objectivity (positivism), upon knowing only objectively,
neutrally, impersonally; it does not accept male construction of reality
as given, inevitable, or real. Instead, it emphasizes the idea that social
knowledge is always interpreted within personal and biographical
contexts, and that the truths are, therefore, concrete rather than
abstract, and contingent, rather than categorical. Truths are grasped
through the intersubjectivity of meaning of subject and object.

In looking carefully at Schutz's concerns with subjectivity, we see
that his main recommendation as to how sociologists can obtain
objective results about subjective activities is to search for the meaning the action has for the actor. The key to that understanding is the
scientific study of meaning contexts, thus divorcing the subjective
experience of the person studied from that of the scientific observer—
the knower from the known. In contrast, intersubjectivity from a
feminist perspective does not mean the separation between subject
and object, but it does accept their dialectical relationship. Thus, the
questions feminist researchers ask grow out of their own concerns
and experiences where intersubjectivity of meaning takes the form of
dialogue from which knowledge is an unpredictable emergent rather
than a controlled outcome.

CHOOSING AMONG ALTERNATIVES

For Schutz, all action necessarily involves choosing among projects.
Without alternatives among which to choose, there is no project with
intentions for completion. Action of this kind for Schutz is reduced to
"mere unconscious doing." This notion is more reflective of men's
situation in society than women's, implying a condition of freedom
(which admittedly varies by race and class) for men to implement
action through choice. What has so often been true about the choices

for women is not only that they are not genuine alternatives, but they are not the choices that women would present to themselves.

> The experience of marriage, of immigration, of the arrival of children, of employment, etc.—all these were moments in which I had in fact little choice and certainly little foreknowledge. I had little opportunity of calculating rationally what it means to have a child, what it means to leave home and live among strangers, what it means to be married, and how each of these experiences would be a major transformation. When I read in autobiographies or fiction of the lives of other women, I find these same qualities and the surprises in store for the subject about whom she may become. I do not find them in the same way in the autobiographies of men (Smith, 1977:115).

One of the great contributions of feminism has been its insistence that women have the right to identify their own projects and choose accordingly—such as where, when, and how to birth their babies—rather than merely deciding among alternatives that have been presented to them by the social structure.

Freedom to choose, then, emphasizes the crucial importance of women's experience in patriarchal society in at least two ways. First, women's experience as segregated from intentionality without alternatives from which to choose can be viewed as reactive behavior. Although it occurs within a sphere of freedom for some, it is a sphere that exists simultaneously with unfree, conforming behavior.

Second, the idea of women's dissociation of meaningful experience from mere doing suggests a tension between consciousness and behavior. For the meaning women ascribe to their own behavior is derived from women's consciousness, which is influenced by the cultural values of men. But it is, nevertheless, uniquely situated and reflective of women's concrete position within the patriarchal structure. In stressing purposeful, rational conduct Schutz makes little or no reference to nonrational behavior. While presumably accounting for subjective elements of experience, he discusses only the rational elements of meaning and conduct. Thus, given the profound association of women with the seemingly irrational side of nature, Schutz's focus is quite specifically on the ontogenesis and consequences of wide-awake, mature, adult *male* behavior.

Schutz presents stocks of knowledge as a normal competence of a social actor who also has the capacity to operate within multiple realities—to transfer from one province of meaning to another. There are not one but many provinces of meaning, and it is likely that individuals experience these, not similarly, but as conflicting demands. According to Schutz, we remain within the paramount reality as long as we choose to cognitively perceive the world in this way.

This occasional departure from the common-sense world into a new province of meaning is performed by a shocking experience that shifts the accent of reality from the former to the latter. Falling asleep or mental illness may be examples of different finite provinces of meaning, but they are hardly of one's choosing. Also, that we unquestionably accept the new reality based on consensus of simply a practical agreement—that is, that we act "as if" we have the same perspective and understanding as others, ignores the fact that only those ideas, attitudes or behaviors held by the powerful become dominant and that these rarely reflect mutually agreeable perspectives.

The consensual model of multiple realities nullifies the social forces that compel women to acknowledge and accept the understanding and perspectives deemed significant by others. Schutz's emphasis on our altering the cognitive style of our consciousness so as to perceive the world differently implies that realities change as individual behavior changes, with structural change following. The phenomenological interpretation of paramount reality as a social construction, for example, suggests that social institutions are not fixed stabilities but rather alterable affiliations. It sees social structures and social institutions not as products of material conditions or deterministic forces but, rather, as the outcome of value considerations. Hence, to understand phenomenologically the structure of any society, it is necessary to understand the values that gave rise to the directions, meanings and goals of these structures.

> One may change the material aspects of society's institutions, but if the values are not changed, the institutions remain the same. Or one may retain the material aspects of society's institutions while changing the values upon which they are based, with the result that one will experience them as different institutions. A case in point is when royal palaces are made into museums. In short, phenomenology insists upon openness to the full range of social reality, including the various levels of social objectivity, which includes values, goals, and meaning, as well as material objects (Stewart and Mikunas, 1974:129).

Schutz's framework is not concerned with changing the larger system. Phenomenological sociology may be able to deal with larger-scale social structures, but that remains to be demonstrated.

Thus, as women begin to reject the taken-for-granted notion that our world must exist in the form that it takes, and that change is not only possible but an inextricable element of our social life, we escape the common-sense-world of our pre-reflective, everyday lives into a new finite province of meaning.

CHALLENGING THE TAKEN-FOR-GRANTED

Schutz's investigation of the natural attitude of the world of daily life or the "life-world"—the world in which we live, work, and act in common with others—is taken for granted by us as our reality. We take it for granted that this world existed before we did and will continue to exist until after our death. In our natural attitude we take it for granted that others exist and that they will act in ways typically similar to ours, will be motivated by typically similar motives, and will interpret our actions in substantially the same way as we meant them. And we assume that others, in turn, interpret our own actions and motives as typically similar to theirs. This commonness of our world experience has several dimensions.

> There are, in the first place, my contemporaries, with whom I am interconnected in mutual action and reaction and who thus live "at the same (historical, objective) time" as I; secondly, my successors, of whom no experience by me is possible, but toward whom I may and do direct my actions; thirdly, my predecessors, on whose world I cannot act, but whose actions and products are handed down to me in the form of tradition that I can modify, partially reject, accept, or take for granted (Zaner, 1961:75).

Within the lived-world, the reality of the world is never called in question, neither is any theoretical foundation given for it. Daily life is considered ours from the outset in that all elements of the world are taken as real for you as for me. The real is not based on empirical or logical reference or a predicative judgment, but on a prepredicative understanding of the world (Stewart and Mickunas, 1974:126). This taken-for-granted commonness of the world of daily life is fundamental to intersubjectivity as an "intramundane" problem in understanding women's experience. "How is a common world," Schutz asks, "in terms of common intentionalities possible?" Feminists ask, how is an intersubjective world, in terms of women's and men's immediate and direct perception of each other's mental life, possible? For feminists the "problem" of intersubjectivity is here encountered in full force.

First, if women assume an interconnectedness among our (male) contemporaries we camouflage both the anatomical differences between women and men and conceal the manner in which our actions and reactions are male-defined in all forms of existing social organizations. On the one hand, denial of difference among women and men, men and men, women and women, who live at the same (historical, objective) time leaves the way open for a reduction of human potential. On the other hand, there are many obstacles that prevent women from seeing our common identity. What it is about male experience that prejudices conceptions of reality is best summarized by Rowbotham:

> The particular image of a particular oppressed group sometimes even serves to magnify the world of the oppressor by projecting itself at the expense of others who share invisibility. For example, male-dominated black and working-class movements can falsely define their "manhood" at the expense of women, just as some women define femaleness at the expense of men. They thus cheat themselves and lose the possibility of man-woman-hood (1973b:29).

What has begun to be revealed about women's experiences, which serves as a contribution to feminist theory, is the notion of a diversity underlying the commonality of our experience. The individual lives of women vary considerably. Our situation in a particular setting—home or workplace—our age and the generation to which we belong, our social class and racial and/or ethnic and religious background, our sexual preference, and the customs governing particular experiences are variables that make for great diversity of details and nuances of each woman's personal experience. Nonetheless, certain common elements can be discerned. These will be discussed in the following chapter.

Second, in directing our action toward our unknown successors, women, as an oppressed group, cannot create an alternative. By accepting and reproducing a predefined malestream notion of human experience, we are prevented from imagining in which experiences transformation might occur should the present realities surrounding them be changed. What is required, then, is a new orientation that deconstructs and reexamines what "appears" to be gender-neutral; that transcends the limitations imposed by male culture; that maintains the fundamental insight of phenomenological sociology; and that constructs reality by starting from women's perspective. This orientation may or may not need to be modified as men are taken into consideration. The "data" of women's experience in male-defined realities do not emerge unless we start with a woman's perspective. Instead of maximizing the polarization between feminine and masculine, an orientation of "back to the personal" would identify and describe women's experiences that are potential sources of strength and power for women, and, more broadly, of liberation and pride.

Third, that of our predecessors, provides some basis for a transformation of reality by modifying, rejecting, accepting, or taking for granted the culture as it has been handed down to us. Feminism challenges the reality of perception by considering in a new way what may otherwise pass as normative. Feminism challenges the process by which content emerges as knowable by validating individual personal experience and the historically articulated experience of other women. Any mode of analysis that asserts the presence of women must challenge the prevalent social organization of knowledge. Thus by taking the everyday world as a "sociological problematic" (Smith, 1974), methods may be developed for expressing women's knowledge.

In addition, feminists may borrow from that tradition of predecessors any theories, methods, and concepts needed for the development of a women-centered orientation. Some ideas of George Herbert Mead, for example, have been accepted, some have been rejected, and still others have been modified to provide new and illuminating reappraisals of the more "encrusted tenets of malestream thought" (O'Brien, 1981). Feminists have also used insights of Marx, Engels, Manheim, and others, about ideology, to create a feminist methodology that consciously locates social experience in a set of social relations. Thus, a feminist perspective does not automatically reject the tradition, but rather, uncovers contradictions in traditional thought.

> We . . . work in a dialectical way. We seek to . . . root these contradictions in the realities of male experience; to point out that they have been valid in specific historical circumstances; to say why they are no longer valid; to conserve what is valuable and to transcend what is history and creative of a future (O'Brien, 1981:12).

Thus, what is not being suggested is a rejection of Schutz's notion that the world of daily life into which we are born is intersubjective. However, that it is a common system of ideas, typifications, and relevances is one notion that becomes problematic within a feminist perspective. Schutz is aware that structural constraints go far to define the everyday world, but their existence is viewed as external to the individual in the form of "imposed relevances" (those interests that are not freely chosen by the individual). Clearly, however, there is frequently an objective or structural component to the imposed relevance. It is concealed within Schutz's theoretical orientation, which apprehends it only from the standpoint of the individual. Individual minds come to know objective reality through an understanding of universal propositions grounded in the external world. Also, an individual is buffeted by powerful imposed relevances that (although the individual subjectively constructs their meaning) have no subjectivity of their own (Sallach, 1973:29). By heightening our awareness of the subjective existence of the individual, Schutz extracts all concreteness from the imposed relevances. Paradoxically, extracting concreteness results also in the removal of subjectivity.

In contrast, when moving from a high level of generalization to the concrete, feminists undertake to analyze the historical situation. Rather than employing imposed relevances as a general category, a feminist analysis, following the Marxist approach, requires that generalizations have an historical element. The result is that the feminist analysis of a specific situation (e.g., women in childbirth) takes into account the personal and subjective aspects of social structure.

CONSTITUTION OF THE OTHER

Returning to the phenomenon of intersubjectivity, we find another major difference between feminist and Schutzian analyses: that of communication with another. According to Schutz, communication occurs only in the reality of the outer world and for this reason constitutes the core of "paramount" reality. Accordingly, any encounter with the Other is possible only through the medium of events occurring in or produced by the body as a "field of expression" with meaning and intentionality.

> "Appresentation," the means of which one object, or state of affairs, now presented is "paired" *(gepaart)* with another state of affairs that is now presented. By virtue of "pairing," the non-presented state of affairs becomes "appresented" (Zaner, 1961:79).

Schutz's claim that appresentation provides the clue for understanding how the Other is first constituted as such in my experience becomes problematic when considering that the body of the Other is given in my experience originally, immediately, as a purely physical thing, as an object of sensuous perception.

> By means of the automatic synthesis Husserl class "associative transfer of sense," the Other's organism is automatically constituted for me as an organism similar to mine, and, more particularly, as a bodily organism *(leibkorper)*, such as I would have an experience (in the way I now experience my organism) were I over there where that physical body now is (Zaner, 1961:79).

What is important is that once the Other is apprehended as Other by means of this appresentational reference, a communicative common environment (the paramount reality) is established out of which higher-level communications—the main social relationship, the "face-to-face" relationship—become possible to develop. By setting up this relationship as one which is obtained between any two or more consociates whose worlds, with their corresponding manipulatory spheres, partially overlap and are thus shared, held in common, implies intersubjective understanding in a Weberian sense. That is, within this relationship the human activities as well as the products of these actions, which intrinsically refer back to the subjective meaning given them by the actors and producers, are understood by me as they are interpreted by the Other. This co-presence of individuals (family, friends, strangers) implies a community of time and space among consociates without regard to differences related to gender (or class or race). What is not examined is how what we are interpreting is consistent with the accepted definition. Although women and men might be in a We-relationship, a relationship of mutual need, for example, women do not have equality with men. Thus, when women are the actors who produce the subjective meaning of their actions to be interpreted by the Other (men), two basic problems arise.

First, the influence of the male-defined Other is the perspective of the male subject as he views woman as Other. Not having established her separate identity, woman-as-Other reflects the established male view of what women are and what they should be. Second, when women challenge the conventional definition of themselves and attempt to advance their own, the perspective of the Other might be eliminated. The influence of male-defined experience on menopausal women, for example, is the source of the arguments within the health movement for a new self-image for women. Also, as women gradually move forward in reclaiming the experience of childbirth as our own and in defining our own situation, the reciprocity of perspectives is less characterized between women and men (and even less between birthing women and male physicians). Conflicts arise as women propose solutions to problems based on our stock of knowledge at hand, our typifications and generalizations, which may not correspond in meaning with those of the dominant group whose language we are using. For until recently, only a small part of our stock of knowledge at hand originated with us; most of it was socially derived. We were taught how to define our situation—that is, how to define, in regard to the natural aspect of the world, the typical features that prevail in the in-group as the unquestioned-but-always-questionable ambit of things taken for granted until further notice. And we continue to be taught how typical constructs have to be formed in accordance with the purpose at hand and its system of relevances accepted from the anonymous viewpoint of the in-group (ways of life, recipes for acting). For this socialization, the typifying medium has been the common male vernacular, a language of named things and events primarily of the typifications and generalizations prevailing in the in-group whose vernacular it is.

The relation between the sexual stereotype (ideal type) women believe in and our actual experience is a very complex one. It is crucial, however, to make a vigilant effort to distinguish between belief and reality, even, or especially, when the reality that emerges is so different from our perception of it. The conditions for the creation of feminist theory are, in fact, grounded in the acknowledgement that social reality differs according to the kinds of activities and social relations in which individuals engage. Because of the uniqueness of the Other's biographically determined situation and the Other having been taught how to define her situation and construct plans of action in accordance with the typifications peculiar to the Other's in-group, Schutz argues that one can never totally experience the consciousness of the Other. Even in the face-to-face relationship, my experience of the Other's consciousness is influenced by my Here and Now and not that of the Other; likewise, the Other comes to know her own experience more immediately upon reflection. Since I am not able to reflect on the experience of the Other, I can only know it by positing that the Other's subjective stream of thought shows the same fundamental structure as mine, implying that our respective perspectives can be exchanged, that in certain typically pre-defined situations the Other, following certain pre-defined procedures and recipes, will behave in one way and not in another. According to Schutz, this interaction, like all social interaction, is thus founded on the general thesis of the existence of the alter ego, and, as such, the ground for the commonness of the social world. This means that the belief in the Other, as another like me, is never itself brought into question, never itself made thematic within the natural attitude. All doubtings and questionings regarding the Other and the common, intersubjective world are left unexamined while this fundamental belief in the Other, "our" world and its objects is maintained. In fact, for Schutz, individuals in their everyday life, natural attitude make constant and unthematic use of a specific *epoché*. They suspend all doubt of the world, its objects, and Others; they refrain from the doubt that they might be otherwise than they are assumed to be.

Accordingly, feminists must set aside the natural attitude in order to get to the most basic aspect of our consciousness. The natural attitude, to Husserl, is a source of bias and distortion for the phenomenologist. But to Schutz, it is a basic subject of phenomenological investigation to "see" the phenomena as clearly as possible and as they are given in immediate experience, in one's consciousness of those things. In this manner, all experiences can never receive equal attention. Thus bracketing, the *epoché* of the natural attitude, may enable feminists to expand our view and to include more aspects of "our" world for sociological investigation. The question remains whether the epistemological tools provided by Schutz can contribute, in accordance with feminist principles, to research on women's subjective experience.

CHAPTER 6

Women as Agents of Knowledge

DICHOTOMY IN RESEARCH

THE PREVAILING IDEOLOGY within sociology interprets the social world through theories that claim allegiance to "pure" (positivist, objective) science. These theories have been shaped by values reflecting the interests and attitudes of "male" culture. Recent feminist scholarship confirms that prevailing common sense and prevailing science are often formulated in such a way as to deem or exclude the experiences of women in favor of the experiences of men, the dominant gender. When men are dominant, they censor women's ideas and explanations. This censorship influences not only how women explain the world but also what happens to our explanations. Being able to generate, validate, and control our own knowledge about ourselves and society is of critical importance to women in general and to feminist sociologists in particular; for we have been "victims" in so far as we have been dependent on males for public knowledge of ourselves. In a male-dominated discipline, the interests of men are not always and perhaps not often compatible with those of women, but while men control information with an eye to their own interest, the knowledge that they produce about women is all that is publicly available, and we are forced to draw upon it to "make sense" of the world, even though it may do little or nothing to reflect or enhance our lives.

The system of values and beliefs that prevail in sociology is no longer taken for granted as "natural" and reflective of the way things are. The false dichotomy between male research as scientific and female research as unscientific not only is unrealistic but also perpetuates some of the less laudable research of men while obscuring some of the more valuable research of women. As Elizabeth Fee reminds feminists:

> We need not, however, go so far as to reject the whole human effort to comprehend the world in rational terms, nor the idea that forms of knowledge can be subjected to critical evaluation and empirical testing. The concept of creating knowledge through a constant process of practical interaction with nature, the willingness to consider all assumptions and methods as open to question, and the expectation that ideas will be subjected to the most unfettered critical evaluation are all aspects of scientific objectivity that should be preserved and defended. The hope of learning more about the world and ourselves by such a collective process of knowledge production and testing is not one to be abandoned; the idea of individual creativity subjected to the constraints of community validation through a set of recognized procedures preserves the promise of progress (Fee, 1983:16).

What passes both for common sense and science may thus be a way of justifying and thereby reinforcing the invisibility of women's viewpoint in theory.

> For the most part, science is the most respected legitimator of new realities. However, what is often ignored is that science does more than merely define reality; by setting up first the definitions—and then specific relationships within them—it automatically renders suspect the same experiences that contradict the definitions (Hubbard, 1983:46).

Sociology is more than ideology, more than a particular cultural production and representation. As Dorothy Smith (1974, 1977, 1978) notes, the contribution of sociology to the governing of our society is its conceptual procedures, models, and methods by which the immediate concrete features of experience, transposing the actualities of people's lives, are transposed into the conceptual frameworks and relevances that are given in the discipline. Smith also underscores the basic limitations of a sociology where women's place is subordinate, ignored, invisible, and where women appear only as they are relevant to male principles and interests. Oakley (1974b) claims that sociology is solely concerned with the acitivies of men and, as such, its subject-areas are artificial constructs that distort women's experience. Both traditionally and as a matter of occupational practices, the governing conceptual mode of the everyday life-world, the natural attitude, has been appropriated by men. In short, a male-oriented conceptual framework has dominated the questions by which the past of culture has been organized.

> The theories, concepts and methods of sociology claim to account for and to analyze the same world as that which women experience. However, sociology is not capable of analyzing its own relation to its

conditions because the sociologist as actual person in an actual concrete setting has been cancelled in the procedures which objectify and separate him from his knowledge. Thus, the linkage which points back to its conditions is missing (Smith, 1974:10).

Indeed, conceptions of scientific inquiry are deeply distorted by their linkage to cultural stereotypes of masculinity. Also, when experience is taken to be gender-free—when the male experience is taken to be the human experience—the resulting theories, concepts, methods, inquiry-goals and knowledge-claims distort human social life and human thought. Moving beyond these stereotypes requires renaming the charactistics of women, not in terms of deviations from the male norm but as patterns of human responses to particular social situations. In this view, female behavior and male behavior are merely different possibilities that emerge from our particular biographies.

One might argue that masculine perspectives are not only distorting because they are partial, but they are also inherently distorting because they must invert some of the reality of everyday life. The consequences of relying on this partial and distorting perspective of experience as the foundation of all knowledge claims will be the focus of this and the following chapter. Also, women's experiences that could be grounded in a phenomenological understanding will be described. These descriptions begin to disclose how a distinctively feminist perspective on women's experience can reshape the most fundamental and most formal aspects of systematic thought in phenomenology. Perhaps a more reliable and authentic understanding of women's experience will evolve by relating phenomenological concepts central to a feminist thought that accurately reflect women's consciousness.

SUPREMACY OF KNOWLEDGE

Feminist research has begun to transform the way a number of disciplines (anthropology, history, literature) systematically ignore or eliminate the significance of women's experience and the structure of gender by changing the fundamental assumptions, categories, and conceptual frameworks that are fundamental to the discipline. Sociology and political science are those that yet remained immune to this transformation, but the transformatory research is indeed in progress. Feminist research in sociology is shifting to categories generated from those expressive of women's experiences, and it is using these experiences and categories to rethink the concepts and assumptions of malestream thought. Feminist researchers seek to develop and to reconstruct conceptual frameworks based on detailed examination of the facts or phenomenon to be explained. We are looking for an approach that combines the analysis of substantive work with the theory arising from this, rather than separating theory (which is experientially based) and experience. We want women's point of view to be given official status so that it can be more easily sought and found. Feminists are therefore particularly interested in looking to those approaches that share with feminism its interest in the personal and its focusing on everyday life as a topic in its own right. One difficulty for feminists doing research within these new boundaries is that few adequate models from the past exist. Until recently, the research of sociologists was sharply separated from their lived experience. Now, as feminists begin to develop their own research topics and interests, they have to check them against their own personal and collective experiences as women.

What, then, is the best strategy for gaining a better understanding of women's experience? What approaches shall we adopt or reconstruct toward women's experience and what methods of analysis shall we use? These questions are, to some extent, independent, but they also overlap because the orientation we adopt toward any study of women's experience becomes an important determinant of our methods of analysis. This contrasts with positivist approaches that assume that there is only one general set of criteria for scientific validity or truth and that it is embodied in the scientific methodologies of the social sciences. Rejecting the assumption of male standardness has opened important avenues for research on women's experience. We begin to understand not only how women's experience compares with men's but also whether women's experience includes qualities present and not present in men's experience.

This "new" reality is constantly being created through scholarly work, and as this occurs a more important transformation has engaged us. In short, a revolutionary movement has begun to break the hold of the dominant group over theory and method by structuring its own conceptual frameworks and connections with our everyday-life experiences as a direct source of knowledge. This suggests that the feminist researcher's own experiences are an integral part of the research and should be described as such. It also suggests that the researcher stop merely reacting to existing social science investigation by using traditional ideas about how "science" should be conducted, and that the researcher must enter herself as the subject of sociological statements in order to fully participate in the declarations and formulations of sociology's mode of consciousness.

In proposing that feminist research be grounded in the researcher's actual experience, I am not recommending that we ignore the concrete conditions and practices upon which experience depends, but rather, that we take our directly and spontaneously experienced everyday life as our point of departure, our problem for our investigations; that we begin from our own original knowledge, from our acts; that we make our acts and experience observable and understandable within "our" culture.

The contemporary women's movement has stressed women's need to know our history and to know our bodies. Indeed, significant feminist contributions to our understanding of reproduction as a social and a biological phenomenon as well as a political and personal issue have begun to appear. Our experience of our bodies has yet to receive adequate emphasis. In order for this to occur, we must understand ourselves and know our bodies and our minds, not as unrelated cultural entities but as related parts of an integrated feminist consciousness. This change of attention coincides with what Belenky *et al.* (1986) call "subjectivism" or "subjective knowing," dualistic in the sense that there are no "right" answers; "truth" is within the individual and can contradict, reject, or deny that which male objectivity provides. They suggest that "as a woman becomes more aware of the existence of the inner resources for knowing and valuing, as she begins to listen to the voice within her, she finds an inner source of strength" (Belenky *et al.*, 1986:54).

Significant feminist contributions to our understanding of reproduction as a social as well as biological phenomenon and as a political as well as personal issue have begun to appear. But for the most part, the female body is an invisible object. That is, there are few authentic literary testimonies to it. Menstruation and pregnancy, as cycles of life, have been partially detached from taboo and turned into literature only with the rise of the feminist movement. As feminists have opened these topics for research, the problem remains—how can we make known our bodily experiences without the bias of centuries of male distortions.

It is surprising that so little feminist research has been done on the impact of pregnancy, childbirth, menstruation, and menopause upon women from women's point of view. Equally, little feminist research has been done on the impact upon women of medically managed childbirth. There is a vast literature on the relation between hormones and women's behavior, but little has been done to extend the understanding and the meaning that we attach to these cyclical changes in our lives. Although the feminist research in this area is sparse, it provides a base for undoing the male cultural devaluation and distortion of these experiences. I will refer throughout this chapter to the research that inspired me and informed and encouraged me to go "back to the personal" in an attempt to begin to illustrate how well the theoretical framework of phenomenological sociology "makes sense" of uniquely female experience.

Abandoning the male standardness of objectivity has not only expanded women's knowledge of experience, but has also altered our assumptions of the social order. For example, several researchers describe women's experience during childbirth as subordinate, passive, low-key, and non-dominating. Such findings might be interpreted as rationale for advising that birthing women become more assertive, a predictable response given the assumption of male norms and the tendency of men "in control" to be assertive. Rejecting the equation between male experience and "correct" experience would allow women to ask whether low-key involvement/interaction is particularly effective in some situations and/or with certain individuals. As researchers, we also might investigate the impact of low-key behavior on medical and technological intervention in a hospital setting, staff/physician relations as well as birthing women's satisfaction, fulfillment, investment in the task at hand, and so on. Researchers need to begin to ask questions that do not presuppose male experience as the standard by which effectiveness, satisfaction, and fulfillment are determined.

Conventional research on women's experience of childbirth, for example, too often assumes that the critical influence on personal satisfaction and effectiveness is women's behavior. The assumption is that women who had a positive experience during labor did so because they enacted the appropriate behaviors, while women who had negative experiences are those who had not "mastered" the requisite behaviors and attitudes. The pragmatic implication of this assumption is that women are viewed (and view themselves) as having major responsibility for the outcome of their birthing. If they succeed in traditional male arenas—on schedule, submit to the typical routines and procedures, acknowledge the expertise of the physician, follow orders—they are entitled to pride; if they fail or are only marginally successful—prolonged labor, premature labor, resistance to medication, pain at irregular intervals—they must look within themselves for the cause. Also, the traditional literature indicates that the "appropriate time" of life-course stages and changes are socially defined and that women are aware of these age expectations. Thus we evaluate our own experiences against the normative standards. The importance of timing and the consequence of deviation from age norms, for example, are two significant influences on how women experience menstruation and menopause (Reitz, 1977; Weideger, 1977).

Certainly we do not want to argue that women's "expected" behaviors are inconsequential to our feeling about our experiences. Neither, however, do we accept the assumption that overt behaviors are the only or primary influence on individual impact. Experience *per se* is neutral. Its value and impact are derived from the interpretations placed upon it; in turn, interpretations arrive out of frameworks of expectations, perceptions, and values that exist prior to the behaviors. These evaluative frameworks have at least as much to do with a researcher's interpretation of women's experience as do an actor's behaviors.

AFFIRMATIVE APPROACHES

Social sciences have tended to regard women's life-cycle experiences as prior and irrelevant to the more interesting questions of the history of the family or the processes of child development that have been treated in serious and scholarly ways. The general neglect of experiences such as menstruation, pregnancy, childbirth, and menopause, is itself an historical phenomenon of great interest to feminists.

A traditional goal of scientific research is generalization. To generalize, it is necessary to define and think in categories. Science bears the imprint of its generalizations not only in the way they are used, but in the very definition of reality they offer—even in the relation of the scientist to those descriptions. To see this, it is necessary to examine more fully the implications of attributing masculinity to the very nature of human experience. In the area of human experience, the basic categories have been women's experience and men's experience, represented as distinct from each other and relatively homogeneous within races and social classes. A large portion of research in sociology on women's experience begins by separating subjects into two realms of humanity—women and men; next, some designated behavior of the subjects is observed and measured; then, the observed behaviors of the female subjects are compared to those of the male subjects; finally, findings, laced with value judgments, are noted. From this prototypical form of research comes identification of differences characterizing women's and men's experience.

The comparative approach indeed provides insufficient insight into women's experience. The research tells us more about how women's and men's experience (measured against or accepting only a male standard) than about the nature of women's with the result that "emphasis on the male work-rhythm has been an emphasis on a defined pattern, on limitation" (Mead, 1949:45). There has been little consideration of women's realities. Instead, when women's reactions to menstruation and menopause have been observed, they have been interpreted as reflections of an underlying (stereotyped "feminine") personality structure, or as an outward manifestation of (inevitable) psychosexual processes. In the late 1960s and early 1970s feminists began to challenge the medical authority by questioning the legitimacy of the disease model of menopause. They argued that menopause is not a disease or sickness but a natural process of aging, through which most women pass with a minimum of difficulty. Some feminists traced the roots of the disease definition back to the synthesis of estrogens.

Also, the question of whether menopause is a psychologically stressful phase of women's life has been researched in recent years. According to Mary Clare Lennon (1982), a major theme among those who argue that menopause is psychologically stressful is that menopause signifies loss—physiological loss of estrogen or the social and cultural losses of "femininity" or youth. Other research indicates that in general neither the male physician nor the female patient respects the experiences of menstruation or menopause. As a result,

> while Western women do not walk about in the drapery of Purdah, the veils of secrecy, shame, and disrespect similarly constrict the female personality. The unknown and hidden aspects of women's life are sometimes described as the riddle of female identity and sometimes derided as the soiled evidence of corruption (Weideger, 1977:8).

Thus, an important consideration of this research is how a given experience is authorized as *that* experience that must be treated by others as what it is. A correspondingly important piece of information is concerned with who is allocated the privilege of definition and how other possible versions or sources of possible disjunctive information are ruled out. The denial of menstrual and menopausal realities, whether by women or by men, leads to the further denial of the pleasure of psychosexual development—the acceptance of one's self, along with the accomplishments that follow from this feeling.

As the above examples indicate, social action is largely a product of the situational demands and constraints of the present that are mediated but not determined by what has occurred previously. This means that in any situation, with its nearly infinite number of things that could be noticed, only the behavior that is important for the researcher's immediate purposes are noticed, the rest is ignored. But in the present, these areas that have been ignored may be thrust upon one's consciousness by someone who points them out. First, one has to admit they are there (Berger, 1973:56–57). As suggested earlier, it is of questionable appropriateness to compare women's experience of anything to that of men. One problem with most male research of women's experience appears to arise from the absence of a sociological frame of reference that, in Peter Berger's terms, "with its built-in procedure of looking for levels of reality other than those given in the official interpretations of society, carries with it a logical imperative to unmask the pretensions and the propaganda by which men clock their actions with each other" (1973:38). To apply a sociological perspective, to ask sociological questions, presupposes that one is interested in looking some distance beyond the commonly accepted or officially defined goals of human actions. It presupposes a certain awareness that human events have different levels of meaning, some of which are hidden from the consciousness of everyday life. It may even presuppose a measure of suspicion about the way in which human events are officially interpreted by the authorities, be they political, juridical, or religious in character. What is called for is a more radical turn in research, one that redefines the fundamental approach we take in doing research; one that affirms women as women by identification of the neglected strengths, values, and positive functions of our experience.

It is difficult to know where to obtain this knowledge on childbirth, for example, since women did not write books; and the real history of the development of birthing as an art, the expertise accumulated and passed on by the actual practitioners, is blotted out in the history of male obstetrics (Rich, 1977:123).

> If we turn to mothers to tell us stories about themselves and their experience we are confounded by silence. For so many centuries not a syllable. The great silence results, in part, from female silence . . . Beyond that is the denigration of female experience by women themselves, the cultural taboos against speaking of childbirth, of mothering—along with several subjects—in truthful, non-sentimental ways, in ways that disturb patriarchal myths . . . that come packaged in a peculiar vagueness that we have yet to penetrate (Bernikow, 1980:44).

Talking to women about our own experiences of everyday life can transcend this denegration and silence, especially as we begin to unravel what we share and what is specific to us—what men would not always notice and what men could not always know from their experience or from their research on our experience. Phenomenologically speaking, such intersubjective shifts have begun to alter the typical situation in which a woman's every description of any experience specific to her as a woman is confronted by the male's own experience, which is defined as "normal." More than this, his experience of how he sees the "norm" is reinforced by the dominant ideology that tells both him and the woman that he is right (Rowbotham, 1973b:35). Such an affirmative approach represents a long-missing and needed complement to the work on "weaknesses-of-women" research, in general, and the disappointment and dissatisfaction with research on the female body in particular. Research from this perspective encourages more realistic and more critical awareness of the adoption of male standards and the simultaneous denial of female standards. It also encourages women researchers to think more carefully about what have been the implications of articulating our ways of knowing, being, and doing through male metaphors. We cannot analyze our life-cycle experiences from the standpoint of any existing methods. What we must do, therefore, is turn to the fundamental biological stages themselves—pregnancy, childbirth, menstruation, menopause—and subject them to analysis from a female perspective. As we have observed, there is no sociology of birth, and yet it is of birth that we must theorize. What this means is that we must not only develop a theory, but we must also develop a feminist perspective and a method of inquiry from which such a theory can emerge. And as feminists have discovered, by holding close to women's experience and by bracketing the powerful patterns male culture has infused into the literature and into our intellect, women can move "from passivity to action, from self as static to self as becoming, from silence to a protesting inner voice" (Belenky *et al.*, 1986:54). This kind of change is central to the interpretive approach taken in the analysis in this chapter.

SUBJECTIVE KNOWLEDGE

The women's movement has led many women to question our role as childbearers, and the results of that questioning have begun to appear. Defining pregnancy and childbirth as topics of research does not imply that they are experiences common to all women. What is implied is that pregnancy and childbirth are visible and communally understood signs of female potency, of the unity of potential and actual. All women carry the consciousness of this unity. Women do not need to bear children to know themselves as women, for women's reproductive consciousness is culturally transmitted (O'Brien, 1981:50).

Everything in a girl's socialization and training has been designed, explicitly or implicitly, in the expectation that she will become a mother, and the chances are great that she will. Although the proportion of young women who say they plan to have no children is increasing, it is still small. Most are going to have at least one child. When we talk about the female world, we are talking about a world in which most adult members have children. One important reason for interpretive research in these areas, then, is to further what we have begun to know about our consciousness and the construction of knowledge. That is, if our reproductive consciousness is to be derived from "our" culture, then it is essential that the sources of what is "true" for women who do experience pregnancy and childbirth be revealed. Thus, to avoid the historical isolation of women that has so obscured our cultural cohesiveness, all women, whether or not they give birth, need to understand, to know, birthing women's relations with their bodies as inner resources for knowing and valuing, their concerns, realizations, hopes and fears, and the ways in which they coordinate their emotions and their relationships. The same result can be gained by sharing knowledge about experiences of menstruation, menopause, and abortion, some of which will also be considered in my analysis. Such research would further Alice Rossi's regarding that of becoming "more attuned to the natural environment, in touch with, and respectful of, the rhythm of our body processes" (Rossi, 1977:15).

If, in fact, feminists hope to dislodge our externally-oriented assumptions about our consciousness in acknowledgement of new conceptions of truth as personal, private, and subjectively known, we need to actively seek knowledge about all female experiences from the view of the subjective knower. It is impossible to reconstruct the varied experiences of millions of women, much less to do so from various perspectives. It is equally impossible to claim that any one woman's experience speaks for all women. Since everyone's subjective experience is unique, no one can speak for others or judge what others say about their experiences. In writing about women's subjective experiences, then, I am admittedly and necessarily skimming the surface of the potential depths of riches they hold, piecing together what I have gleaned from various sources of women's writings on their experiences. What follows is an attempt to move away from the external/public perspective on knowledge to a first-hand/private perspective on experience.

At some time in a woman's personal history, she has experienced events that have propelled her into a reappraisal of her life as a woman; generally, it was the power of those experiences and the "shock" of her appraisal, as well as the phenomenological reflection of these experiences, that led to an experience of self-awakening, a shift in consciousness perhaps, when things no longer appeared the same as they were. Experiences of self-awakening are not frequent and involve a number of difficult obstacles—not only regarding their emergence through reflection—but also as barriers that are intrinsic to the experience themselves. Three in particular are emphasized by Zaner (1970). First, although any experience of self-awakening is strangely compelling, not to say intricate and fascinating at the same time, only in rare instances does the intense immediacy of the experience retain its impact and vividness. Thus, we must rely on our recollection of the experience, a circumstance that introduces the real possibilities of distortion. Even when a sense of its significance remains, distance and other concerns enter in and further obscure the content of the happening. A more serious barrier, according to Zaner, is that the self feels compelled to articulate the experience; yet language resists this effort. Hence it becomes difficult to "find the words" capable of retaining the true sense of what happened. A final barrier, an encounter of further incongruity, occurs between our experience and the context of concerns prevailing in the world of daily life (within which we soon learn to "keep to ourself"). Women's experience of self-awakening, that often leads to and changes our sense of self and the content of our personal relationships and commitments, must first overcome this incongruity. Not only must the study of such experiences take note of such difficulties as these, but it must also "reckon with the subtle and complex dimensions of subjectivity" (Zaner, 1970:176).

The statement of the women's movement—that the personal is political—indicates one barrier between a woman's description of her changed ways of relating to herself and others that she is trying to effect in the here and now, and a society that does not support such change. Expressed in this ferment, women's experience is not just a measure of change but also a sensitive guide to the future. Such barriers notwithstanding, the study of these experiences and disclosures of self is not only possible but positively necessary as part of the process of personal and political change. Feminist research can go further in recovering knowledge of women's experience viewed subjectively. Having accepted that part of the "means" lies within what is already immediately available to us—our consciousness of ourselves as women and feminists within a male culture—is the first step necessary to discover and reveal some aspects of women's experience that have been ignored.

The creative experiences of pregnancy and childbirth are female experiences totally alien to male creative experiences. As Margaret Mead (1949:236) noted several decades ago:

> Women's attitudes towards childbearing and men's attitudes toward childbearing have complex and contradictory elements in them, and . . . a society may pick up and elaborate any one, or sometimes even a contradictory, set of attitudes. And as with all learned, culturally elaborated behavior, the farther away from the biological base, the freer the imagination. There seems some reason to believe that the male imagination, undisciplined and uninformed by immediate bodily clues or immediate bodily experience, may have contributed disproportionately to the cultural superstructure of belief and practice regarding childbearing.

We should not be surprised that discourse on childbirth omits subjectivity, for the specific experience of women has been absent from most of our culture's discourse about human experience and history. While a substantial amount of writing and research has been done on the broad social trends related to childbirth, little had been done until recently on the actual women's experience of birthing. Since most of the literature on childbirth and its aftermath has been written by men (obstetricians) as observers who have reflected upon the experience as if it were their own, the emphasis very obviously has been mostly on its physiological, biological and medical aspects. Also, as Adrienne Rich reminds us:

> It is important to remember that the writers were by no means disinterested and that they were engaged in both a rhetorical and political battle—and that the one groups whose opinion and documentation we long to have—the mothers—are, as usual, almost entirely unheard from (Rich, 1977:19).

Menopause was defined as a deficiency disease by physicians in the 1960s, when synthetic estrogen became widely available and highly recommended to women by physicians. By the mid-1970s feminists agreed that menopause was a normal aging process and that women's health care was a social problem. Frances McCrea (1983) studied how those opposing definitions of menopause evolved and examined the efforts of women to fight off the "stigma" of the disease label. The labels of pregnancy as an illness and menopause as a disease are not neutral. These labels, like any illness or disease, reduce the status and autonomy of the woman-as-patient while increasing the status and power of the physician-as-expert. Phenomenologically, the knowledge comes from the perspective of the dominant group. "True or false the knowledge, disinterested or interested the motives, claims of knowledge function as ideologies . . . and . . . it is highly unlikely that they can remain neutrally descriptive (Freidson, 1971:30). Thus, by cohorting the authority to define the experience, the physician obscures any interpretations of women. How women feel about ourselves largely determines the nature of our experiences. To deny how we feel denies our existence.

It is not only the attitude that our medically and technologically advanced culture has adopted toward these experiences that is important but also what women experience as individuals. Since the subjective meaning one bestows upon certain experiences of one's own spontaneous life necessarily differs from the meaning the observer attaches to them, what appears to the observer objectively to be the same behavior in several persons may have very different meanings or no meaning at all for the behaving subject (Schutz, 1973:210). As such, our experiences remain at a particular level of description that denies women's creativity and projects onto women descriptions not considered in need of further analysis. It also denies the possibility that anticipating, understanding and knowing an experience—*a priori* culturally described and prescribed—may be one thing; it is quite another to experience it. But a change in attention—a "suspension" of established definitions and descriptions—can turn something taken-for-granted into something problematical (Berger and Luckman, 1967:24).

For feminists the lack of description of women's subjective experience of childbirth became a matter of great concern. It is an experience that belongs to a women's stream of consciousness, that is remembered and reproduced by her, and that must be reclaimed and controlled through her reflection and recollection.

> As soon as a woman knows that a child is growing in her body, she falls under the power of theories, ideals, archetypes, descriptions of her new existence, almost none of which have come from other women (though other women may transmit them) and all of which have floated invisibly about her since she first perceived herself to be female and therefore potentially a mother. We need to know what, out of all that welter of image-making and thought-spinning, is worth salvaging, if only to understand better an idea so crucial in history, a condition which has been wrested from the mothers themselves (Rich, 1977:84).

Viewing childbirth as central to our lives, other feminists (Arms, Kitzinger, Rothman, Shaw) are contributing to the rediscovery of women's capacities in birthing that are juxtaposed against conventional interpretations and distortions of pregnancy, childbirth, and lactation as natural functions in which no project is involved. For hundreds of years, women have been denigrated so completely that we have not thought our knowledge of our experience special enough to bring to the level of consciousness. In the last hundred years, waves of feminism have occurred as women have adopted male individuation as a way to fuller personhood. Now, there is a new movement of women trying to find out who in fact we really are.

UNIQUENESS OF EXPERIENCE

In reclaiming her interpretation and meaning, a woman need not reject the necessity and the significant contributions of medical technology. Recognition of the importance and value of technology and services provided to some women by physicians does not necessarily eliminate an examination of the particular nature of the immediate antagonisms and contradictory tendencies that they generate. For the barriers that confront birthing women are real, not merely the conjurings of our imagination.

Like oppression in other phases of life's experience, oppression in childbirth and menopause is a social and historical experience. Its forms and expressions have changed as the advances in medicine and the relationship between women and men have changed. Women who were disadvantaged by lack of knowledge in dealing with their bodies, for example, are now demanding the choice of whether to birth or not birth, where to birth, who shall attend, and by what means they will be assisted.

> For in order to create an alternative, an oppressed group must at once shatter the self-reflecting world which encircles it and, at the same time, project its own image onto history. In order to discover its own identity as distinct from that of the oppressor, it has to become visible to itself (Rowbotham, 1973b:27).

The medical behavioral aspects of childbirth and menopause have been studied almost exclusively from a clinical rather than a sociological perspective, with the consequence that emphasis has been limited to women's physical condition—to determine either the presence or absence of pathology—rather than on social roles, social relationships, and patterns of social interaction. There are physiological considerations. But as bodily experiences unique to women, they cannot be judged on merits based on comparisons with male experiences; there is no way to assign them on the basis of the relative qualifications of men and women. For example, although a man's writing a novel restricts his leisure, his decision to pursue the project in the first place was his free choice. The man writing the novel can also choose to set it aside and return to it another time, or abandon it completely. The project is predominantly an intellectual endeavor. Although the man's body is involved in its creation, the novel's completion is not determined within his body, nor is it dependent on another human being for its beginning or its completion, nor binding to his life in terms of commitment. The same is true in relation to the writing of this book.

Once pregnant, a woman who has made a commitment to follow through with her pregnancy may not so easily terminate, interrupt, or for that matter "forget" about her pregnancy; there are changes that serve as constant "reminders" to her of her project, and there is always the potentiality of physical damage to herself or to the foetus. Also, for the most part, a woman is dependent upon another human being for her creative activity as childbearer, and as a consequence of this activity will have another human being dependent on her. In other words, female consciousness knows that a child will be born, knows what a child is, and speculates in general terms about this child's potential. Yet pregnant women and novelists are quite different. The woman cannot realize her visions, cannot make them come true, by virtue of the labor in which she involuntarily engages, if at all. Unlike the novelist, her will does not influence the shape of her product. Like the novelist she knows what she is doing; unlike the novelist she cannot help what she is doing. This aspect of women's experience exposes the deep inadequacies of the interpretations of experience as a description of women's reality. A woman does not (cannot) "produce" another human being in anything like the way a person produces a novel. The development of a foetus, the birthing of a baby, the gradual relinquishing (surrender) of control, and the experience of the human limits of and limitations on human actions are fundamental characteristics of childbirth (and later child care) experienced exclusively by women.

Women's own body, not only nature, is an available ground of being that is in this way fuller than the masculine sense of body seems to be. A woman's body is rooted to cosmic reality in a way the male body is not. To have a child is a much more significant experience for a woman; she has a lot more to lose. Rich (1977) argues that the medical management of childbirth has "separated" us from our bodies by depriving us of a power that would otherwise be ours. She criticizes modern obstetrics for preventing women from "knowing and coming to terms with our bodies." Similarly, Rossi (1977) criticizes the medical profession for interfering with the natural relation of women to our bodies, for interfering with the "natural" process of birthing.

Throughout history, male writers and thinkers have socially and medically defined childbirth as formally much closer to what happens in male reproductive experience, despite the fact that the books are intended for women (O'Brien, 1981). For example, physicians analyze and predict sequences of pregnancy, labor, and delivery as types, with their technological means/ends relations and their particular motivations. The segment of the female population that appears in the hospital during childbirth becomes the object of scientific study that constitutes data for the construction of "ideal-patient types." Also, by looking at "products' (birth rates, population growth, annual statistics of hospital births) as "objective" science, the subjective activity of birthing women is not referred back to. The danger is that these ideal types or typolgies are not considered as abstractions but as absolutes. As "unexamined myths," they maintain a "subterranean potency": they affect women's thinking in ways we are not aware of, and thus undermine our capacity to resist their influence (Keller, 1983:87).

Part of "claiming reality" of female bodily experience, then, is to study and peel off masculine phantasies that distort women's sense of our bodies and how we experience them. This activity is in the sphere of mundane apperception, that particular process of understanding by which newly observed qualities of an event are related to past experience. Thus the methods and interpretations available to feminist sociologists may be derived from a far-reaching investigation of a constitutive phenomenology of the natural attitude.

CHAPTER 7

Phenomenological Reflection on Women's Experience

MEANING OF ACTION

IT HAS BEEN NOTED that women had been left out of most phenomenological scholarship; that the standard approaches to the study of phenomenology made more than token inclusion of women's perspective difficult; and that phenomenological sociology would have to undergo serious rethinking if it were to be applied to feminist research. What follows, then, is a consideration of the specific ways that phenomenological sociology can address the concerns and questions pertaining to women's everyday-life experience, in this case the experiences primarily of childbirth and menopause.

If women are to do more than perform roles assumed by a particular culture to be our obligation as women, we must first establish distance from those roles, reflect upon them, and then decide whether or not they are our own; for social roles are not merely social consequences of biologically determined reproductive differences between women and men. My analysis starts here, where I choose from all the interpretive schemes in the story of past experience the one that is relevant to the problem.

As a starting point of reflection, established theories and all traditional prejudiced and "metaphysical" views are suspended in order to gain access to pure and primordial experience in which the "things themselves" appeared to me in a genuinely original way (Kockelmans, 1967:225). A special motivation—a special condition of interest demanding a transition from a naive attitude to a reflection of a higher order—is needed in order to induce me, the naive person, to question the structure of my lifeworld. To make up my mind to observe scientifically this lifeworld means no longer to determine to place myself and my own condition of interest as the center of this world, but to substitute another null point for the orientation of the phenomena of the lifeworld (Kockelmans, 1967). This null point and how it came to be constituted as a type, the phenomenology of childbirth, depends upon the particular chosen problem-situations that I chose—women's demand for control over their lives, women's interpretation of bodily experiences rather than the meaning others— physicians, nurses, society in general—have attributed to it.

A woman decides that she wants to have a baby, and she becomes pregnant. For her, making love in order to become pregnant becomes the purposive action leading to the act of birth. For the purpose of this analysis, we will consider the decision to follow through with the pregnancy.

First, there is the process of deliberation. According to Dewey (1922:179), a deliberation is "the dramatic rehearsal in imagination of various competing lines of action." Phenomenologically, such action is "covert action": an attempt to solve a problem mentally. Such action tried out in imagination is neither fatal nor final; it is retrievable. In the process of deliberation, each habit and each impulse involved in the temporary suspension of overt action takes its turn in being tried out. At this point, we could say that my deliberation had ceased and that a choice, a decision had been made; I had decided not to become pregnant. My choice was what I really wanted, what was "an emergence of a unified preference out of competing preferences" (Dewey, 1922:181).

A few years later, as I reflected upon the phantasy, the idea of pregnancy turned into a real possibility that touched me at that very moment (Wild, 1965:69). I was able to picture the alternations that would take place in my life and, in imagining that I would carry out my project, I had hit upon an object that furnished adequate stimulus to the recovery of covert action. I, in fact, had chosen to become pregnant, a choice which was not possible until I felt no annoying hindrance, repulsion, or dissatisfaction from the consequence of my action in the future. It is the outcome of the action that was anticipated in my projection: that I will have become pregnant and that I will have given birth. In order to project my future action as it will have progressed, I had to place myself, in my phantasy, into a future time—that is, into a time when the projected action will have been accomplished. What was thus imagined in the future was not the future action, but the intended act as already accomplished and it was imagined in the Future Perfect Tense, *modo futuri exacti* (Schutz, 1973:69) and determined by the "because motive".

The events of pregnancy and childbirth became congruent to me in the present, as I imagined they would be in the future. What is implied is that the projected action, its ends and its means, remained compatible and consistent with these typical elements of the situation in accordance with my knowledge at hand at the time of projecting. The simplist complex of meaning in terms of which this action was interpreted by me was its motive. The motive for me to become pregnant was an "in-order-to-motive" (Schutz, 1973), for it will have become the end for which the action to bring it about will have been undertaken. In-order-to motives refer to the future; to the state of affairs to be brought about by future action. They are identical with the object or purpose for the realization of which the action itself is a means. Thus the action of my pregnancy was determined by the project including the in-order-to motive, the idea of the setting various reactions in motion in the present. Some of these shared the passive character of waiting, others aimed at actively preparing for the future. I did not, however, merely wish for something to happen. Rather, I engaged in its active counterpart, in considering steps to make it happen. The in-order-to motive, then, influenced the decision of starting to act, starting to bring about the action. Sexual intercourse, for example, had not been associated previously by me or by my husband with a wish or an intention for pregnancy. But once the decision had been made, there supervened in this intimate aspect of our relationship the intention to carry out the project, to bring about conception. The activity of carrying out the intention did not entail the notion of sheer "mechanism"; for within the project itself there was room for spontaneous expression. Also, if a woman and a man frequently make love to each other, the exact moment of conception, or the particular occasion when it occurred is rarely known. Hence, the intention may continue to present itself even if the goal, albeit unknowing, has been reached.

People acting rationally must also make the judgment as to the means, the action, for achieving their goals. Schutz distinguishes conscious from unconscious action.

> An action is conscious in the sense that, before we carry it out, we have a picture in our mind of what we are going to do; it is unconscious when we do not retain nor continue to reproduce the picture (1967:63).

Then as we proceed to action, we consult our life-plans to the extent that we have mapped them out, allowing the flexibility which the performance of our activity implies; or we retain the act pictured as completed in the future. Nothing else constitutes for the actor the unit of her act other than the "span of her project" that includes also the actor's consistent life-plans as far as the concrete future state of affairs to be realized by the projected action is concerned. The latter has its more well- or less well-defined position within these life-plans; more or less well defined.

First of all, the whole system of life-plans, although at every moment consistent with itself, necessarily changes with the transition of the actor's self from one moment of his [or her] inner life to another . . . Secondly, the system of life-plans is only partially known to the actor in full explicitness and is only partially caught by the ray of actual attention and thereby rendered relevant. Both together constitute the explicable though not explicate background against which the projected concrete act stands out. And . . . it is the span of the project, thus determined, which for its part creates the unity of the act (Wagner, 1976:41–42).

I had a picture in my mind of what I was going to do before I did it— my "projected" act. My thought was directed at the act as being fulfilled in the future, and "only if the future act is thus assumed or posited can the means be selected" (Schutz, 1973:61).

The unity of the action was constituted by the fact that the act, already existing in projection, in phantasy, would be realized step by step through the action. The phantasy in projection was a real lived experience that could be reflected upon. Even though it still remained abstract as a new possibility, the phantasy drew me away from my established life. As I reflected upon the phantasy, I saw it contract into a real possibility. My apprehension of this possibility became illuminated by a consideration of what ought to be. My situation was first understood in terms of two physical states: not pregnant and not yet pregnant. In the second state, a possibility existed that could negate and radically transform the first state. I apprehended certain features of social reality as unacceptable as each state appeared in imagination, and I chose in favor of a transforming project for the future. As I conceptualized a different state of affairs, new considerations came into my grasp. When the new possibility, that of "having a baby" became accepted, it called for specific action.

But all this is open only to me as the actor; it remains beyond the observer's control and evey beyond her approach. For the observer has no other access to my action but the acts once accomplished. What the observer can observe are only segments of my performed activity. If she were to describe what happened in my mind in performing the action, she would have to enter into the whole process of my stream of thought with the whole history of my personality, with all my subjective life-plans, with all my experiences, and with all my anticipations and expectations of future states of affairs. To be able to do so, the observer would have to run through all stages of her inner life in the same succession and at the same pace and experiencing it in the same fulness as I did. That means that the observer would have to be one and the same with the observed. Thus, for the observer, the unity of my act, its beginning and its end, is no longer identifiable with the span of the actor's project; it is defined by the segment of the actor's activity the observer has selected as the object of her consideration. The observer then decides whether my observed action must be integrated as accomplished or as part of a work in progress. The observer, on the contrary, decided whether the observed action must be interpreted as accomplished or as part of a greater work in progress. For her, then, the unity of the act, its beginning and its end, is no longer identifiable with the span of the actor's project; it is defined by the segment of the actor's activity the observer has selected as the object of her consideration. In this manner, the term "unit-act" located in subjectivity, assumes quite a different meaning if it is interpreted from the objective point of view. "By no means can we speak of the unity of action from the subjective point of view and accept at the same time the supposition that the limits of the unit are constituted or demarcated by the observer" (Wagner, 1976:42).

The phenomenological meaning of "working" is action geared into the outer world based upon a project and characterized by the intention to bring about the projected state of affairs by bodily movements. It differs from mere thinking. Mere mental actions are revocable; if our anticipations are not fulfilled by the outcome, as when we are dissatisfied with the result, the whole process of mental operations may begin again. Such was the case when I first considered the idea of pregnancy, rejected it, and then entertained it again at a later point. Working, not only within but upon the world, modified by my actions—my becoming pregnant—changed the outer world (of which my body was a part). Although my husband and I were relying on the knowledge of what was possible with a certain probability, it was not merely a question of physical conception, but of whether together we would be able to make more certain that what we had decided we wanted to happen would, in fact, happen.

Before this work had been carried through in the outer world, it was still open to modifications. Once I had changed the outer world by my actions, I might have restored my initial state of affairs, my state of non-pregnancy, by a countermove such as abortion, but *I could not make undone what I had done.* My reflective act of attention to an action phantasized as over and done with preceded the action itself—my becoming pregnant; and action based upon a preconceived project and referenced to the preceding project make both the acting and the act meaningful (Schutz, 1973:216). Thus when I projected my action in imagination—my becoming pregnant—I was rehearsing future conduct (my projected act) as that that will have been completed. I was also anticipating the future outcome of my conduct—an act, childbirth—that was also projected into the future as having been completed. Thus, phenomenologically speaking, my action at this point may be defined as conscious or purposive, for it had a goal of optimum clarity—I had a picture in my mind of what I was going to do before I did it. And as my action proceeded, I consulted that which I had "mapped out," projected rational action that had been planned some time in advance, the goals of which—in terms of the means, the ends, and the secondary results—had been clearly anticipated.

THE LIVED-BODY

The dominant culture defines feminine beauty as shapely and slim. To the degree that a woman derives a sense of self-worth from looking "sexy" in the manner promoted by dominant cultural images, she may experience her body as ugly and alien. On the other hand, or at the same time, the pregnant woman may experience a heightened sense of her own sexuality. Also, whereas our society often devalues and trivializes women, regards women as weak and delicate, the pregnant woman may gain a certain sense of self-respect (Young, 1984).

> This bulk slows my walking and makes my gestures and my mind more stately. I suppose if I schooled myself to walk massively the rest of my life, I might always have massive thoughts (Lewis, 1950:83 in Young, 1984:52).

On the other hand, if a culture defines pregnancy as a vulnerable, fragile, or even polluting, a woman may feel anxious, isolated, or undesirable. In our society, it has been shown that men's attitudes toward pregnant women are often filled with conflict. Not infrequently, men living with pregnant women feel competitive and will become particularly active in creating something themselves. Most societies have sets of rules and beliefs that dictate how a woman ought to feel and act during pregnancy. In many societies, pregnancy involves numerous taboos such as prohibitions on certain foods. Finally, in a society that still too often narrows women's cultural roles to motherhood and the producer of heirs, the pregnant woman often finds herself looked at with approval.

> As soon as I was visibly and clearly pregnant, I felt, for the first time in my adolescent and adult life, not-guilty. The atmosphere of approval in which I was bathed—even by strangers in the street, it seemed—was like an aura I carried with me, in which doubts, fears, misgivings, met with absolute denial. This is what women have always done (Rich, 1976:6 in Young, 1984:53).

By about the fourth month of my pregnancy I felt an increased sensuality, a radiance being projected from myself, and a sense of uniqueness—that I had become special. I thought about the fact that there were more nonpregnant women in the world than pregnant women, and that I, as a pregnant woman, "stood out" among other women. This feeling was, however, of short duration. I soon became overwhelmed with another thought: all people whom I encountered had been born of mothers. My mother had been born of a mother and so had her sister, and my father and my husband and his mother. I had always thought that birth and death were common experiences to all human beings, but I had never thought in terms of everyone having been born from the bodies of pregnant women, bodies just like mine. I began to feel a greater connection between myself and women in my everyday life. And as I continued to think about "special," I no longer related it to myself; but there was a growing sense of the extraordinary of all women whenever I thought about the women who had birthed humanity.

I became convinced that talking about my pregnancy would make the experience more positive for me and at that point my life began to change. I went out of my way to speak to woman who had birthed—recently, within a year, or several years ago. I learned what other women experienced and felt about their pregnancies and the births of their babies. I became fascinated at discovering that other women were fascinated, too; and they were always willing to talk about their experiences in great detail, often commenting on how vividly (to their surprise) they recall their experience, especially since they hadn't talked or thought about it for some time. I remember one woman in particular; I had ordered some take-out food in celebration of the acceptance of a paper for journal publication that I had written on childbirth. She owned the catering/take-out business and claimed that what had allowed her to go into business for herself was what she had learned about herself during her childbirth experience. That had been a new awareness of her self—her strength, her courage, and her sense of having overcome—a seeing and a coming-to-know of her self that she didn't even realize she had until then, twelve years before.

The experience of thinking about myself in relation to other birthing women, to other women, and to men was a self-presentedness to myself. On the one hand, I am discovered to myself-my self is at the same time the discoverer, the discovered, and discovering, and experienced itself as such. What happened was the unfolding of my self in its reflexivity. My self, in short, recognized itself; what was revealed was "what I am." I recognized me as myself, as having been me all along, although I did not notice it until then.

One aspect of pregnancy that has not been emphasized in the literature on childbirth is that of the foetal movements, which served as a stimulus for my conduct. For example, although the shifts in my body weight, the nausea, and other physical manifestations of pregnancy enhanced my awareness of their having been caused by another, my response was not only a bodily one. I could not, for example, control the enlargement of my abdomen or breasts; they were responding to the foetal needs independent of my will. But the uninhibited foetal bodily movements of which I was aware served as stimulae for my activity as well as a response to my activity. In other words, some of my intentional bodily movements were responses to the foetal movements that I felt, and some of the foetal movements appeared to be responses to my bodily movements. For example, when my body remained at rest—standing, seated, reclined—I frequently felt the shifting or turning activity of the foetus within my body. I was also able to observe the movement of a foetal limb protruding at the surface of my abdomen, and moving across it or from an upper corner diagonally to a lower corner. Often if my body had been active, the foetus responded with activity. The point to be made is that I felt that this mutual reacting to and upon each other through these early movements served to familiarize and prepare me (and possibly the foetus) for the other's reactions. Whether the foetal activity be regarded as actions and reactions that, according to George Herbert Mead, might have arisen under the stimulation of the bodily movements of each—or might have been the outflows of "nervous energy"—they, too, served as a stimulation to my appropriate reaction. That is, whenever I felt the foetal movement, I felt inclined to pause and feel it to its completion.

Iris Young speaks of her reflection of the experience of pregnancy revealing a body subjectivity that is decentered, herself in the mode of not being herself:

> As my pregnancy begins, I experience it as a change in my body. I become different from what I have been. My nipples become reddened and tender, my belly swells into a pear. I feel this elastic around my waist, itching, this round, hard middle replacing the doughy belly with which I still identify. Then I feel a little tickle, a little gurgle in my belly, it is my feeling, my insides, and it feels somewhat like a gas bubble, but it is not, it is different, in another place, belonging to another, another that is nevertheless my body (Young, 1984:48) . . . I feel myself touched and touching simultaneously, both on my knee and my belly. The belly is other, since I did not expect it there, but since I feel the touch upon it, it is me (cf. Strauss, 1963:370).

Adrienne Rich also describes a different sensation:

> Nor, in pregnancy, did I experience the embryo as decisively internal in Freud's terms, but rather, as something inside and of me, yet becoming hourly and daily more separate, on its way to becoming separate from me and of-itself. In early pregnancy the stirring of the foetus felt like soft

tremors of my own body, later like the movements of a being impris-
oned in me; but both sensations were *my* sensations, contributing to my
own sense of physical and psychic space.

Without doubt, in certain situations the child in one's body can only feel
like a foreign body introduced from without; an alien (Rich, 1977: 47–
48).

This part of the discussion might be one area that will enable male
readers to come closer to understanding how a woman's experience
of "self-in body" differs from a man's experience of it. It has been my
notion that the male representation of self-in-body has been likened
to the driver in the driver's seat. It is true that he does the driving and
can choose the direction and destination. The body retains a some-
what fixed position except as manipulated and directed by the driver.
Yet, although a woman may manipulate and direct a foetus—albeit to
a limited degree—she also becomes the one manipulated and directed
from the other wihin.[22]

Phenomenology argues against any reductionist tendency that
would reduce all explanations about the body to explanations of
physical phenomena; that the human body cannot merely be understood as another thing in nature or an object among physical objects
such as trees, stones, stars for the reason that the body of a persons is
that from which and the means of which all such natural objects are
experienced (Stewart and Mickunas, 1974:96).

Although phenomenologically one can never view his or her lived-
body as another object due to the fact that the lived-body is the
necessary condition for any experience whatsoever, thus constituting
an irreducible standpoint for any natural experience, if the lived-body
is also the means by which consciousness experiences the world, how
might my body as the lived-body be understood in relation to the
project being described? And how might the foetal body be interpreted? It would appear that the body, which one lives and the body
which one encounters, is in relation to a body living within it,
encountering itself and the other.

There existed a relationship between my lived-body and the foetal
lived-body that made me aware of the other to the degree that my
awareness of the other was correlated with my experience of that
other's body, and that other's experience of my body. And just as my
lived-body is my only access to the world—not considering the world
apart from the perspective offered by my body—so, too, is my lived-
body the foetal body's access to the world as well as the foetal body in
its analogy to myself, my access to the world. Accompanying the
changes in my body there appeared a consciousness of my pregnancy. I experienced a particular "entity"—a changing body in size,

shape, color, radiance, and so on. All of these were unified in experience in such a way as to account for my perception of an object, a foetus, for without it there would be no pregnancy. Also, I experienced this object as the same object through a series of perspectives that occurred in a succession of time.

Young also speaks of pregnant consciousness as

> animated by a double intentionality: my subjectivity splits between my awareness of myself as body and awareness of my aims and projects. To be sure, even in pregnancy there are times when I am so absorbed in my activity, that I do not feel myself as body; but when I move or feel the look of another I am likely to be recalled to the thickness of my body. (1984:48, 50, 51).

In Demetrakopoulos's discussion of the spiritual experience that women derive from the "great experiences" of our bodies—menstruation, childbirth, and breastfeeding, she notes of pregnancy:

> Probably it is difficult to experience the individuality of the foetus during a first pregnancy, but during later pregnancies many mothers know through foetal movement, rhythms, and sometimes a kind of telepathy, what sort of person they are going to birth. Women have been forced to repress this knowledge by a culture that in its masculine orientation prefers to see pregnancy as purely physical and mechanistic (1983:27).

MODES OF UNDERSTANDING

In contrast, from a medical point of view a pregnant woman may be regarded as one who is "ill." The pregnant woman may regard herself or be regarded by others as a person who is "normal," experiencing a normal life interlude. The controversy lies both in the medical as well as in the social implications of pregnancy and childbirth. It may be viewed as a social role that may be attached to the status of the pregnant woman. The concept of role is one important means for the development of a solid structure for an understanding of the behavior surrounding pregnancy and illness. As Irving Zola points out,

> by the very acceptance of a specific behavior as an "illness" and the definition of illness as an undesirable state, the issue becomes not *whether* to deal with a particular problem but *how* and *when*. Thus the debate over . . . [pregnancy as illness] . . . becomes focussed on the degree of sickness attached to the phenomenon in question or the extent of health risk involved. And the more principled, more perplexing, or even moral issue of *what* freedom should an individual have over [her] own body is shunted aside (1972:19).

Eliot Freidson presents a fairly refined delineation of the "sick" role based on his definition of illness:

if the label of illness can be attached to a "problem" it receives extensive support and also becomes dominated by medical institutions even when there is no evidence that medical institutions have any especially efficacious way of dealing with the problem (1970:149).

Treating pregnancy as an illness or disease can also produce alienation for the pregnant woman because she often has a bodily self-image of strength and sometimes an increased immunity to common diseases such as colds and flu (Young, 1984). While her body may signal one set of impressions, however, her entrance into the definitions of medicine may lead to the opposite understanding. First, being sick implies deviance but is distinguished from other deviant roles by the fact that the sick person is not considered "responsible" for the condition. With the current acceptance and disposition of contraception, legalized abortion, and in-utero fertilization, however, the possibility that pregnant women make conscious decisions about their pregnancies has increased. Yet the fact that pregnancy does not merely "happen" to a woman, but rather, may result from motivated interaction is precisely what constitutes the pregnant woman's condition as an illness and not a "natural phenomenon . . . like the vagaries of the weather" (Parsons, 1951:430). So what might be regarded as private and personal by the woman becomes redefined in the public sphere as illness, even though neither the pregnant woman nor the expectant father (for it then could be concluded that he contributed to her illness) regard it as such.

Women are encouraged by our culture to enact a similar role during menopause. Male physicians have written, until recently, almost all the books on menopause; and they are the ones who have defined it through an array of symptoms. While physicians put a great deal of emphasis on changes in menstrual experience in the years just before the expected onset of menopause, they do little to learn the nature of specifically menopausal symptoms from women. In the absence of concrete information, it is not surprising that the worst experiences have taken precedence over the commonplace but less dramatic experience of the majority. This justifies to physicians the necessity for attaching to menopause the label of "illness" that, of course, requires medical "treatment." That reality has meaning for men and certainly for women, for if we are viewed negatively, we respond to that. The stages of women's life cycles are made to appear as a neat unilinear affair going on in women's bodies. We claim that is not enough and that part of reclaiming the female body is to study and dissolve masculine phantasies that have distorted women's sense of our bodies. McCrea notes a similar situation between the menopausal woman and the physician:

By individualizing the problems of menopause, the physician turns attention away from any social structural interpretation of women's conditions. The locus of the solution then becomes the doctor-patient interaction in which the physician is active, instrumental, and authoritative while the patient is passive and dependent. The inherent authority of physicians is institutionalized in ways that minimize reliance on explanation and persuasion (McCrea, 1983:113).

The intervention of the physician must be considered an effort to control an dominate the birth process.

The doctor is director—he makes all the important decisions in the delivery room. This practice is supported legally and institutionally. The doctor decides the kind of anaesthesia to be used, the amount of and kind of drugs, the timing for the birth, the use or not of forceps. (Shaw, 1974:85).

The control of obstetrics by male physicians has also come to mean the power to determine what care one should get, as well as to evaluate what one has received. Male professional dominance, then, is one analytical key to women's discouragement and dissatisfaction with their experience; for,

the factors leading to self-determination by women facing childbirth are, in the first place, those which prevent the excessive dominance of any other person or institution outside the woman or her control (Shaw, 1974:144).

It has been a persistent part of male professional ideology to insist that no matter how knowledgeable women are, we are incapable of reliable judgment. In some cases, the physician's advice is accepted because it happens to coincide with what the woman expects or desires, whether or not the grounds for her expectations are the same as those of the physician. In other cases, the woman becomes persuaded in the course of her interaction with the physician that his advice is in her best interest, whether or not it happens to conform with what she initially believed she needed. "But here the danger is greater, for not only is the process masked as a technical, scientific objective, but one done for her own good" (Zola, 1972:21). In general, the alternative desire and the one often demanded by the medical profession is that birthing women obey and remain passive and not contradict the physician's authority. Insistence on obedience and passivity constitute other instances of the woman giving up her role as an independent and responsible adult, the effect of which is aggrandisement for the physician and alienation for the woman.

In addition, one of the basic conditions and traditions of obstetrics is the social distance in the doctor-patient relation, which serves to maintain the physician's aloofness, dignity and status vis-a-vis the lay patient. In his theoretical analysis of the doctor-patient relationship, Friedson points out that a requisite for the maintenance of the professional self-image and, therefore, professional behavior toward patients, is the maintenance of an effectively neutral orientation toward the patient. The birthing woman, then, must be regarded as a medical or clinical phenomenon, rather than as a person, in order for the physician to behave as a professional. Dacia Maraini (1979:691) speaks of Adrienne Rich's (1979) tracing of the history of the relationships between birthing women and physicians:

> Was hospital delivery truly useful, functional, and progressive? What about the losses in human solidarity, emotional participation, and psychological security in the brutal passage from "hands of flesh" to those of "iron?" One thing is certain—and women know it even if they cannot always express it with ideological precision—the great rhetoric about motherhood functions, above all, to hide the process of reification of the female body which is necessary for the appropriation of human reproduction by the patriarchy. Laughably, this forced renunciation by a woman of her own needs is portrayed as a "free choice"; the myths function even if they are cruel. The mother, with her flowery cradle, her little layette, her lullabies, her anxious and unselfish love, believes she is having a baby for herself, and instead she is having it for others.

The perspective of birth mothers who protested to physicians after their birth experiences is reflected in the following comments:

(B.D.)   What a joy it was to have a daughter! . . . Yet, something was not quite right. Some sadness and regret tinged my joy, and I couldn't dispel those feelings . . . Now I feel compelled to express my feelings to you . . . I felt robbed at Sharon's birth. Cheated. Manipulated. Ripped off. Something terribly important was missing, and I felt its loss. At first, I couldn't explain what was gone, but suddenly I knew: it was *me* . . . There I was, laboring to birth my first child, awed by the miracle of life within me . . . I felt soaring pride in us [my husband and me], and I felt amazed by my own strength. But then, suddenly, when labor speeded up and birth seemed close, you took over. *You took over* . . . You took away my right to give birth and gave me instead a delivery. You took away my autonomy, my sense that I was birthing my child . . . I was forced to lie passively and uncomfortably, to push at your command . . . You told me to relax, that you'd take care of everything . . . Well, *I* wanted to take care of everything. And then, when my uphill pushing wasn't effective [lying on my back], you sliced open my perieneum so you could deliver my baby.

(L.P.)   You have taken such a "holier-than-thou" attitude about your technical capabilities and have failed to look at the humanistic side of things . . . I feel that my case was mismanaged . . . Needless to say, I was devasted when I came out of the anaesthesia.

(D.K.) Instead of letting me go with the contractions and push like my entire body was doing, you made me hold my legs together and you said, "Don't push, we're not ready yet." My baby and I were ready! I had to fight against all the natural responses of my body so the anaesthesiologist could put a needle in my spine . . . When I moaned because it was so difficult *not* to push I heard you say, "See I told you natural childbirth was painful; the spinal will take effect soon." You were right. Very soon I felt nothing (Panuthos, 1984:57–59).

The use of instruments and technological intervention—foetal heart monitor, sonogram—objectifies pregnancy and alienates birthing women because they negate our own experience of those processes. As the previous section described, phenomenologically, the pregnant women had a unique knowledge of their bodily processes and the life of the foetus. They felt the movements of the foetus with an immediacy and certainty. Reliance on recently-invented machines encourages medical practitioners to objectify this knowledge as well as to devalue women's own experience in favor of more "objective" information. When obstetrical medication or mechanical devices interfere with her project, the woman's actions become unintentional. Absorbed by the bureaucratic and technological management of the hospital organization, she becomes uninvolved and cannot identify with her state of being and her action. She is no longer in control of her action; she is reduced to the status of object, a mass of organs and pathology, while the machines and equipment involved in her labor and delivery take on human attributes.

(Anonymous) The doctor arrived—I had never met him before. He inserted a fetal monitor and then he got a heartbeat. It was slow for a baby. Later, they realized it was mine (Panuthos, 1984:162).

Since pregnancy and childbirth are not diseases or disorders from the point of view of women, the intervention of the physician may be regarded as an effort to control and dominate the birth process.

The doctor is director—he makes all the important decisions in the delivery room. This practice is supported legally and institutionally. The doctor decides the kinds of anaesthesia to be used, the amount of and kind of drugs, the timing for the birth, the use or not of forceps (Shaw, 1974:85).

Birthing women's behavior within the doctor-patient relationship, of course, was structured long before the woman's encounter with a physician during her pregnancy. Her "training" for submission oc-

curred throughout her socialization. Thus, we see in this relationship
further evidence of women's point of view devalued.

> When a woman goes to her obstetrician she encounters his ideas about
> attitudes and behavior appropriate to a female patient. The relation
> between doctor and patient is basically an asymmetrical one, and he is
> the dominant partner. So his view of her role, both as patient and as
> mother, forms the basis of their interaction. Her preconceptions about
> what doctors are like and how they behave operate in the transaction
> too, but are expressed less often (Kitzinger, 1978:116).

While both the physician and the pregnant woman have come
together with a specific end in mind, each has a different perspective
as well as the means of managing it and controlling it. If the description of the lived-body experience of pregnancy in the previous section
is valid, pregnancy and childbirth entail a unique body subjectivity
with which it is difficult to empathize unless one is or has been
pregnant. The rational technique of physicians is consciously and
systematically oriented to the experience which for them consists in
scientific knowledge and technical skill. For them, the meaning of an
act lies in its technical result, and the means applied to this area are
their "techniques"—medication, forceps, monitors.

It is not merely a difference in perspective that enters into the
relation between the physician and the birthing woman but also a
difference in what is brought to that perspective. Most physicians
believe more fully in their scientific expertise and technological skills
than in the natural process of birth, and are more likely to reach for
forceps than wait for even the slightest complications to correct
themselves. The physician is trained and expected to act, not merely
to be a passive observer of what goes on. "It is very difficult for a
person trained in technical know-how to do technically nothing
during a normal birth" (Arms, 1973:55). Also, the same educational
process that teaches women to wait, watch, be compliant and submis-
sive, trains men to act, intervene, and initiate. The male physician
cannot be expected to do otherwise—particularly when confronted
with "turning sloppy old nature into a clean safe science" (Arms,
1973:53). Another explanation suggests:

> Perhaps it is the combination of the medical perspective, a man's
> inability to experience labor and his consequent awe of it, and the
> hospital setting—a location for experiencing and overcoming bodily
> crisis—that produces this perspective and action (Arms, 1973:115).

Thus the physician's abstract knowledge leads him to prescribe a
treatment that seems to the woman to have no direct connection with
what she is experiencing. What becomes relevant to the physician is
that which bears on the achievement of *his* particular outcome. And

the woman, by definition as a "patient," must either be persuaded to accept the physician's ministrations or be placed in a position where she has nothing to say about *her* particular outcome. Physicians need patients to carry out their work and must convince a birthing woman that she needs a physician to carry out hers. In either case, she is not likely to be self-directing, for she cannot control any production and particularly any application of knowledge and skill in the work she is performing through her body even if it is not the first time. Her work cannot be completely autonomous because the physician and the hospital staff can legitimately criticize and otherwise evaluate her performance, as well as assume the credit for whatever work she does. As one obstetrician admits:

> We obstetricians are so clever with our tools and gadgets that we have rewritten the obstetrical drama in such a way as to make us the stars instead of the women. We even accept the congratulations of husbands and then wonder why women are resentful of men (Arms, 1975:88).

After assisting a birthing woman who refused medication in the hospital, another obstetrician exclaimed:

> Well, no stitches, no problems. Three minutes. That's the quickest one I've done yet! (Arms, 1973:202).

L. R. Willmuth (1975) interviewed couples to discover what factors made them feel most positive about their birth experiences. Feeling of autonomy and a sense of control were isolated as being most important. These factors are among those that have frustrated and angered birth women over the medical management of childbirth in traditional hospital settings. In addition to demands for control and autonomy, the need for individual, private control of our birthing within a supportive communal setting have led to a gradual drift away from the resistance to standard hospital routine in favor of birthing at home or in those hospitals or maternity centers where midwives or nurse-midwives assist (Arms, 1973; Levesque, 1981; Rothman, 1979, 1982, 1984; Shaw, 1974).

(L.L.) There isn't one thing about her birth that I would change—except maybe to have shared it with a few more good friends of mine . . . For a while I chose to labor in a warm bath and that was great . . . The hot compresses to the perineum and the massage with vitamin E oil were both soothing and so helpful to the stretching process needed for birthing. I had it all [at home] (Panuthos, 1984:61).

(H.S.) Childbirth is a very sensitive time for me; I am preparing to take care of this tiny, fragile person coming into the world, completely dependent on me and on her father. So, I want to be treated gently, not like an object. In the hospital I never got the feeling that anybody except Ray [my husband] was concerned about me. The way they scrub at you and get you ready—as though you have no feelings whatsoever. Everything went just as smoothly at home without all that prepping. In the hospital they made me feel afraid I was going to contaminate my own baby (Ward and Ward, 1976:92).

CENTRALITY OF EXPERIENCE

For many women, how the baby is born is extremely important. Even the birthing woman who recognizes her capabilities in childbirth may not be able to count on encouragement and fair treatment in the hospital setting. She may, in fact, face a difficult decision in weighing whether to enter a setting that almost inevitably will involve her in a conflict with traditional images of her place in society, and, perhaps, with her own images of personal fulfillment. Once past the initial barriers, she may be forced repeatedly to review her decision as she faces successive conflicts between her personal life and her professional care. This indicates further recognition by women that aspects of our seemingly individual and personal life remain embedded in and deeply affected by social institutions that are independent of our immediate control. Thus, it is not difficult to understand why a pregnant woman can feel that she is merely a container for a foetus, the development and safe delivery of which is under the control of obstetric personnel and machinery, and that her body is an inconvenient barrier to easy access, and that if she were not around, the pregnancy could progress more efficiently (Kitzinger, 1978).

This statement takes a particular side in two important contemporary debates pointed out by Mitchell and Oakley (1986): the debate about whether medicalization of childbirth *has* brought about real gains for women and about whether women "need" to experience autonomy or control in the process of controlling our births. Tremendous positive satisfaction can be derived from the experience of childbirth even without its significance being magnified and complicated so as to relate to a pathological condition. In fact, the magnification of its significance and satisfaction may contribute to the sense of fulfillment and accomplishment for the birthing woman. Rather than experiencing a kind of emotional "shock," as often is experienced at the beginning of a serious illness (Parsons, 1951), women who have been anticipating the onset of labor are more prominently delighted and joyful at its realization.

(V.B.M.)   When I went into labor, I prepared my room . . . I couldn't quite decide how to have the baby. Should I draw the curtains and give birth in the serene tranquility of semi-darkness? I couldn't get over the feeling that it was a rather natural event, so I ended up leaving the curtains and windows open to let in the warm air and sunlight.

(E.R.)   I knew I was in labor, but Jeff had an old college friend coming over for dinner. I had prepared a big pot of spaghetti and meatballs; and I was determined to sit down and eat dinner with them, even if I delivered right there in the middle of the dining-room! After I straightened up the kitchen, I went up and took another warm bath . . . Then I got into bed and timed the contractions (Ward, 1976:111).

From the descriptions thus far we see that we cannot generalize about the process of making the decision to become pregnant, nor can we assume that women have the freedom to make that decision; we cannot generalize about the choices available to women, nor can we assume that women have the freedom of choice. There are many variations in the lives of individual women that impact on how we view our experiences and how we experience them.

Many cultures regard childbirth, like motherhood, as a major source of fulfillment and satisfaction for women and disapprove of negative attitudes toward childbearing and childrearing. Some cultures set such high standards and expectations, and so strongly oppose dissent, that feelings of incompetence and frustration would appear inevitable. In societies that are still untouched by modern technology, women receive more honor and credit for giving birth than do women in our society. In this culture a woman can be made to feel foolish for emphasizing the centrality of birthing to her identity or personhood (Demetrakopoulos, 1983). Despite cultural biases, an increasing number of women the world over have begun to express feelings of ambiguity, dissatisfaction, fear, resentment, inadequacy, and anger about these experiences. Here are some comments from mothers regarding such feelings:

(Anonymous)   Thoughts of failure, of lost control, of intensified labor—all of these plagued me. Yet I took the Demerol . . . He [the physician] stressed that I was "still the same woman."

(Anonymous)   This [delivery] also recalled my previous delivery, and I remained very tense. I was terrified of losing my self-control (Chabon, 1966:135, 165).

(M.G.)   I've never expressed the rage I feel toward everyone about my birth . . . I didn't know what to ask for. I gave all responsibility away and gave up (Arms, 1973:86).

A growing literature by women protests the process by which pregnancy and childbirth have been "stolen away" from us, transformed into a male-dominated orientation of birth experts and medical professionals—an orientation that has led us all to believe the myth that drugs and machines save lives and carry no potential harm. Pregnancy is clearly significant in terms of women's under-

standing of our reproductive capacity. Like menstruation and menopause, it has visible manifestations, a fact that can bring pride or
shame to women in societies where male values prevail. This is one
reason why women must develop different modes of understanding
and expression of female experience.

Many women know that things are not what they seem to be.
Uncertainties such as these make it difficult for us to decide how to
struggle and against whom to struggle, but the very possibility of
understanding one's own motivations, character traits, and impulses
is also at stake: first, the realization that what is really happening is
quite different from what appears to be happening; and second, the
frequent inability to tell what is really happening. Since many things
are not what they seem to be, and since many apparently harmless
sorts of things can suddenly exhibit a sinister dimension, social
reality may be reviewed as deceptive. In this view, some women
experience a "double ontological shock": first, the realization that
what is really happening is quite different from what appears to be
happening; and second, the frequent inability to tell what is really
happening at all (Vetterling-Braggin *et al.*, 1977:28–29).

> (M.B.) I lay there listening to women all around me scream. I wasn't in
> pain. As soon as the nurse left me alone I had my first real
> contraction and I screamed right through it. She came back and
> asked if I was in bad pain. I said, "I don't know because I don't
> know how bad it will get." She said, "We'll make you feel comfort-
> able;" and gave me two pills. I don't remember another thing until I
> woke being shaken by a nurse . . . When I took Linda home I began
> coming unglued. They gave me four pills every four hours, but I felt
> worse every day . . . Before my birth I thought only dummies do it
> without drugs . . . I feel very different now (Arms, 1975:50).

"In the hosptial they made me feel afraid I was going to contaminate
my own baby. I wish they had treated the birth process as what it is: a
fact of life, not a disease" (Ward and Ward, 1976:93). Thus, many
women know that there is more to childbirth than merely the production of a live baby and a live mother. For many women, birth will
occur only once or twice in a lifetime and is too significant to not be
named by us as a healthy, safe, and powerful natural event that
magnifies our relationship with our bodies and our minds. As Rich
(1976) declares:

> Childbirth is (or may be) one aspect of the entire process of a woman's
> life, beginning with her expulsion from her mother's body, her own
> sexual suckling or being held by a woman, through her earliest sensa-
> tions of clitoral eroticism and of the vulva as a source of pleasure, her
> growing sense of her own body and its strengths, her masturbation, her
> menses, her physical relationship to nature and to other human beings,

her first and subsequent orgasmic experience with another's body, her conception, pregnancy, to the moment of first holding her child.

Women are beginning to appreciate and respect our similarities and our differences, and we are struggling to have what we know about female experience respected by others. The knowledge that has come from these struggles has particular application to pregnancy and childbirth, as we have seen, and also to menstruation and menopause. These cycles of life are events that are basic in every woman's life, yet our knowledge about them has not been shared and respected, but hidden. Since the last decade, women have been actively seeking knowledge about their bodies and about experiences specific to them from a subjective point of view. As we are coming to know the truth about ourselves in our society, we have begun to reject the prevailing opinion that our bodily experiences are negative. As with all our experiences, what holds true for one may not hold true for another. But there are facts about these stages of our life cycle that apply to all women. But the image of uniformity and standardness that is projected results from the prevailing male definitions of women, and it is deceptive.

Weideger's survey of 558 women reveals variance in the physical, emotional, and social attitudes of women toward menstruation and menopause. The taboo against menstruation, she argues, leads to the cultural belief that it contains an element that is not acceptable to other people. Examples of responses to her questionnaire confirm this:

(V.M.)   It's pain—literally and figuratively.

(M.W.R.)   During the time I was menstruating, which was from age eleven to age fifty-three, naturally I would have preferred no menstrual flow.

(M.R.C.)   I didn't know that I had started and was afraid to ask my mom or anyone. I don't know how long (it seemed like years) that I went on not knowing what was going on with my body . . . It was really a traumatic experience for me.

(D.J.H.)   I wasn't even sure it was my period when I began to menstruate . . . I was scared to tell anyone. I thought something was wrong with me, until I asked my girl friend about it. She said not to worry about it because that's how her first period was, too.

(J.M.P.)   I thought my first cycle was the only one I'd have. Imagine my shock to find this happens every month.

(B.P.)   I expected to turn into a beautiful fairy princess—felt ugly when I did not.

(H.M.L.)   I had no information whatsoever, no hint that anything was going to happen to me, and then to make everything nicer, I had been suffering from a severe kidney infection. When this mysterious gush of blood appeared, of course, I thought I was on the point of death from internal hemorrhage. (Weideger, 1977:5, 8, 169).

Women who have begun to consider menstruation as legitimate parts of their lives responded differently.

(M.P.W.)   It [menstruation] makes me very much aware of the fact that I am a woman, and that's something very important to me . . . It's also a link to other women. I actually enjoy having my period. I feel like I've been cleaned out inside.

(M.C.B.)   The menstrual cycle has become such a part of my life by now, I don't want to change it. It is part of being a woman, which I am proud to be.

(R.J.C.)   I really like it. It's difficult to explain, but it's the same way I like the changing of the seasons. I guess the monthly cycles are "earthy" and symbolic to me (Weideger, 1977:4, 5).

Menopause partakes of the menstrual taboo by preventing women from experiencing the full dimension of their being. Women have begun to speak to one another and to publicize their experiences and their connection to their own personhood.

In looking for the approach that leads best to women as knowers of our experience, we need to detect and correct the inadequacies, errors, and biased information that have filtered through to us by collective cultural representations, while recognizing that the efforts to develop a feminist perspective on women's experience from a subjective point of view assumes that there are some things common to all women in Western societies. This chapter has begun to confirm empirically that, indeed, variation is one of the first rules toward our subjective knowing.

ATTENTION TO THE PROJECT

A woman's body begins to prepare for childbirth from the first day of pregnancy. At the moment of delivery "the upper portion of the uterus gradually pulls open the cervix . . . the lower end of the uterus containing the opening into the vagina . . . and pushes the baby's head through it" (Miller, 1963:100). This, in essence, is what happens during labor. Although it is a natural process requiring considerable effort and energy on the part of the birthing woman, it is not the task of a woman's body alone that is responsible for that conscious and deliberate progress of her labor but also the task of her mind, which orders the appropriate movements of her body when they are needed. I felt that I was developing the capacity of my mind to control my body. Learning to direct my muscles required active mental and physical effort on my part. As time went on, I realized that the conditioned reflexes would be created only through constant, daily repetition of the exercises. Thus, I began to regard my preparation as a learning process, one that once learned, would not have to be thought about in terms of "how to do it." By the time I would be in labor, I expected to be fully rehearsed with my mind free to respond to my bodily sensations.

It is thought that labor has a sudden onset occasioned by the rupturing of the membranes at the opening of the cervix; rather, it is a culmination of nine months of physical and psychological preparation and anticipation; this was evident to me toward the end of the ninth month of my pregnancy when my attention was again drawn back to my action. It was as if my entire pregnancy had been a gradual crescendo toward the days that remained before birthing.

Once labor began it continued independent of my will. It was as if my body was taken over by an unfamiliar and independent force. I could not will the onset of labor, nor could I consciously or intentionally alter its pattern once it began. It proceeded inexorably to its end regardless of my desires, but as the word "labor" implies, I did not need to assume a passive attitude toward it. In fact, I experienced myself as a source and a participant in this creative process. Although I did not plan and direct my labor, neither did it merely wash over me; for I, the person, was the process, the change; and I was fully conscious of my active contribution. My mind and my body became my environment and each was in communication with the other. The last few contractions, before the cervix was fully dilated were the most difficult, demanding my sustained patience, endurance, and strength. The interval between each contraction diminished to the point where it seemed that there was no interval at all; one contraction seemed to follow powerfully and closely upon the other with exact precision. My body took over in a tremendous sweep of physical energy. It was as if I had "exploded . . . into extraordinary concentration and tensions and the joy of being 'gathered'!" (Wolff, 1974:24). As I turned into the rhythm of my body, my husband explained to me afterward that he could only be in awe as he observed me thrown onto awareness of my body, surrender to the power of my body.[23] He could see of course that I was still in the hospital room with him—that was the everyday, "paramount" reality—but I had moved into another reality. I had experienced what Schutz (1973:232) refers to and what Kierkegaard has called a "leap" or a "shock"—a radical modification in the tension of my consciousness founded in a different *attention à la vie,* as well as a specific *epoché*—namely the suspension of doubt that I would be able to "ride above" the contractions and remain in control—which implies a transition from a paramount reality, the world of everyday life, to another finite province of meaning (Schutz, 1973:232). This does not imply a separate state of mental life; it is merely a different tension of one and the same consciousness, and it is the same life, the mundane life, but it is being attended to in a different modification (Schutz, 1973:258).

I willfully turned away from whatever I had been doing in the everyday world—resting, walking, chewing ice chips. I did not experience a "leap" back to my paramount reality, but rather, a gradual "coming back" or "returning to" with the fading of each contraction. When I did turn to the everyday life-world, I was different from when I had left it: my body was warmer and more perspiry; sometimes my mouth was dry; and I was temporarily exhausted although more "wide-awake," still attentive to my project.

The metaphor of a great wave is often used in describing the muscular contractions that occur during labor. If you are standing on the shore and a great wave begins to gather up far from the shore and grows higher as it gathers force, to remain facing it in an attitude of fear, rigidity, and helplessness would make you become tense. When the wave struck, you would be swept under. But to swim above it with the calm alertness necessary to time your strokes and to use your strength to its greatest advantage would allow the wave to pass beneath you. If you had panicked, you would have been submerged by the wave, but by "tuning in" to its rhythm you would have ridden its crest and allowed it to pass. Such an encounter would have required advance preparation and anticipation during the early stage of labor.

Feminists have criticized the optimistic, even heroic terminology of "natural" (prepared, little or no medication) childbirth as related to the ideal of doing it "like-a-man" (Jones, 1985: Morgan, 1984) referring to women doing whatever it is impressively. Indeed, it must be submitted that the criteria for measuring and judging the human accomplishment of birth denies and, in fact, inverts the concept of "like-a-man." The feminist objection to the techniques of breathing and muscular relaxation, for example, that a pregnant woman may learn in order to control her body during contractions are rooted in the notion of additional male inventions being imposed on women only so that we might more easily accept male-dominated procedures. Margaret Mead pointed out:

> Natural childbirth, the very inappropriate name for forms of delivery in which women undergo extensive training so that they can cooperate consciously with the delivery of the child, is a male invention meant to counteract practices of complete anaesthesia, which were also male inventions (Arms, 1975:138).

On the contrary, we can become aware of ourselves as body and take an interest in its sensations and limitations for their own sake. My awareness of my body did not impede the accomplishment of my aims. My experience of the controlled muscular activity was exactly what allowed my labor to continue as something I was creating. The breathing supported my confidence and was the integrating force between my mind and my body. These actions did not draw my attention away from what my body was experiencing; on the contrary, they tuned me into my body through the knowledge they revealed to me of what was taking place within my body. My body was attending to itself at the same time that it was enacting its project that was also my project. There remained no basis for preserving the exclusivity of the categories subject and object, inner and outer, I and world. There was, in fact, a unity that might be viewed as anti-Cartesian in its opposition to the division between mind and body. Also, the classes on "prepared childbirth" provided confirmation that I could learn and know my body and trust that knowledge.

My body had a rhythm all of its own and, with my mind calling signals, intentional movements "tuned in" to that rhythm. Although it required concentration and a very conscious effort at first, my mind and my body were interacting, one responding to the other. My feelings at this point were mixed—excitement, fear, relief—at knowing for sure that "this was it." As my labor moved ahead much more rapidly I became strongly associated with my immediate, present, bodily experience of the contractions. I felt that I was meeting my first real challenge and that my mind was being tested by my body in new ways. Also, I knew that if I could not manage the contractions now, I would not be able to manage them later, when they would be more intense and longer-lasting. Therefore, once I knew that I would be able to repeat my activity again and again as long as the contractions kept coming, I was actually thrown into a joyful state of pride in having mastered the contractions on my own (without medication). I felt a satisfying exhilaration and optimism in realizing that contractions did pass (I had feared that each would last "forever") and that I could just let them consume me; there was no reason to be afraid of them. I knew now that I could trust my body; it would continue telling me what to do and I would continue doing it . . . for as long as necessary. A much greater realization, however, was of the fact that I really was "having a baby."

At about 5:45 A.M., in a sitting-upstraight, comfortable position, I felt a sudden, surging, intense pressure and thrusting sensation—as if my body had been taken over by its own force. And in one huge push, coming from my concentrated effort and the natural movements of my body, the head of my baby was expelled to below a chin.[24] This was a moment of triumph, exhaltation and astonishment—looking down and seeing my baby actually sliding out of my body. In another one or two minutes (an amazingly long time for me to see only my baby's head outside of my body) I responded to an urge to bear down—though not too hard—birthing first one shoulder, then the other. The rest of the little body—trunk, hips, legs—merely followed effortlessly and quickly. My first external physical contact with my baby was the feel of myself being touched and touching simultaneously of a warm, damp arm resting on my thigh at 6:02 A.M., just the right time. This moment entailed the most extreme suspension of the body distinction between inner and outer.

Rich has reflected and stated:

> Nothing, to be sure, had prepared me for the intensity of relationship already existing between me and a creature I had carried in my body and now held in my arms and fed from my breasts . . . No one mentions . . . a heightened sensibility which can be exhilarating, bewildering, and exhausting. No one mentions the strangeness of attraction . . . to a being so tiny, so dependent, so folded-in to itself who is, and yet is not, part of oneself (Rich, 1977:17).

SELF-ENCOUNTER

Although the action was still in progress, my attention was already on the act as if it had been completed. It was as if I had birthed my baby while my baby was birthing herself. Thus, if the sensation, which corresponds to the sensualists' concept of happiness, is release from pain rather than its absence, then the intensity of the sensation of giving birth is beyond doubt matched only by the sensation of pain itself (Arendt, 1958:98). Also, if it is true that in order to think creatively women and men need the stimulus of contrast (Mead, 1949:43), no contrast in my life had been greater than that between the moment before and the moment after the spontaneous birth of my baby.[25] Within minutes I had come to know the truth about myself. Also, I knew that my feelings about myself had been shaped by this event and that my sense of my self had been altered dramatically. I also knew that the change was irreversible; I would never be the same. There was an immediate sense for me of an intense reciprocal and cooperative relationship between my baby and me. At that moment I realized "We did it!"

What had taken place was not merely unusual to me but remarkable ("marked-out" and hence to-be-taken-note-of) and astonishing. My astonishment was not only astonishment-over, but "astonishment-at"; My self was astonished "at" the very happening, that it could ever happen. My self, familiar and intimate to me, surprised itself at that moment. My experience of self-awakening, in short, was a disclosure of my self to myself, a disclosure that was doubly-reflexive. Indeed, what happened in my self-encounter, the doubly-reflexive astonishment, was that my self was not only intentionally familiar with itself but at the same time unfamiliar and strange.

This double reflexivity is what stood out as self-awakening in my experience. It was a decisive experience for my self, for my self was no longer the same. The experience was transforming: seeing my baby that I had birthed were both set off from and seen in a different new perspective that fascinated my self. My body seemed at the same time strange and new, yet familiar and well-known to me. As Zaner suggests,

> self-encounter is essentially *self-awakening* and *self-transforming* . . . The experience "wakens" the self to itself, and not only as being itself and alone, but as inextricably bound to its world, things, others, its own body, in the setting of authentic wonder. In these terms, the transforming power of the experience and the grounds of its significance for the maturation or growth of self is that this maturation becomes genuinely possible through it (Zaner, 1970:183–84).

This discovery-as-recognition has several aspects. I was able to "tell" that it was me-myself who had been discovered and revealed to me (it was me, I realized, and no one else). On the other hand, I experienced myself "as" what I had been all along, even though I had not recognized this before. I thus discovered myself "as myself" and "as" previously not noticed until now. I was suddenly and unexpectedly presented before myself, given to myself as "what I am" and as such experienced myself. It was the beginning of a self that can be called my own.[26]

DIMENSIONS IN TIME

There is a distinction between the time dimensions in which labor occurred. According to Schutz following Bergson:

> We experience our bodily movements simultaneously on two different planes: inasmuch as they are movements in the outer world we look at them as events happening in space and spatial time, measurable in terms of the path run through; inasmuch as they are experience together from within as happening changes, as manisfestations of our spontaneity pertaining to our stream of consciousness, they partake of our *durée* (Schutz, 1973:211).

Just as a real thing or the real world is not a phenomenological datum, so also world-time, real time, the time of nature, is not such a datum. The moments in question were not ticks on a clock, nor were they movements in the idealist sense of abstracted instants in the flow of subjective consciousness.

The inner time or *durée*, the medium within which the labor proceeded for me, was where my actual experience was connected with the past by my recollections and retentions about my pregnancy, and with the future by the protentions and anticipations of my birthing. In and by my bodily movements I performed the transition from my *durée* to the spatial time, and my working actions partook of both. I experienced my working action as a series of phases— simultaneously in outer and inner time, unifying these phases into a single experience. For me, it was not true that the time I lived through while feeling the slow movement of a contraction, from its beginning to its end, was of "equal length" with the one that had just preceded.

In speaking of the temporal character of objects of perception, memory, and expectation, it may seem as if I assume the objective flow of time, and then really discuss only the subjective conditions of the possibility of an intuition of time and a true knowledge of time. What I accept, however, is not the existence of a concrete duration but time and duration appearing as such. To be sure, I also assume existing time. This, however, is not the time of the world of experience but, to use Husserl's (1964:23) term, "the *immanent time* of the flow of consciousness"—the evidence that consciousness of my bodily movements, rhythmic motions, exhibited a succession even as I felt senseless to make every doubt or denial appear.

Similarly, the two or three "clock" minutes between each contraction seemed for me like several seconds; whereas during my pregnancy time stretched out, and moments and days took on a depth and length as I experienced more changes in myself, in my body. During labor, however, time shrank and was condensed. There was not the sense of growth and change, but rather of total involvement, my mind attending to and surrendering itself to the activity of my body. My labor, then, was experienced in a dimension of time incomparable with that that can be subdivided into homogeneous parts. The outer time was measurable, and I myself was aware of it. It was of interest to me in fact to determine the objective time of my lived experience through one that was time-constituting. Occasionally I asked my husband what time it was according to his watch. (My concern for the clock time was in keeping account the length of my labor and wanting to know the exact "time" of the birth of my baby.) Each time I was astonished by his response, by the fleeting of standard time. My reaction to that phenomenon varied, however. On the one hand, I was very eager for the outcome; on the other; what was occurring was so tremendously exhilarating and there was a timeless sense about it; I did not know when the contractions would stop, when labor would cease, when I would give birth, or in what manner.

> Living in the present does not have to do with knowing who one is, but that it also has to do with appreciating that timelessness denied by the modern world in its preoccupation with superficial change and senescence; with making a friend of eternity. For most of us there are moments when we do feel timeless. Those are the moments in which we feel we are truly alive, but they are rare (Oakley, 1984:146).

This relationship to time varies among birthing women as evidenced by others' descriptions:

> During labor . . . there is no sense of time. There is no intention, no activity, only a will to endure. I only know that I have been lying in this pain, concentrating on staying above it, for a long time because the hands on the clock say so, or the sun on the wall has moved to the other side of the room (Young, 1984:54).

> Time is absolutely still. I have been here forever. Time no longer exists. Always. Time holds steady for birth. There is only this rocketing, this labor (Chesler, 1979:16).

There was no gauge of measurement for the dimensions of inner time in which I lived during the contractions.

> Because standard time coincides with our sense of inner time in which we experience our working acts, if we are wide-awake, inner time governs the system of our plans under which we subsume our projects (Schutz, 1973:222).

We must go on to elaborate the way in which the time dimensions differ from "stages" of reproductive process, the ways in which they interact; and we must also develop a methodological framework for the analysis of the social relations that constitute a relation in which the contradictions with and between these moments are worked out.

Although standard time for the physician elapsed along with my *durée*—as when he measured the length of the transition phase by the clock—the physician and I were not united by a common time dimension. This does not imply that I was not sharing a sector of time and space with my husband, however, My sounds, facial expressions, and gestures, for example, geared into the outer world as an expressional field open to interpretation, and could be grasped in immediacy. Although most of the activities of performing occurred within standard time as measured by his watch, he also sensed the activities as part of the *durée* in much the same way in which they occurred for me. The contractions of my body, then, were lived through in simultaneity by two streams of consciousness, mine and my husband's. This living through a vivid present shared by us in genuine face-to-face relation constitutes what Schutz (1971:173) refers to as the mutual tuning-in relationship, the experience of the "We." In this instance, my husband and I "tuned-in" to one another—living through the same contraction, growing old together. And it was within this experience that my conduct became meaningful to my husband as he was "tuned in to me." That is, my body and its movements were interpreted as a field of expression of events within my inner life. Certainly his participating in simultaneity in the ongoing process of my communicating established a new dimension of time.

REFLECTIVE ATTITUDE

All our acts and actions can be explained phenomenologically. To do so, however, required a change of attitude from a non-reflective to a reflective attitude. Since I wanted to use my memory for liberation, an interpretation of an experience in the everyday life-world was traced back to its original constitution of lived experience in pure duration—which called for an act of reflection. This presupposed that particular kind of *attention à la vie*,

> *attention to life*, the basic regulative principle of our conscious life. It defines the realm of our world which is relevant to us; it articulates our continuously flowing stream of thought; it determines the span and function of our memory; it makes us—in our language—either live within our present experiences, directed toward their objects, or turn back in a reflective attitude to our past experiences and ask for their meaning (Schutz, 1973:213).

It also presupposed that it was important to me that a particular truth become not only clear to me, but be perceived by me as a viable operational basis for my emergence from the experience as a newly or partially autonomous person.

In establishing myself as the disinterested observer within a reflective attitude, I did not turn away either from the whole of experienced reality and actuality or from certain areas of it; I only suspended judgment concerning the reality and validity of what was experienced. The *epoché*, the suspension of all natural belief in the objects of experience, was the precondition for reducing the natural world to a world of phenomena. The world that I had transformed into "mere phenomena," therefore, did not differ in content from the world of the natural attitude, but the way in which I was related to them was different.

Although I consider my experiences of pregnancy and childbirth as central to my life, I attribute part of my vivid memory of it to its status of a first-time event. Phenomenologically, first-time events have specific qualities.

> They present the first problems that will be encountered within a setting and generate the first tactics to deal with those problems. Because of their very first-timeness, these problems and tactics have the potential of high drama and memorability for the actors and become the base on which they will define future situations within the setting (and perhaps other settings) and develop future tactics. These first problems may eventually be reformulated or solved, and the first tactics discarded, but they must be dealt with, one way or another . . . . Generally, the problem presented by a dramatic first-time event is that of quickly learning a new world of meanings and developing effective techniques for doing so. Concretely, the problems have to do with the meanings themselves as they are "discovered" and the development of situationally appropriate tactics effective in affecting those meanings toward desired ends (Stewart, 1977:53).

I had always been able to describe some of these "first-time problems" and "generated tactics" within the context of my first pregnancy and childbirth experiences, but I had never reflected; I had not asked myself whether I had wanted to become a mother; whether it was really true that to have a child or not to have one had been options for me; or whether in fact I had changed as a result of the experience.

Caught in my feelings of responsibility and love for my daughter, as well as my commitment and response to her needs, I never "stood back" and "reviewed the situation" with any detachment. In my emotional attachment there had not been an opportunity for a "sense of proportion" in relation to other experiences. As one interested in phenomenology, the opportunity for reflection provided that opportunity; as one interested in contemporary women's issues, the political and social contexts of pregnancy and childbirth were put forth for critical examination; and as a mother who participated with a particular awareness in the birth of her baby, the topic of and the opportunity for reflection attracted my interest and attention.

Once I began to reflect on my experiences, I still thought about myself, but I thought about myself in a different light. For example, putting aside for a moment what I believed to be my mere recollection of the experience, I thought more about what I actually had done. The scope of my reflection about myself, therefore, became considerably wider than that of my previous thinking since it included facts about my relations to others and about myself which were unnoticed before or had appeared irrelevant. Also, I had to raise the question whether the world I had taken to be immediately experienced was not, at least in part, the embodiment of my own wishes and the product of my imagination. Again, reflection required suspension, and the scope of inquiry was thus widened.

The *epoché* thus rendered questionable what I had previously taken as certain and self-evident. This does not mean that I rejected the experience as a whole, since "to question something is not to deny it" (Schmitt, 1967:65). I did not say, for example, that I was not really happy; I did not deny that my socialization was influenced by sexist biases; but rather, I allowed my experience to become ambiguous and open to question. The certainty I once possessed as a result of immediate experience came into doubt as if it might have been an interpretation of a first experience. That it was a "first" for me presented a problem: a presupposition of a reference back to the schemes I had on hand the validity of which were thrown into question. Thus, the criterion by which one interpretive scheme is chosen is dependent upon the particular attentional modification that happens to be operative at that time, thereby producing the paradox that the lived experience itself decides the scheme into which it is to be ordered. Thus, the problem that is chosen proposes its own solution.

The interpretive scheme itself should be thought of as something dependent on the Here and Now as it existed for me, for "no lived experience can be exhausted by a single interpretive scheme. Rather, every lived experience is open to numerous interpretations" (Schmitt, 1967:85). Berger suggests that the course of events that constitutes one's life can be subjected to alternate interpretations. In fact, we interpret and reinterpret our own life. According to Bergson (1974), memory itself is a reiterated act of interpretation. As we remember the past, we reconstruct it in accordance with our present ideas of what is important and what is not. This means that in any situation with its near infinite number of things that could be noticed, we notice only those things that are important for our immediate pur- poses. This also means that our past is malleable and flexible, con- stantly changing our recollections reinterprets and re-explains what has happened. Thus, when I tried to distinguish those aspects of my experience that were genuinely evident from those that I merely assumed to have existed, I was examining the world in relation to myself; when I inquired into the beliefs, feelings, desires, and atti- tudes and habits, which shaped the experience upon which I was reflecting as the subject, I, too, was the object of examination in relation to my cultural world.

Also, it was the describing of those new facts, instead of explaining them, that was phenomenological, made possible by reflection; the reflection has preserved for me the memory and the feelings, before and after birthing, that I was the person having the baby. I am sure that those who attended and assisted during my birthing experience did not understand the huge challenge that I had felt presented to me at the point of the decision to become pregnant, and that they had no idea of how I really felt about the outcome (they had hardly noticed the impact it had on me)—that I had emerged with an unpredictable discovery—knowledge that in my life I would encounter new challenges, new tests of my capacity and ability, but that they would be met by a different self than I had been before.[27]

> Only in the reflective attitude do we begin to separate what is given to experience, what close and attentive scrutiny reveals to be "really there" from what was merely added to this experience by the observer, as interpretation or anticipation . . . It is here, in reflection, that the distinction between true self and knowledge is first drawn (Schmitt, 1967:98).

I wanted to do more than merely rewrite the past from memory. To do otherwise, to describe myself to myself, necessitated my critical awareness of the limitations of my sources. That is, as an individual located in a particular culture, what I noticed and how I described it depended to a great extent on my biographically determined situation, my knowledge at hand, my perception of my culturally defined social role and my expectations of an individual in our society. Therefore, as I moved from the public personal to the private I may not always have been aware of the effect of the values and ideology on what I was able or willing to perceive as real about myself and those around me. Like other reflective accounts, I expect that mine contains social biases that are built into the reflection of an experience that I deem mine. What I have documented can be at best only partial, but others are putting together other parts of which Rich refers to as "this immense half-buried mosaic in the shape of women's lives" (Rich, 1977:XIX).

REVELATIONS AND TURNING POINTS

To be honest to myself, to reveal the person I am to myself and indeed to everyone else implied a willingness to share not what male culture has designated as "private" (the precept that women must keep these experiences hidden) but what feminists have claimed as private (the precept that women must know and to share). Like Elizabeth Cady Stanton, I believe that every truth we see is ours to give the world, not to keep for ourselves alone, for in so doing we cheat humanity out of our right and check our own development (Stanton in Schneir, 1972:156). Moreover, feminist principles reject analyses that ignore or deny the level of reality most immediate for individual women, such as that it is through the unity of mind and body that childbirth occurs. Indeed any analysis becomes false insofar as it disregards the immediate, sensual reality of individuals altogether. In order to make this connection, a methodological orientation has to have recourse to other conceptual frameworks, particularly those that assert women's right to and need for bodily self-determination. For as women are revealing their own conscious meanings through their experiences as their own, they are also shaping the tools by which to interpret it. They are also finding their own consciousness.

The described experience therefore, belongs to my *durée*, my stream of consciousness. It can be remembered and reproduced by me; it can be communicated to all people in ordinary language, and it can show that other forms of possible communication can be explained as being derived from this paramount situation. I devised a plan of action that developed into a plan for life for me. I experienced something for myself, the experience itself, not as dictated by a book, social opinion, or cultural attitude, but through the assertion of my body and my mind.

Through my experiences of pregnancy and childbirth, I revealed myself to myself in my singularity, in my uniqueness. I also revealed to myself the connecting threads between my life and my daughter's life, between our lives and the lives of other women and men. The validity of my knowledge of my experience may be underscored by the corroboration of other women. That other women have had comparable experiences and feelings heightened my new knowledge about myself. The impact of this experience for me was a kind of transformation of consciousness, a redefinition of identity, in which my sense of myself became adjusted to fit the new reality that I encountered. While the idea that I had changed or become a "different" person contributed to putting closure on my past experience and helped me to move on to new situations—taking care of a new-born baby—the notion of transformations is also significant to this analysis because it emerged from my bodily experience in everyday life. In chapter six, we spoke of Kierkegaard's "leap" when the taken-for-granted becomes problematic (open to examination) through a change in attention. The experience of childbirth just described was one of those situations where I stopped and took stock of myself. In this sense, my experience provided a juncture for personal change and development. Strauss has written on such junctures as "turning points":

> Some transformations of identity and perspective are planned, or at least fostered, by institutional representatives; others happen despite, rather than because of, such regulated anticipation; and yet other transformations take place outside the orbits of the more visible social

structure, although not necessarily unrelated to membership within them . . . [There are] certain critical incidents that occur to force a person to recognize that "I am not the same as I was, as I used to be." These critical incidents constitute turning points in the onward movement of personal careers . . . When the incident occurs it is likely to strike with great impact, for it tells you: "Look! you have come way out to here! This is a milestone!" Recognition then necessitates new stances, new alignments. (Strauss, 1959:92–93).

Childbirth may not constitute a turning point in the lives of all women. However, it represents for me a deep significance in shaping transformations of identity.

(Anonymous) I regained faith in myself, even though I was physically exhausted. The contractions got very fast, intense and long. Imagining their productivity and their ability to open my body gave me strength to go on. I don't feel like "thanking Dr. Lamaze." My son was born after forty hours of labor and I thank *"myself!"* . . .

(P.) I enjoyed my labor, and even spent several hours of solitude. I watched the lunar eclipse, examined my feelings, and meditated. I felt really in tune with nature. During each contraction I did a visualization of reaching down to help birth my baby. It really opened me up, and gave such a push it was incredible . . . I feel I'm still floating. I got it all—the best that could possibly happen . . . My body, I love it! It's a good strong, healthy body and it's true to me. For the first time, I feel truly whole, not just because I had a vaginal delivery [after four Cesareans], but because I learned to trust my intuitions, my body's wisdom, and for the first time I really believed in myself. It took me a long time but I learned so much (Panuthos, 1984:113, 149–150).

Each process for each woman is unique and none deserves to be categorized, timed, judged, or criticized. For example, when a baby dies, a birthing woman loses not only the baby, but herself as a parent, a mother, and the new images of self and other that had been built up through the months of her pregnancy.

(I.) Dear Mothers of babies I don't have,
There are days when I want to walk up to you and say—"I lost my babies. Do you know what that is like?" It's a horrible, endless nightmare. It never stops completely. When I go shopping and hear your babies crying and gooing, I hate the sounds. I look at my groceries and think, "Where's my baby? I did all the right things." . . . Your babies remind me of the hole in my belly, empty hole. The hole in my heart is probably even bigger. It's so embarrassing to face people who think you've done it and then you

fail. . . . Some days I hate my body. I wish it worked. It just won't.

(Anonymous)   Finally, after weeks of inner torture, I decided that I'd done my best. I don't really know why. It doesn't make a lot of sense. But I was sure glad, because I've since given birth and I'm really pleased with my son, Allan, and with myself.

Also, women's consciousness can assist us in warding off self-recrimination brought on by our not being able to muster the strength to confront our individual physician or the system.

(J.)   Anyway they gave me gas. I was so "sick" after that I didn't even want to see the baby, and don't remember when I did. Here transformed was a parent that had taken natural classes and had the tape recorder and camera ready . . . I had come to the hospital with one spot of poison ivy on my wrist. I told the doctor that before the "op." He said it didn't matter. They put the I.V. there and the poison ivy spread all over my arm. It was so oozy the nurses didn't want to touch it. So here I was, a first time mom: C-section with poison ivy trying to nurse a baby. Nerves—husband perfectionist—and nervous about the situation over critical in-laws. Me—a people pleaser—Help! I criticized myself for years, feeling that I *should* have stopped my doctor from cutting me; stopped the nurse from putting the I.V. into my poison ivy; stopped my in-laws from criticizing me; stopped my husband from harassing me. I finally realize that I should stop punishing me for doing my best in the first place.

(C.)   When I got to the hospital, I was told that I wouldn't be allowed in the birthing room because I'd had a previous Cesarean. Although the birthing room was empty and located only a few feet from the labor room, I was placed in the labor room with another couple. It was awful. I begged to be moved but didn't have the strength to labor and fight at the same time. I felt punished as I knew VBAD's [vaginal births after Cesareans] weren't well received . . . I had a vaginal delivery but not without unnecessary upset. I left the hospital almost immediately because I ruffled so many feathers I was afraid of further retaliation on my son and me. I'm angry still and hope someday to stop punitive policies (Panuthos, 1984:77, 80–81).

(L.A.)   I worked hard to get my home birth. I searched for months to find a doctor or a midwife. Never once did I feel I was in danger. I never had any serious doubts that I could do it. The actual birth experience was worth all the effort. It's the most wonderful thing we have ever done.

(J.L.)   They kept insisting, "Are you *sure* you don't want anything for the pain?" I said, "No. I don't want anything." It seemed as if there were eighty-eight different nurses in and out and half of them couldn't have cared less about me (Ward and Ward, 1976:114,122).

The new scholars of women's history have already begun to discover that the social institutions and prescriptions for behavior created by men have not accounted for the real lives of women, and that any institution, in this case the medical institution, which expresses itself so universally, ends up profoundly affecting our pregnancy and birth experiences and even the language we use to describe it. Thus, the discovery that masculine intellectual systems are also inadequate because they lack the wholeness that female consciousness could provide, calls up before women a different description than the one we have known; it primes the imagination of women living today to conceive of other modes of existence as part of a drive to self-knowledge. In particular, it signals an impulse that acknowledges the authenticity of the individual and insists on freedom from a predefined standard.

> Truly to liberate women, then, means to change thinking itself: to reintegrate what has been named the unconscious, the subjective, the emotional with the structural, the rational, the intellectual . . . and finally to annihilate those dichotomies (Rich, 1977:66–67).

Thus, paradoxically, the "unique" and "special" woman that I had considered myself gradually revealed how systematic the process was by which male cultural attitudes had categorized me and other women who birth, and by this categorization, had isolated and alienated us from one another. Coming to see things differently then led to a development of consciousness that was apprehended by me through an experience of liberation.

NEW CHOICES, NEW POSSIBILITIES

With few exceptions, sociological research on childbirth has parenthood as its focus. Most of the literature deals with the impact of childbirth on marriage, on the marital relationship, and is limited through adherence to gender-divisive notions of parenthood, both explicitly in the framework and conclusions and implicitly in the instruments of inquiry.

> The general rewards and difficulties of maternity: its contribution to personal growth or to personal disintegration; its capacity to dislocate preexisting social-political identifications and to provide functionally inferior (within a sexist capitalist society) alternatives—all these have been conceptualized as dimensions of wifehood, as contaminating the marital relationship, rather than as influencing the status, identities, and experiences of women. Moreover, the analysis of reproduction as a parameter of marriage reduces the sexual dimension of maternity to the

sexual component of wifehood, instigating the same wedge between maternalism and sexuality found in Western industrialized culture generally (Oakley, 1979:623).

In the area of medical sociology, prior to the 1970s, the main theoretical interest to sociologists of reproduction was the relationship between pregnancy and illness as distinct social roles. In 1967, Illsley contended that reproductive events can only be understood contextually as components of the woman's life experience. As we mentioned previously, sociological research at the level of the person experiencing pregnancy and childbirth is very scarce. What few studies do exist have tended to lack a clearly stated theoretical or conceptual focus. Hence, they are either purely descriptive and, therefore, analytically weak, or else they lack central findings. One exception is within the arena of ethnomethodology where women sociologists have begun to offer insights into the management of reproduction and the effect of paradigmatic conflicts between doctor and patient from the perspective of subjective experience as valid data. Other women are building on these findings by recounting experiences that groups of women hold in common. In listening to other women, we gain new insights into the significance of our experience. In general, however, the sociologist's contribution has not been to investigate women's experience but to extend the limits of the medical model and propose a more elastic conception of the variables that can be seen to influence the biological outcome of maternity.

> Clearly what the sociology of reproduction has lacked to date is a repertoire of first-hand accounts. Until very recently the reproducers themselves have been represented merely as statistics, and/or they have been manipulated to fit the contours of a largely "ungrounded" theory. The feminine paradigm has been less visible in sociology than in psychology and medicine, for sociological representations of women are more a matter of subtle theoretical distortion or simple omission than dogmatic rhetoric. . . . Paradigmatic representations of women as mothers are bound to obscure the subjective reality of their reproductive experiences. To uncover this, a nonparadigmatic approach is needed that would enable the reproducer to be restored as the central figure in the biocultural drama of birth (Oakley, 1979:628).[28]

The possible alternatives of meaningful existence do not emerge from coercion or force. They belong to the human condition in which women find ourselves and we must work out a version of the world which both fits the facts and is meaningful to us. Our membership, as it were, in a particular culture no longer need be evidenced by an acceptance of devaluation of women's experience. In both the public sphere and the private sphere, challenges are being addressed to the cultural emphasis on childbearing and childrearing as the destiny of all women. Indeed, the willingness or unwillingness of women to bear children has become a political issue. The fact that some women do choose to birth does not eliminate them from this struggle. On the contrary, feminism and motherhood are only contradictory aims because of contradictions imposed on women by malestream culture. Feminists must break this code. We must reestablish reproduction as meaningful, authentic, and purposeful. By examining our own experiences as childbearers from the time of making the decision to become pregnant or making the decision to follow through or not follow through with our pregnancies to the time of lactation, by reinterpreting them in terms of meaning that they have for us, we are seeking to gain control over the use of our bodies for reproduction in the first place. We do not imply that all pregnancies or births result from women's deliberation, decision, and choice. Nor do we assume that all women possess the freedom to make decisions about whether, how, and where to bear our children. We insist that birthing women rewrite our history as we are rediscovering that birthing can be different from culture's "institutionalized" version that violates the potential of meaningful experience. "The question rests with women themselves (as to what is or what is not their vocation)—to be decided by their own experience, and by the use of their own faculties" (Mill, 1970:27).

For birth women, the freedom from externally-oriented conceptions and definitions implied in the move toward subjective knowledge represents a move toward emancipation. It is also a step toward connected knowing, an orientation toward understanding and truth that emphasizes a "joining of the minds."

CHAPTER 8

Phenomenological Sociology Reconsidered

EXPANDING CATEGORIES

THE TERM "RECONSIDERED" has more than one meaning. First, it refers to the fact that phenomenological sociology and its plausibility as a methodological orientation for feminist theory has previously been considered. Dorothy Smith (1977) writes from the Marxist perspective in which she works that it had been suggested to her that a phenomenological sociology is a feminist sociology merely because it begins within the consciousness of the knower and is therefore "subjective." She argues that the phenomenological perspective remains within the conceptual abstracted world and begins from there, taking for granted the material and social organization of the bifurcated consciousness, and does not render its organization and conditions examinable. Second, from the perspective of this book, we can begin to see how the knowledge-claims of phenomenology are founded on distinctive and often distorted masculine understanding of experience. We can also begin to see how feminist research and analyses of particular experiences lead us to new philosophical and other theoretical insights. Keeping this in mind, we must now determine what relevance phenomenological sociology as introduced by Schutz may have for feminist research.

The absence of women as subjects in sociology and philosophy gives, as has been pointed out, a distorted impression of social reality. The placing of women's experience in predefined categories has misrepresented interpretations and definitions of our experiences and their personal and social importance. Yet, when we begin to account for the partial and often inadequate treatment of gender in social theory and social research, it is clearly not enough to blame particular techniques, especially those that are conventionally identi-

142

fied with "positivism"; nor is it enough to say that it is because the foundation of the discipline is based on conventional male-oriented values of sociological inquiry—such as "rational," "scientific" and "scholarly." In creating universal values, traditional sociologists have often left their specifically masculine impression on them. Those of us whom Germaine Greer labels "intellectual escapees" have too often denied our own experience and accepted only the ideas and procedures defined by men's thought systems. So it really is a question of separating one from the other and ridding ourselves of this confusion without necessarily rejecting all aspects of the model. Male orientation may influence the organization of a discipline so that the invisibility of women is, in fact, a structural weakness. When a woman is defined she is defined through the "maleness" of culture and language exclusively in terms of her relationship to men, and through a male perspective of who women are and what they experience. In the last six or seven years, many women, including myself, have struggled to redefine the grounds of feminist methodology. This new body of work owes a great deal to the women discussed in this book, and to many more.

The common focus of a feminist perspective is on making women visible, on bringing women out from under into twin spheres of social reality and cultural belief systems. Feminists have recognized for some time that one of the characteristics of male culture is the insistence that all forms of experience be studied objectively, i.e., as a face that exists independently of personal experience, as an institution. I agree fully that the positivistic ideal of a scientifically valid knowledge is insufficient for the explanation of women's and men's experience. It must be admitted that this problem of dealing with the subjective phenomena in objective terms is *the* problem of the methodology of social science. The male demand for objectivity presents the following questions for feminists: which of the elements pertain to the experience when the references are really categories in the mind of the actor and are, therefore, subjective; and which ones are but appropriate schemes of interpretation by the observer and are, therefore, objective? Gouldner, Keller, and others have argued cogently that value-freedom or objectivity is not possible, the former arguing that sociologists must take sides. Schutz suggests that it not be a goal of subjective research.

> The idea of scientific knowledge is incompatible with the subjective point of view which [is correctly said to be] a fundamental element of the theory of action. It is true that the term "scientific" does not mean that the so-called scientific elements of knowledge of the actor must have been verified by empirical science. It is sufficient that the actor in the social world presumes those elements as verifiable by empirical

science. But verified or verifiable: both categories of the observer's knowledge and more precisely of the knowledge of the scientific observer's knowledge of the scientific observer of acts and actor's within the social world; both are therefore categories peculiar to the objective point of view (Wagner, 1976:36).

To reject classical objectivity does not mean that we must or should relinquish our search for objective knowledge. It means, rather, that we must modify our theory of knowledge and our conception of objectivity.

Feminists are concerned with the objectivity of our findings but place less emphasis on this than on getting at the subjective meanings of things to the actors. Feminists claim that the reference to the subjective approach is an indispensable prerequisite for feminist theory and feminist research. This raises the broader theoretical question of how it is possible to deal with subjective phenomena in terms of objective conceptual schemes. I hope to determine that phenomenological sociology, as a subjective approach, is not only a possible means of description of the social world but also one that is adequate to the reality of women's experience.

We begin our reconstruction of the meaning of scientific objectivity by seeing that all human thought, at least that in the wide-awake state, is intentional or purposeful. As Schutz argues, it is primarily intentions at any time that order human thought, that determine the relevance of information and ideas about the world and ourselves. To begin from direct experience and to return to it as a constraint or "test" of the adequacy of the systematic knowledge is to begin from where we are located bodily. The aim of phenomenological sociology as an alternative would be to develop precisely that capacity from precisely that beginning so that it might be a means to us for understanding how the world comes about for us and how it is organized so that it happens to us as it does in our experience. And if we are to correct a profound and long-standing imbalance,

> we cannot do it without jumping rather brutally and without invitation on the end of the philosophical seesaw which has lingered too long in the rarefied heights of the complacent taken-for-granted of male conceptions of the nature of man (O'Brien, 1981:12).

ARTIFICIAL DISTINCTIONS

Marxists have criticized the idea of objectivity and challenged the positivist idea of generalizing science and the notion that truth can be expressed in causal relation independent of time and place. The Marxist critique is also concerned with women as agents of knowledge, arguing that the methodological norm of objectivity is itself socially and historically constituted, rooted in an ideology that attempts to mystify the social relations of the knower and the known through the procedures that appear anonymous and impersonal. It claims that the ideology expressed within sociology by theories and methods ignores sexual divisions and does not "see" the experience or situation of women. Similarly, feminism insists upon the use of personal experience in sociological accounts in opposition to the claims of positivistic rationality. To be sure, some men can do research on women, particularly those men who adhere to feminist principles.

It is important to note, then, that questions of gender do not occupy specifically a central place in Schutz's phenomenological sociology. This, of course, is not just a matter of concern for those interested in feminism or women's issues, but it affects everyone involved in this perspective. "Taking gender seriously" is not simply a recognition of the justice of feminists' charges against "normal" sociological practice, but an exploration that can raise new issues and point the way to new solutions (Morgan, 1981:94). Furthermore, social situations (project an end that defines the elements relevant to its attainment) from the subjective point of view, as part of the social world, are male-dominated arenas; women have historically been tangential to them. Most of the models upon which phenomenological sociology focuses are derived from traditional masculine concerns and settings. The concealment of women exists throughout the phenomenological literature. It extends from the classification of the subject-areas and the definition of concepts through the topics and methods of research to the construction of models and theories generally.

A methodology for woman-centered research should have two requirements: first, to give rise to a different definition of women's experience as social actors; and second, to investigate subjective aspects of experience as they are experienced only by women. The need to grasp theoretically the significance of women's subjective experiences of pregnancy, childbirth, menstruation, and menopause, a need that is at least partially articulated in this book, is emerging as one of the main concerns of feminist theory and practice. I have argued that, in spite of its limitations, the Schutzian view of subjective experience offers a sound and adequate conceptualization of experience from the perspective of the person having the experience. This being the case, the phenomenological sociological approach, reformulated by a consideration of woman-as-researcher also offers some insight into the general issue of women's role in society. The question of what light can be shed on the issue of women's oppression and women's liberation through a phenomenological sociological perspective has been addressed, for the most part, within the specific experiences of pregnancy and childbirth, and, to a lesser extent, menstruation and menopause. They are intended to serve as only a model for defining and describing those aspects of women's experience that go beyond or contradict the cultural definitions.

Thus, one justification for a phenomenological perspective on these particular experiences is that they are bodily experiences common to a great many women; men do not experience them. In turn, women have limited access to certain male bodily experiences (although women generally do not reflect on them and describe them as if they were ours). Phenomenologically speaking, neither women or men can be presently included under the general heading "human" experience. Rather, the biological distinctiveness, as well as the social experiences resulting from this distinctiveness, must be acknowledged and described in order that experience be less masculine and, therefore, more human.

Phenomenological sociology has to do with descriptions of people living in-the-midst-of-the-world, experiencing themselves and the world in their prereflective state; and it describes the foundation of structure of the world on the basis of consciousness. Hence, from the foregoing descriptive study of women's experiences viewed subjectively, we can say that a feminist phenomenological sociology would work to illuminate artificial distinctions between thought and feeling, between subject and object, or between expert and non-expert. It would not be based on the separation between subjectivity and objectivity, but rather, would seek to integrate all aspects of our experience into our understanding of the natural world. Childbirth, therefore, may be regarded as a subject and object of an integrative feminist phenomenological sociology. A new value for this activity, the goal of feminist praxis, is a goal that means the breaking down of the distinction between female and male perspectives.

Let us take the doctor-patient relationship as a single example of the contrast in perspectives. The physician has been trained to perceive objective reality according to a specific set of medical theories. If the woman's (patient's) experience does not fit readily into this trained perspective of objective reality, then her experience is discounted. By refusing to accept the physician as unquestioned authority and by insisting on a more active and reciprocal relationship between doctor and patient, the Woman's Health Movement has given a new visibility to women's actual experience during childbirth and menopause, and thus has provided for the possibility of raising new questions that can potentially expand the boundaries of scientific knowledge in medicine. This has led to changes in our understanding of what is "real"; it has required a shift in the previously rigid boundaries between objective and subjective phenomena; and it has required a different consideration of the relationship between mind and body.

Acknowledgement of such contrasts has not resulted in rejection of medical science or the denial of everything that has been achieved through previous paradigms. But it has resulted in the possibility of moving towards an expanded and more complete form of knowledge. The possibility of this kind of shift within medicine suggests the possibility of opening up and expanding the range of subjective knowledge of women's experience within the social world. Such breakthroughs allow further for the possibility of seeing "objective" tension in the object of knowledge. From this perspective, women as objects of knowledge are viewed not as passive recipients nor as active ones confirming reflections of society. Instead, the tension which informs the method suggests a concept of women in society that also expresses a negation: women opposing the very conditions to which they conform. This tension requires a reconsideration of the assumption in phenomenological investigations that there is a basic continuity between consciousness and activity.

ALTERNATIVE CONSTRUCTIONS OF MEANING

The idea of women simultaneously conforming to and opposing the conditions that deny our freedom suggests that a breach between consciousness and activity does not exist for men who have the dominance over cultural imperatives to implement consciousness through activity (projects, plans, action) and to create concepts that reflect their position. Such a dissociation of consciousness between conforming behavior and consciousness emphasizes the significance of not examining women's consciousness in phenomenology in at least two ways. First, consciousness can be viewed as it is split off from activity, freed from conforming behavior, imagining and phantasizing oneself in a life-world free from oppression and alienation. In short, consciousness can be viewed as women's sphere of freedom, a sphere that exists simultaneously with unfree, conforming behavior. Second, women's reflective consciousness sets in process modes of thought that may be the very opposite of that taken-for-granted consciousness that binds us to the objective characteristics of what we are experiencing. Reflection prompts awareness, self-awareness, analytical and evaluative scrutiny, theoretical understanding, and a systematic grasp of causation (Lengerman and Wallace, 1985:121). These modes of seeing the everyday established routines of women's sphere make possible mobilization for change. Also,

> like new social history, the study of the female world demands the
> redemption of the everyday . . . Ordinary as well as extraordinary lives

compel scrupulous attention . . . To understand them both, interpretation of their subjective experiences matter (Stimpson, 1984:19).

Theories also change in a variety of ways. Knowledge may increase in an incremental way in which we add small bits of new knowledge to that which is already known. Or, we may gain knowledge as we clarify more precisely that which is already known. Finally, Kuhn (1970) suggests that theories may change through revolution in which new information that runs counter to the prevailing knowledge precipitates a crisis and leads to the development of a new paradigm. As important to recognizing how theories change is the acknowledgement that theories do change. A phenomenology for women, where women inform the knowledge it seeks, does not suggest an opposition to existing theories and to the very facts that they discover. The difficulty has been knowing where to start. Consideration and acknowledgement of differences in the way women and men experience the world would reveal different, perhaps contradictory facts. Indeed, my experiences are not the same as another person's nor are my reflections on those experiences. Reflection is subjective, active, and creative. Events and objects do not have inherent meaning, nor are they remembered in exactly the same way by everyone. In fact, according to Schutz, all lived experiences,

> whether passive or active, are lacking in meaning and discrete identity. At the same time they are actually lived through, they are not given to us as separate and distinct entities. However, once they have receded a slight distance into the past, that is, once they have "elapsed," we may turn around and bring to bear upon them one of the aforementioned Acts of reflection, recognition, identification, and so forth. Once it has been caught in the "cone of light" emanating from the Ego, an experience is "lifted out" of the stream of duration and becomes clear and distinct, a discrete entity. It is at this moment and by virtue of the Act of turning-toward that the experience acquires meaning (1967:XXIII).

This means that when a woman as actor finds a different meaning in an entity, she will alter her behavior toward it, even though the physical properties of the entity may have changed very little or not at all. But changes in meaning may reveal new facets of the entity to the public (Tiryakin, 1973). Women's experience of childbirth in a hospital environment is now a complex entity manifested in a variety of things, from medically induced labors, to routinely performed episiotomies, to totally anaesthetized women; these routine procedures have been performed for several decades, yet for the most part were treated with indifference by most women and physicians. But once the dehumanization, alienation, and degradation of the situation was revealed by many women, a vast number of other factors came to be perceived as part of the same phenomenon (alienation, coersion, isolation). This realization has led to a variety of social, political, and personal actions and changes in how women birth (home births, hospital-affiliated maternity centers, family-centered hospital maternity care, midwife-assisted births). What is of phenomenological and feminist interest in this situation is the noematic structuring of the collective perception and experience of childbirth. This example shows us that within a phenomenological orientation the distance between the object of social consciousness and its subject can be overcome. Here, the transmission of knowledge is not simply from expert to nonexpert but is reciprocal; the problems and issues are defined by mutual dialogue. In principle, the same kind of process has begun to be established between social science research and feminist scholars who are raising various aspects of women's experiences as a scientific problem for investigation. As women identify the subject-categories that represent our actual experience in the life-world, we are also revealing discrepancies between the way we are studied and the way we study ourselves in sociology. Again, in the case of childbirth, the omission of subjective research clearly conveys a distorted impression of women's consciousness. No account is taken of the importance to women of planning, choosing among projects and actions, or the personal meaning that reflection has for women.

In becoming active subjects in the creation of knowledge about ourselves and the world around us, women can utilize feminist principles as tools for liberating selected scientific approaches from the inherited habits of male thought that separate human experience into contradictory realms. According to the feminist view,

> science itself must be transformed not simply to permit the acceptance of women, but more importantly, to conceptualize new kinds of relationships between human beings and the natural world, by overcoming an alienation between culture and nature built into our current social experience and thus into our existing forms of knowledge (Fee, 1983:14).

The tension between describing and transforming, which is first perceived by the knower, the subject of knowledge herself, implies a concomitant. And in describing the meaning of experience, when one shares the same gender-socialization and critical life-experiences, differences may be minimal; but when women and men grow up and live in radically different social realities the differences abound. Thus, what is "brought to bear" upon women may differ greatly from men or men's perception of it. While feminists have warned of thus assigning attributes on the basis of gender, it must be pointed out that a phenomenological sociology that recognizes gender differences and values, both male and female, would create a more holistic perspective.

Another conceptual distinction that Schutz discusses is the role of objectivity versus subjectivity in the social sciences. Although some feminists have cautioned against uncritically accepting the linking of subjectivity, irrationality, or the idea of a life force as female (Rothschild, 1983:xxi), there is an element in Schutz's way of thinking with which feminism can agree. Feminist thought has criticized incisively the so-called rational and objective characteristics of sociology. Like the philosophers who challenged positivism or scientific objectivism, feminists have sought to show how the subjective, intuitive, and irrational can and do play a key role in our experience. Current scientific operations (separating, ordering, quantifying, manipulating, controlling) and the implicit criteria of sociological well-being underlying such inquiry (ego-strength, reality orientation, objectivity) are male features that feminist research has also identified as distinctively masculine and that may or may not be modified to accommodate feminist research considerations. In contrast, more communal kinds of scientific inquiry that involve naturalistic observation, sensitivity to intrinsic structure, and qualitative patterning of phenomena studied, and the greater personal participation of the investigator can be accommodated with the phenomenological sociological approach.

Within the particular models of subjectivity and objectivity that have been presented in this book, we can begin to see the interconnections between subject and object that relate to feminist research. The subject/object dichotomy in sociology—the distinction between the person conducting the research and the person about whom the knowledge is being developed—begins to be resolved when women are the agents of knowledge in research on women from a subjective point of view. A phenomenological sociological perspective on women's experience in which the researcher and those being studied are women attempts to demistify the social relations of the knower and the known through procedures that appear less anonymous and more personal—that is, more subjective. The knower in this methodological framework is not "abstract knower" but "knower." Although throughout the book I have assumed a relation between the two, it is evident that a fuller and more detailed conception is necessary, and that we need to continue looking at the ongoing dialectic between subjectivity and other levels of social reality.

TYPIFICATIONS OF EXPERIENCE

Returning to Schutz's acceptance of Weber's insistence that objectivity is made possible only through "ideal types," we see that in questioning how ideal-typical concepts penetrate to the subjective meaning of individuals he went beyond Weber in arguing that all sciences, including sociology, are ultimately bound to construct modelled conceptions of their subject matters and then conduct their analysis within the limits of those models. He questions how individuals can be free if their action is somehow determined by their ideal types, and how social science can pursue subjective meaning by being objective about that which is by its nature subjective (Schutz, 1967, 1973). Like Weber, Schutz considered ideal types (typifications) essential to the constitution of the objects of sociological consciousness, and necessary for social-scientifically disclosing the social world as a "structure of intelligible intentional meaning" (Schutz, 1967:7). However, ideal types vary and shift in accordance with the observer's point of view, the questions being asked, and the total context of the observer's experience (Schutz, 1967:92). Necessarily, then, some of the meaning the social world has for individuals is omitted in the traditional ideal type. Something that appears to be as natural, as universal, as timeless as our bodies, for example, may have a malleability, a history, a meaning that changes. Thus, social science has meaning only within certain limits. The consequence here for feminists is the highly necessary inclusion of women's point of view.

Feminist research shows how ideal types of experience change when the observer's point of view is feminist or woman-centered and the individuals' experiences and interpretations are women's. Bringing women's experience into the description of social life creates a necessary balance to scientific inquiry, and feminist perspectives bring an experiential and holistic approach that transforms such inquiry into an integrated paradigm. Research of this kind, in which the content is expressly identified with women and women's roles and activities, has indeed begun to pave the way for feminist phenomenological sociology; and for feminist phenomenological sociologists *our* world relentlessly invites rigorous attention and informed respect, and *our* world, reminds us that as sociologists we participate in a common effort. In the stepping back lies a promise of return, an enlargement of our existence in the direction of both a widened sense of the world and deepened sense of ourselves. Thus, we acknowledge to ourselves and to others our understanding of our own experience in the lifeworld.

The significance for feminists of the idea of the lifeworld in Schutz's thought is that it was used, not to define the phenomenological project, but to define the project of social science: this was to be the empirical study of the lifeworld. Study of the present, local lifeworld—that is, of sociology as distinct from history and anthropology—can lead feminists in two directions. It can lead us to define a new type of phenomenological sociology or it can lead us to redefine phenomenological sociology traditionally conceived. We go in the first direction if we question what in the given world, the lifeworld, makes intersubjective understanding possible: people are capable of understanding others. How is this possible? (Schutz, 1973). We go in the second if we ask how the idealized world of phenomenological sociology—such as, the world of spontaneously creative women— relates to the actual lifeworld: can and does the researcher refer to the same social world that appears to the actor? (Schutz, 1973). There has been much discussion in this book of both questions.

Thus, it is not only the construction of the ideal type in phenomenological studies as an *a priori* framework for sociological empirical investigation to which feminist principles oppose, but rather, its claim to lead to universal ideal types that are developed through procedures that are interpreted and constructed from a male perspective. By ignoring study of women's consciousness, for example, women are reduced to actors without consciousness, or at least without the capacity to be creative. As such we are totally constrained by external events and, therefore, from a scientific point of view, we are totally predictable and capable of being studied scientifically. This framework awaits an integrated feminist paradigm.

The following serves both to illustrate by contrast the nature of subjective meaning and to emphasize the implications of objective meaning, according to Schutz, which are important to our discussion:

> Objective meaning consists only in a meaning context within the mind of the interpreter, whereas subjective meaning refers beyond it to a meaning-context in the mind of the producer . . . What is essential to this further knowledge is a knowledge of the person being interpreted . . . Every interpretation of subjective meaning involves a reference to a particular person. Furthermore, it must be a person of whom the interpreter has some kind of experience . . . whereas objective meaning is abstracted from and independent of particular persons (1967:134–35).

FEMINIST CRITIQUE

Most social scientists believe that they may restrict their attention to what the social world means to them, ignoring the question of its meaning for mundane actors. Although Schutz concedes that that viewpoint can lead to "real scientific work" that bypasses the problem of subjectivity, he opposes the varieties of "objectivity" and quantification that substitute the researcher's viewpoint for that of the subjects without acknowledging that substitution and taking its consequences into account.

A major premise of Schutz related to the subjective is that subjectively meaningful action is shaped by an unquestioned acceptance of socially derived and approved "recipes," prescribing typical behavior used in typical circumstances. Feminists would agree that social behavior is caused by factors independent of the subject. While it is true that women and men constrict their social reality, they are also affected by the social forces and social systems in the societies in which we live. However, as has been pointed out, women and men have experienced the social world differently; their taken-for-granted-ness, recipes, typifications, and systems of relevance vary, as do their values, goals, purposes, and meaning orientation. Feminism, then, introduces a political element into Schutz's work by its insistence that the world of public affairs and political struggles be included in an interpretation of the lifeworld, along with the experiences and attitudes of the private sphere. These ideas are not actually in conflict with Schutz's interest in the orientations of social actors. In fact, it is often the case in his work that when he is looking at the subjective (recipes, knowledge on hand) constraints of the actor, he is looking at them from the point of view of the actor, from the actor's orientation to those constraints. Schutz consistently implies that we always can and sometimes must refer to the subjects' activities and their interpretations of those activities by considering projects, life plans, available means, relevances, situations and knowledge on hand among other things (Schutz, 1973:35). More broadly, we can say that given his phenomenological position a major intellectual concern of Schutz is the subject orientation of the actor. In this view, although we may not fully agree with Schutz and although he may not fully satisfy a feminist perspective, he does present a more holistic view of the meaning of social action than Weber does. There is undoubtedly a great deal to be learned from phenomenological sociology about create consciousness. Social consciousness for Schutz involves the suspension of doubt that the world is as it appears, that the world is intersubjective. Both purported "laws" were the outcome of an investigation framed in a male context and thus deny the fundamental dualism in Western culture. Thus, their application to analysis of people is experience of the social world makes that analysis and investigation incomplete.

Through the process of intersubjective "comparing of notes" with men's experience, feminist scholarship in sociology has begun to explore women's meaningful (reflective) experiences in culture and society with little confirmation. According to the Schutzian model, this may be good reason for putting such phenomena under scientific "quarantine." However, if we accept phenomenology's claim that whatever presents itself to *anyone's* careful and discriminating observation has *prima facia* equal rights, then those experiences have an equal right to exist and be recognized as belonging to our world of lived experience. The implication for feminism on this point is that the debate over whether equality means sameness also touches on the questions of what is to be standard.

The phenomenological method is generally thought of as primarily concerned with description. But it has become evident that it is more than that; for in aiming toward description of the phenomenon, it reflects backwards toward an elucidation of the structures of consciousness; it bypasses all question of the "subject's objectivity" or the "object's subjectivity" by revealing the immediate world as it is immediately and directly known through a prereflective consciousness.

This initial and direct knowledge constitutes the foundation upon which all future knowledge is built (Schutz, 1967). In order to see things as they manifest themselves, phenomenological sociology abstains from viewing things through what Husserl called "the general thesis of the natural standpoint," namely, from the presupposition that there is a factual world that has a being out there, a world that is knowable and measurable by us, and hence objectively grounded in nature or in the nature of things (Husserl, 1962:96). Phenomenology "places in brackets" this "natural attitude." This methodological heuristic device (the *epoché* or abstention from the natural attitude) is not meant to deny the reality of the world, or of what the natural attitude asserts is "out there." Its purpose is rather to reveal the *a priori* structures or presuppositions of consciousness in terms of which what we perceive makes sense or has meaning for us. What the bracketing procedure enables us to do is twofold. First, it allows the sociological observer to relate social phenomena to the way in which we are experienced by subjects in a situation. Since subjects are always in a situation, the phenomenological investigation concretizes and personalizes social phenomena even while it seeks the essences of these phenomena, their fundamental meaning in and for social action. By directing our attention to the primacy of experience, we are returning "to the things themselves." By perceiving how the phenomenon is experienced by the subjects of the situation, we give the emphasis to approaching and seeking to understand the phenomenon from the interior, rather than initially treating it as an inert thing to be manipulated at will.

Second, the bracketing procedure enables us to see the phenomenon more globally, for to be liberated from the natural attitude means to be freed from the restrictions of conventional ways of seeing things and events, including the limitations of our feminist and sociopolitical perspectives. Obviously, this means that the sociologists who take Schutz's methodology seriously and apply it to the social world must be willing to undergo a certain estrangement from their common-sense perception of social phenomena. This may lead to a position of solitude and alienation, but it may also lead to liberation and freedom, much as that described by Rich. In any case, the phenomenological sociological approach leads us to perceive alternative meanings to a given arrangement of social objects or social conditions. Suspending judgment on the validity of the assertions of the natural attitude enables us to see hidden sides of social phenomena and covert meanings to social relationships, so that we may even find that what has meaning in the natural attitude may sometimes appear to have no meaning at all in a more global feminist phenomenological perspective.

We may now begin to see how phenomenological sociology relates to a descriptive study of women's subjective experience. Menopause, for example, is a phenomenon: it, too, gives itself to consciousness; it appears, and the consciousness of menopause is the essence itself of consciousness. A descriptive study of it, then, would have to concern itself with an appearance, a phenomenon which, while existing through various stages remained a totality. Only when the initial phases have taken place does it stand out as a discrete item from the background of the continuum of other lived experiences. Thus, if the phenomenological constructs such as *epoché, durée,* recipe, typification and reflection have been significant in elucidating the structured features inherent in the total lived experience, they have also been significant in emphasizing the paramount importance of the lived experience. Childbirth as described was not only a pre-phenomenal experience that appeared, that presented itself to consciousness; it became a meaningful lived experience through reflection as both a planned and completed project—an act, a *lived* experience. Without returning again and again to this lived experience, we cannot hope to arrive at a valid and meaningful description of it, the nature of, and structures inherent in its appearance, creation, and presentation.

CONTRIBUTIONS TO FEMINIST RESEARCH

The contributions of phenomenological sociology to feminist research are numerous. Its relevance to feminist sociology is most obvious in its tools for dealing with the number of issues that can no longer be taken for granted in our culture. First, a phenomenological approach opens the way toward an understanding of how women's experiences as subject matter relates to feminism. It offers the opportunity to re-evaluate the place of our experiences in "our" culture by elucidating their nature to the end that the cultural values attributed to them emanate from them. For example, as menopause is viewed from more perspectives, the attitudes and the language of menopause change and become richer with positive expressions that more correctly mirror a time of life with respect for its complexity. Also, viewing menopause as one of women's basic realities brings us closer to understanding how and why we respond and behave the way we do to everything around us. From this perspective, menopause leads to self-realization and self-affirmation.

Second, one of the greatest values of a phenomenological sociological approach to feminist research is that it is open-ended. The descriptions of experiences in question might not only provide the basis upon which other studies might be made, it might also be further elaborated by others whose experience goes beyond the original description. This elaboration is possible, however, only insofar as others verify the original description by their own lived experience of the phenomenon under consideration, as it is recalled, and as it is presented in the stream of consciousness of individual women. What might come of such elaboration of the shared experience is continuous woman-centered collective response and challenge to male standards of experience. The value for feminist sociology of such responses that have begun to emerge in the literature is notably evident, not only because they had been conspicuously missing, but also because they provide a much needed arena for discussion leading to a comprehensive and collective (though at the same time thoroughly individualized) approach to the study of women's experience in the everyday world—which opens the possibility for a transformation of consciousness within the context just described.

Externally-oriented positivist frameworks overlook the way that women's experience is devalued and objectified by our being treated in research both the same as and as different from men. One merit of this book might be that it begins to address the ways this difference shapes the research and the phenomenological sociological framework. For this is the phenomenological source of women's resistance to our subordination as subjects of research and as researchers. Consciousness of the contradictions in which women are placed by virtue of our gender is a precondition to feminist research and feminist theory construction. In so far as phenomenological sociology brings about such consciousness, it is therefore clearly relevant to feminist principles. On the other hand, such consciousness does not of itself alter the social conditions that produce it. Individual life is situated in specific social and historical environments. These environments influence not only what our experience is but also how we think about it. As this book has shown, although women's experience encompasses a variety of perspectives, one basic premise of feminist thought is that its interpretation, understanding, and meaning of women's experience emerges from our own stream of consciousness.

The approach taken in this book, therefore, does not deny that individuals are caught up in the institutions of their time; but, rather, it recognizes the social reality that individuals experience within particular institutions. Thus, the relationship between personal troubles and public issues in Mills's sociological imagination that for feminists is the junction between personal experience and social organization cannot come to fruition without adequate knowledge of that personal experience, a new starting point for analysis. It is here that phenomenological sociology and a feminist perspective interact: whereas phenomenological sociology interprets our consciousness of the world, feminism seeks to transform it.

Feminists may disagree about the best way for women to achieve self-awakening, transformation. For some feminists, this is to be secured only through theoretical frameworks that analyze the power relationships between men and women, and practices based on that analysis. For other feminists, transformation emerges with a shift in consciousness through analyses involved in our social situations. These feminists and others are, however, agreed in recognizing the current injustice attributed to women in theories, methods, and conceptual schemes that prevail in sociology. I concede that women's self-awakening, our shift in knowing, will not, by itself, arrive automatically or enable us to transform the concrete social order. A long detour by the analysis of various theoretical frameworks and their application to women's discovery of a knowledge base from which we can investigate social realities is close at hand. It has been part of the project of this book in particular to provide the methodological framework through which women might be transformed from an object of knowledge into a subject capable of appropriating knowledge.

In providing a phenomenological analysis of women's experience that might bring to light phenomenological sociology's intrinsic values for feminist theory, I hope that I have also acknowledged the woman-identified values that can be found in these experiences and how they may be communicated to others. When these experiences are described, the tendency has been to emphasize the woman's description (her expression of her thoughts or ideas about what it was like for her), to emphasize the description of those in attendance (evocation of observers' impressions or ideas of what it was like for her) without describing what the experience was really like as a deliberated-upon and planned (from the woman's point of view) and completed (from the observers' point of view) act. Phenomenological sociology may not solve the problem of truth; but following Berger's definition of a sociological perspective (chapter six), by interjecting the question "Says who?" into our phenomenological analyses, an element of skepticism is also introduced that cautions or guards us against converting too rapidly. "It makes us less likely to be trapped by every missionary band we encounter on the way" (Berger, 1973:65) and brings feminists closer to the truth.

One direct consequence of this book, therefore, may be to encourage sociologists to broaden their standpoint in studies of women to include the subjective with the belief that this will increase the authenticity and validity of their explanation of "human" behavior. Because of its assumptions, a feminist phenomenological sociological approach to the study of women and men would help to abolish androcentricity by not placing the sexual differentiation above personhood. For in its approach to the study of social reality, a feminist phenomenological approach does not assume that one sex can be understood apart from the other, as if it were a complete "essence." While this approach may reassure the powerful that being human is synonymous with being alike and that we all want and need the same things, this is, in the end, untrue. If social reality is not diverse, it will be peopled with individuals whose homogeneity is defined and determined by those who have the power to bring it into existence.

Moreover, if there is any question of bypassing the significance and meaning of women's experiences such as pregnancy, childbirth, and menopause within a medical environment, it may be because they have been taken out of women's private sphere, and the outcome and meaning for others appear quite different from the outcome and meaning for women. If the phenomenological sociological approach to these experiences can clarify the relationship of meaning to experience, it can lay the groundwork for the distinction between experience from the perspective of the woman having it and from the perspective of (male) observers. As phenomenological sociological methods have revealed, any search for knowledge about a phenomenon begins with the direct intuition of the phenomenon, apart from any prejudice, expectation, or reflection. The phenomenologists' attitude toward the phenomenon, then, is prereflective and is neither objective or subjective; it is an attitude of being conscious of the phenomenon "as-it-appears-to-me," without shaping it any way by *a priori* interpretations or beliefs, thereby leading the researcher to describe the (meaningful) "lived experience" of phenomenon, the essential relationship between consciousness and its world. Thus if pregnancy, childbirth, menstruation, and menopause, as examples, are the phenomena, I as the phenomenological sociologist describe women's immediate encounter with those cycles of life and proceed from there to describe the analyzable structures, such as time, action, intersubjectivity, inherent in the total experience. Other phenomena—sexuality, childcaring, working—may also be analyzed in this way.

Obviously, for some feminists there will be problems involved in a phenomenological sociological orientation, but the problems addressed in this book do not lead inevitably to the conclusions that we should abandon its use. Perhaps Schutz's most serious liability as a potential exemplar of a practitioneer is his lack of interest in, and insight into, a paradigm integrated with women's perspective. While such a major omission may serve to eliminate Schutz from serious consideration as an exemplar, phenomenological sociology does have a great deal to offer on the subjective meaning of social reality and on the reflective attitude. Also, the richest aspect of a feminist consideration of phenomenological sociology lies in the interrelationship between consciousness and meaning. Acknowledgement that phenomenological sociology could provide a framework for studying women's consciousness, stands as an indirect invitation to other feminists to consider adopting this approach. In addition, a feminist phenomenology may enable us to expand Schutzian accounts from the subjective standpoint to include all human activity rather than activity more characteristic of males. The development of such an integrated holistic paradigm is a very large task, one that requires the philosophical, phenomenological, and sociological contributions of many feminists. This book addressed only the question of the epistemological underpinnings that such an integrative paradigm would require.

In an exploration of the plausibility of an application of phenomenological sociology to feminist research, I submit that phenomenological sociology is compatible with feminist research and feminist theory construction (and reconstruction). Necessarily many questions remain and clearly many conventional methods remain for our scrutiny. Perhaps this book will serve to provoke others to articulate and pursue these questions. It is my hope that my investigation leads to a reexamination and perhaps reconstruction of conventional methodological frameworks in sociology as well as the development of new ones that will extend women's potential to know, understand, explain, describe, and define our experiences and related phenomena.

NOTES

1. Maurice Natanson's efforts are significant for phenomenological sociology especially because of his emphasis on the concept of social role and his uses of the concepts of social role and typification as a means of analyzing intersubjective consciousness. See Maurice Natanson, *The Journeying Self: A Study in Philosophy and Social Role*, Reading, Mass.: Addison-Wesley, 1970, pp. 8–46; Natanson's collection of essays, *Phenomenology, Role, and Reason*, Springfield, Ill.: Charles C. Thomas, 1974, especially Part 2; Natanson, *Phenomenology and Social Reality*, The Hague: Martinus Nijhoff, 1979; and Natanson, *Phenomenology and the Social Sciences, Vol. I*, Evanston, Ill.: Northwestern University Press, 1973.

2. See Aaron Cicourel, *Cognitive Sociology: Language and Meaning in Social Interaction*, New York: Free Press, 1974; Jack Douglas, *Understanding Everyday Life; Toward the Reconstruction of Sociological Knowledge*, Chicago: Aldine, 1970; Harold Garfinkel, *Studies in Ethnomethodology*, Englewood Cliffs, New Jersey: Prentice-Hall, 1967; and Roy Turner, ed., *Ethnomethodology: Selected Readings*, Baltimore: Penguin, 1974; Suzanne J. Kessler and Wendy McKenna, *Gender: An Ethnomethodological Approach*, Chicago: University of Chicago Press, 1978; Shulamit Reinharz, "Experiential Analysis: A Contribution to Feminist Research," in *Theories of Women's Studies*, Gloria Bowles and Renate Duelli Klein, eds., Boston: Routledge & Kegan Paul, 1983, pp. 162–91.

3. It is one of the subtle ironies of history that phenomenology arose as an attempted response to a general crisis of scientific knowledge (not in its amount but in its validity) as formulated by the methodology of positivism. For positivistic methodology, which traces its origin to Auguste Comte, was itself a historical response to the crisis of knowledge in European society at the beginnings of the industrial-technological social order, which has stamped modern society up to our time.

4. Both Henri Bergson and Edmund Husserl were attractive to Schutz because they each proposed a kind of intuitionist return to pure subjectivity but without at all rejecting the intellectualist aspirations of science. The major difference between the two philosophers, in terms of Schutz's enterprise, is that they stand at different ends of the range of possible mediations between science and subjectivity—Husserl is more objectivistic and scientific, Bergson more subjectivistic and metaphysical.

5. Schutz explains that the term "objective meaning" is obviously a misnomer, insofar as the so-called "objective" interpretations are, in turn, relative to the particular attitudes of the interpreters and, therefore, in a

161

certain sense, "subjective." These terms, then, do not really refer to matters of ontological status.

6. Here we can detect some similarity to the views of George Herbert Mead and his concept of "taking the role of the other," which Schutz also incorporated into his methodological framework.

7. Although Husserl (and Bergson) were interested in philosophizing about what went on in the mind, the question to Schutz was how to turn this interest into a scientific sociological concern.

8. For critique of Schutz's attempt to reveal some of the inadequacies of Weber's differentiation of direct and explanatory understanding, see Anthony Giddens, *New Rules of Sociological Method: A Positive Critique of Interpretative Sociologies,* New York: Basic Books, 1976.

9. Every individual's stock of knowledge consists, in sum, of the fundamental elements common to all human beings, the habitual knowledge common to all members of a given society and subsocieties, and the specific knowledge of a unique biography, all always "on hand," along with the immediate knowledge the individual has "at hand" in the current situation. As the individual's stream of experience progresses, knowledge "at hand" passes into knowledge on hand. Knowledge at hand, then, is continuously absorbed into knowledge on hand, usually prereflectively. Thus, "stock of knowledge," except where noted, will refer to the stock of knowledge on hand.

10. "The common-sense world," "the world of daily life," and "the everyday world" are some of the expressions Schutz uses to describe the world experienced by people within the state of consciousness described by Husserl as the natural attitude. Schutz intends to pursue a phenomenological analysis within the framework of this mode of consciousness. His efforts are, therefore, directed to the mundane, nontranscendental sphere of social life characterized by our everyday existence.

11. Schutz's insights into reflexivity demand that sociologists cultivate awareness of how common-sense assumptions enter their work, and that they then examine the implications, utility, and tenability of those assumptions. "When common-sense assumptions are uncritically admitted into the apparatus of a science, they have a way of taking their revenge. This may appear through equivocations creeping into its basic concepts and thereby working an adverse effect on research. Or it may occur through a failure to see that apparently diverse phenomena are really of the same type, a failure generated by not having penetrated beyond the appearances to the roots of the phenomena in question. If this danger hangs over every science, its threat to sociology is particularly acute. For sociology's task is to make a scientific study of social phenomena. Now, if social phenomena are constituted in part by common-sense concepts, it is clear that it will not do for sociology to abstain from a scientific examination of these 'self-evident' ideas " (Schutz, 1967:9).

12. Phenomenological methods begin with only the imminent object being investigated (the noema) and the particular mode through which it is given (the noesis). In other terms, "to the things themselves" is a procedural admonition to study an object of experience as an object-of-*my*-experience and to exclude everything that does not belong immediately to that object as directly given. In short, phenomenological methods are reflexive. They involve the certainty of "seeing my seeing"

inasmuch as a phenomenon is known as an object-of-*my*-knowing. In these respects, phenomenologists separate "the intentional lines between us and the world in order to uncover the umbilical cord that ties us to the world" (O'Neill, 1974:xxii, in Rogers, 1983:68).

13. A more lengthy discussion of social action appears in Alfred Schutz, "On Multiple Realities," In *Collected Papers, Vol. II, The Problem of Social Reality*, The Hague: Martinus Nijhoff, 1973:207–59.

14. For illustrations of the mutual tuning-in relationship, see Richard M. Zaner, "Theory of Intersubjectivity: Alfred Schutz," in *Social Research*, Vol. 28, 1961:71–93; also Louise Levesque-Lopman, "Decision and Experience: A Phenomenological Analysis of Pregnancy and Childbirth," *Human Studies 6*, pp. 247–77 (1983).

15. In order to keep the distinction between meaningful and nonmeaningful activity clear, the term "conduct" was adopted by Schutz to refer to subjectively meaningful experiences. Also, experience is divided into conduct and non-conduct, which is meaningful and nonmeaningful experience, respectively. Finally, conduct planned in advance is action, and all conduct is either covert (mere thinking) or overt (mere doing). However, the term "conduct" as used in this sense does not imply any reference to intent.

16. For examples of social institutions based on value orientations see David Stewart and Algis Mickunas, *Exploring Phenomenology*, American Library, 1974.

17. However much some sociologists today may be constrained in their thinking by the remnants of nineteenth-century positivism, there is no doubt that almost all of them agree that social actions are meaningful actions—that is, that they must be studied and explained in terms of their situations and their meanings to the actors themselves. The disputes over the kinds of meanings involved and the ways in which they are to be determined are fundamental, but there is not little dispute among sociologists over the proposition that social meanings are in some way the fundamental determinants of social actions (Douglas, 1970:4).

18. One of the early and important influences on Marx was German idealism, particularly the work of Hegel. The Hegelian dialectic was a subjective process taking place within the realm of ideas. Although affected by this view, Marx and the "Young Hegelians" were dissatisfied with the fact that the dialectic was not rooted in the real, material world. Building on the work of Faurebach and others, Marx sought to take the dialectic and extend it to the material world. On the one hand, this meant that he was concerned with "real" actors rather than idea systems; on the other, he came to focus on the material structures of capitalist society, primarily the economic structure—the "real" material structures of capitalism and the contradictions that existed within them. Subjective ideas continued, however, to play a key role in Marx's notions of false consciousness and class consciousness.

19. Contemporary radical, or "left" phenomenologists, eagerly refer to Marx's early assertion, "To be radical is to grasp things by the root. But for a man the root is man himself." Taken literally, these words supply a theoretical common ground necessary for the evolution of a synthetic phenomenological-Marxism. The goal of Marxism, from this perspective, is to expose (to human perception) the truth of man and history there has remained latent, hidden, and grossly distorted in the machinations of

capitalist society. The phenomenological effort to reveal "things them-selves" so that humanity can move toward more reliable knowledge of the world is now intellectually linked to a Marxist critique of Western capitalism. Both attempt the disocculsion of society, the return to a purified human awareness of those naively experienced social structures constituting our own oppression and alienation. The liberation of the working class from their social enslavement of a newly awakened, reflective humanity, no longer submitting to those de-humanizing cate-gories of economic, social, artistic, and intellectual reality created by and for an elitist society (Gorman, 1977:152).

20. In the ensuing discussion, it is important to keep in mind that the ubiquitous "women" does not represent all women of contemporary society nor any specific women (unless otherwise indicated), but refers to more of an "ideal type" as suggested by the theoretical orientation under examination.

21. For the purpose of this writing, when the term "childbirth" is referred to and used in the context of "experience" (singular), it is to be understood to include pregnancy, labor, and delivery.

22. Nancy Hartsock's discussion of Nancy Chodorow's (1978) study of object relations in human development may offer insight to this occurrence. One aspect of the relational existence of the self-in-body may be related to the boundary challenges that Hartsock claims are inherent in the female rather than male body. These challenges make it impossible to maintain rigid separation from the object world. Menstruation, coitus, pregnancy, childbirth, and lactation—all represent, according to Hart-sock, challenges to bodily boundaries. Chodorow concludes in her analysis that through socialization girls' gradual emergence from the oedipal period takes place in such a way that empathy is built into their primary definition of self, and they have a variety of capacities for experiencing another's needs or feelings of their own. That is,

    girls, because of female parenting, are less differentiated from others than boys, more <u>continuous with</u> and <u>related to</u> [Underlining mine] the external object world. They are differently connected to their inner object world as well . . . This early experience forms a ground for the female sense of self as connected to the world . . . (Hartsock, 1983:295).

23. One meaning of surrender, as described by Kurt H. Wolff (1974:20), relates to the "pertinence of everything: Everythingis everything within the awareness of the surrenderer . . . everything is important, but everything else vanishes." I use the expression "surrender to," also suggested by Wolff (1974:28), "as distinct from surrender: Surrender is unforeseeable, unpredictable; it cannot be brought about by an effort of the will; it happens it befalls. Surrender-to, instead, is concentration, dedication, devotion, utmost attention. It has the characteristics of sur-render except that they are aimed at consciously."

24. The greatest difference among the different kinds of voidings is between the orgasm and the rest. Probably the reason is that in all others what is expelled is waste, while the orgasm expels life, as it were (Wolff, 1974:25). In this sense, childbirth carries that occasion one step further: the expulsion of real life, just now emerging.

25. With regard to what has just been described, "Surrender itself . . . cannot occur if the body intrudes. The body must not interfere, for one must be untrameled, free to 'gather' oneself: in both surrender-to and surrender one *is* 'gathered,' one" (Wolff, *op. cit.*, p. 32).

26. "What is caught (comprehended, conceived)[as the result of 'surrender'] . . . cannot be anticipated . . . The result of surrender may not be a concept in the everyday or scientific sense of the word but the clarification of an existential question, a change in the person: ontologically, it always is a new conceiving, a new concept, a beginning, a new being-in-the-world" (Wolff, *op. cit.*, p. 20).

27. Since the surrenderer wants to *know*, he or she must move surrender to 'catch,' must comprehend, conceive, so that he or she can tell others what has occurred (Wolff, 1963:20).

28. Such accounts are presented in Ann Oakley, *Becoming a Mother*, London: Martin Robertson, 1979 and *Women Confined: Toward a Sociology of Childbirth*, New York: Schocken Books, 1980; Louise T. Levesque, *Being Pregnant: There Is More to Childbirth Than Having a Baby*, Ontario, Canada: Diliton, 1980; Louise Levesque-Lopman, "Decision and Experience: A Phenomenological Analysis of Pregnancy and Childbirth," *Human Studies 6*, 247–77 (1983); Iris Marion Young, "Pregnant Embodiment: Subjectivity and Alienation," *Journal of Medicine and Philosophy 9*, 45–62 (1984); Mary K. Zimmerman, *Passage Through Abortion: The Personal and Social Reality of Women's Experience*, New York: Praeger, 1977.

GLOSSARY

Act. The outcome of action based on a preconceived project; the accomplished action.

Action. Designates human conduct as an ongoing process devised by the actor in advance, that is, based on a preconceived project, and it is this reference to the preceding project that makes both the acting and the act meaningful.

Biographical situation. The sedimentation of all our previous subjective experiences; to this situation belongs not only our position in space, time, and society but also our experience that some taken-for-granted elements of the world are imposed upon us, while others are either within our control or capable of being brought within our control, and thus are principally modifiable.

Conduct. Subjectively meaningful experiences emanating from our spontaneous life; refers to all kinds of subjectively meaningful experiences of spontaneity, be they those of inner life or those gearing into the outer world.

Consciousness. Refers to all of perceptual experience, to people's thinking, believing, writing, remembering, anticipating, deciding, and choosing. To be conscious is to be conscious *of* something, a something that then stands to the activity of consciousness as the meaning of its performance.

Durée or inner time. Time within which our actual experiences are connected with the past by recollections and retentions and with the future by protentions and anticipations. Also referred to as time-consciousness.

Eidetic approach. A methodological device of investigation outlined by Husserl for dealing with possibly imaginable things, not concrete real things. It refers to the reference that phenomenologists do not have to do with the objects themselves; they are interested in their meaning, as they are constituted by the activities of our mind. The eidetic approach leads to an entirely new theory of induction and association and also opens the way to a scientific ontology.

Epoché. Derived from a Greek term meaning abstention; Husserl's method for studying phenomenon; a method of radical doubt: the observer suspends judgment about the phenomenon or questions its very existence by "brackeing the objective world." Used by Schutz (differently from Husserl) to indicate the suspension of our belief in the reality of the world as a device to overcome the natural attitude by radicalizing the Cartesian method of philosophical doubt. Differs from the *epoché* of the natural attitude.

Epoché of the natural attitude. Everyday people's suspension or bracketing not in the outer world and its existence, but the doubt that the world and its objects might be otherwise than they appear to us. Differs from the phenomenological *epoché*.

Essence. That intuited invariant quality without which the intended object, the phenomena, would not be what it is. Has as its reference the *a priori* realm of possibilities that precede those of actualities.

Face-to-face relation. The relationship obtained between any two or more consociates whose worlds within actual and potential reach (with their corresponding manipulatory spheres), partially overlap, and are thus shared, held in common. It implies a community of time and space among consociates; it does not imply any degree of intimacy, since it is equally applicable to the co-presence of freinds and of strangers.

Inner time. That aspect in which wide-awake individuals experience their working acts as events within a stream of consciousness. See *durée*.

Life-world or world of daily life. Encompasses the macro-subjective, taken-for-granted background framework of social life as well as its impact on the thoughts and actions of actors; interpreted by others, our predecessors, as an organized world. Includes the totality of typifications upon which all experience, knowledge, and conduct is based; a world that is taken-for-granted by the typical actor; it is simply there, handed down to us by others in the form of "knowledge at hand," which functions as a scheme of reference. The fact that the social world is, to a large extent, predefined by cultural impositions leads, paradoxically, to more freedom for the actor. Because of these culturally imposed patterns, actors do not have to negotiate every aspect of every situation. By relying on definition by type and conduct by recipe, the actor is free to modify knowledge and conduct in regard to particular problematic facets of the social world.

Meaning. The result of an interpretation of a past experience looked at from the present with a reflective attitude.

Natural attitude. The standpoint of all conscious activity except phenomenological reflection; the underpinning of all human experience as the belief in the existence of whatever concerns us; the taken-for-granted frame in which all problems that we must overcome are placed; the "unexamined ground."

Noema. Cogitations subject to modification that originates within the intentional object (of my perceiving) itself.

Noesis. Modifications of the intentional object due to activities of the mind.

Null point. That this world has significance and meaning first of all by me and for me; with respect to a personality.

Outer time, objective or standard time. The time common to all of us; a single supposedly homogeneous dimension of time; time measurable by clocks and calendars. To the natural attitude, standard time is, in the same sense, the universal temporal structure of the intersubjective world of everyday life within the natural attitude.

Paramount reality. As distinguished from the world of dreams, of scientific theory, of games, and so on; the world in which we find ourselves in our "wide-awake" living peopled with others with whom we are acquainted and others whom we know less well or not at all, or groups of others equally well or less well known to us; and a multiplicity of "products" of activities of others, all of which intrinsically refer to others.

Phenomenology. A reflective enterprise in which one questions one's experiences in a skeptical fashion, without necessarily rejecting these experiences. "Essentially the trick of making things whose meanings seem clear meaningless and discovering what they mean. By doing this we reveal meanings that are not actually apparent to the critical mind but which nevertheless are present at some other level of consciousness" (Blumenstiel in Psathas, 1972:189); an effort to explore people and their existence by placing primary emphasis on the self, understood as consciousness confronting a world and engaged in human action.

Phenomenological reduction. The technique of bracketing or suspending not only the existence of the outer world, along with all the things in it, inanimate and animate, including other people, cultural objects, society and its institutions, but also our belief in the validity of our statements about this world and its content, as conceived within the mundane sphere.

"Real" social world. An image held by Schutz that recognizes that people have minds; that they engage in the social construction of reality; and that their constructions set the limits for activity. Social actors construct the social world through their consciously instructed activity. The constructions, in turn, constrain further creative activity.

Reciprocity of perspectives. The open possibility of an interchange of the standpoints, that is—metaphorically speaking—on the establishment of a formula of transformation by which the terms of one system of coordinates can be translated into terms of the other.

Reflection. The process by which we detach attention from the flow of experiencing and turn that attention analytically to the actor (self) and the act. This ability to detach, to "see" self and activity as objects is the "ability to reflect." (Philosophers and social scientists claim that only human beings have the capacity for reflection.)

Social action. Action oriented toward the past, present, or future behavior of another person or persons; a relationship between the behavior of two or more people. According to Weber, that which takes account of, and is oriented to the behavior of others; behavior to which a subjective meaning is attached.

Social world. A world peopled by social actors who have minds and who engage in creative activity; not amenable to scientific analysis.

Stock of knowledge. The storehouse of our consciousness in which is filed away past experiences (presented to us as ordered) and through which we come to know about the world and what to expect. With every moment of conscious life, a new item is filed—all of which are evolved in the conception of a duration that is manifold.

System of relevances. That which governs us within the natural attitude and is founded upon the basic experience of each of us; frameworks of possible or alternative actions as we work toward our purposes and goals; frameworks that are set up by the stock of our knowledge.

Taken-for-grantedness. The commonsense expectation that the world will continue to be much as it has been; the expectation that, until further notice, our past notions, beliefs, concepts, and even our inarticulated anticipations will continue to apply and serve our needs; that we live in an unquestioned matric (but one which can always, under certain circumstances be brought into question) that defines not only those goals achieveable by bodily activities, but also our inquiries and problems in general.

Thou-relation. A theoretical construct specifying the limits of the face-to-face experience of another human being purely as a person, not as a specific individual.

Time-consciousness. See *durée.*

Typifications. Recipes for action that exist in the culture as a whole—that is, that exist macro-subjectively. Schutz's view of typification is essentially similar to Weber's concept of ideal types. As people are socialized, they learn these recipes, these typical actions for typical situations, and come to employ them in appropriate situations. In other words, in any given situation, an action is determined "by means of a type constituted in earlier experiences." In face-to-face relationships, typification is modified to a certain extent by adjusting interpretations and definitions to unique situations. The more impersonal the situation or the more remote the relationship to the other persons, the more typified meanings are employed.

Vivid present. Originates in an intersection of *durée* and cosmic time; the experiencing in simultaneity of the working action as a series of events in outer and in inner time, unifying both dimensions into a single flux.

We-relation. That which occurs when the thou-relation is reciprocal; involves mutual awareness and sympathetic participation in one another's lives for some period of time, whether long or short. Empirically, we-relations involve various stages of apprehension and typification of other individuals.

Wide-awakeness. A plane of consciousness of highest tension originating in an attitude of full attention to life and its requirements. Passive attention is the opposite of full awakeness. The state of full awakeness traces out that segment of the world that is pragmatically relevant, and those relevances determine the form and content of our stream of thought.

Working. Action in the outer world, based upon a project and characterized by the intention to bring about the projected state of affairs by bodily movements; the most important form of spontaneity for the constitution of the reality of the world of daily life.

World of daily life. The intersubjective world that existed long before our birth, experienced and interpreted by others, our predecessors, as an organized world. Now it is given to our experience and interpretation.

BIBLIOGRAPHY

Andersen, Margaret L. 1983. *Thinking About Women: Sociological and Feminist Perspectives*. New York: Macmillan.

Arendt, Hannah. 1958. *The Human Condition*. New York: Doubleday.

Arms, Suzanne. 1973. *Immaculate Deception*. Boston: Houghton Mifflin Co.

Bart, Pauline B. 1972. "Depression in Middle-Aged Women." In *Women in Sexist Society*, eds. Vivan Gornich and Barbara K. Moran. New York: New American Library, pp. 163–86.

———. 1969. "The Sociology of the Middle Years." *Sociological Symposium*, vol. 3.

Bartky, Sandra Lee. 1977. "Toward a Phenomenology of Feminist Consciousness." In *Feminism and Philosophy*, eds. Mary Vetterling-Braggin, Frederick A. Elliston, and Jane English. Totowa, N.J.: Rowman and Littlefield, pp. 22–37.

Belenky, Mary Field, Blythe McVicker Linchy, Nancy Rule Goldberger, and Jill Mattuck Tarule. 1986. *Women's Way of Knowing: The Development of Self, Voice and Mind*. New York: Basic Books.

Berger, Peter L. 1973. *Invitation to Sociology: A Humanistic Perspective*. New York: Anchor.

Berger, Peter L., and Thomas Luckman. 1966. *The Social Construction of Reality*. New York: Anchor.

Bergson, Henri. 1974. *The Creative Mind: An Introduction to Metaphysics*. New York: Citadel Press.

Bernard, Jessie. 1972. *The Future of Marriage*. New York: World Publishing.

———. 1974. *The Future of Motherhood*. New York: Penguin.

———. 1981. *The Female World*. New York: Free Press.

Bernikow, Louise. 1980. *Among Women*. New York: Harper & Row.

Bien, Joseph, ed. 1978. *Phenomenology and the Social Sciences: Dialogue*. Boston: Martinus Nijhoff.

Bierstedt, Robert. 1963. *The Common Sense World of Alfred Schutz*. "Social Research", vol. 30, pp. 116–21.

Blau, Peter and Otis Duncan. 1967. *The American Occupational Structure*. New York: Wiley.

Blumer, Herbert. 1969. *Symbolic Interaction: Perspective and Method*. Englewood Cliffs, N.J.: Prentice-Hall.

Bostock, Anya. 1972. *Talk on BBC Third Programme*. "The Listener." August.

Bowles, Gloria and Renata Duelli Klein, eds. 1983. *Theories of Women's Studies*. Boston: Routledge & Kegan Paul.

Braverman, Harry. 1974. *Labor and Monopoly Capital*. New York: Monthly Review Press.

Buhle, Mari Jo, Ann D. Cordon, and Nancy Schrom. 1982. "Women in American Society." *Radical America* 16(3):34–35.

171

Burnham, Dorothy. 1983. *Black Women as Producers and Reproducers for Profit.* In *Woman's Nature: Rationalizations in Equality,* eds. Marian Lowe and Ruth Hubbard. New York: Pergamon Press. 1983. pp. 29–38.

Carlson, Rae. 1972. "Understanding Women: Implications for Personality Theory and Research." In "New Perspectives on Women." *Journal of Social Issues,* 28(2):17–29.

Chabon, Irwin, M.D. 1966. *Awake and Aware: Participating in Childbirth through Psychoprophylaxis.* New York: Delacorte Press.

Chesler, Phyllis. 1979. *With Child: A Diary of Motherhood.* New York: Thomas Crowell.

Chodorow, Nancy. 1978. *The Reproduction of Mothering: Psychoanalysis and the Sociology of Gender.* Berkeley: University of California Press.

Chodorow, Nancy and Barrie Thorne. 1986. "Letter to the Editor." *Sociologists for Women in Society Network News* 111:5, 3.

Cicourel, Aaron. 1974. *Cognitive Sociology: Language and Meaning in Social Interaction.* New York: Free Press.

Collins, Randal, ed. 1985. *Three Sociological Traditions: Selected Readings.* New York: Oxford University Press.

Comte, Auguste. 1957. *A General View of Positivism.* New York: Robert Speller and Sons.

Cook, Judith A. 1984. Review of *Breaking Out: Feminist Consciousness and Feminist Research,* by Liz Stanley and Sue Wise (London: Routledge and Kegan Paul, 1983). *Contemporary Sociology* 13(2):194.

Cooke, Joanne, Charlotte Bunch-Weeks, and Robin Morgan, eds. 1979. *The New Women.* Greenwich, Conn.: Fawcett.

Correa, Gena. 1977. *The Hidden Malpractice: How American Medicine Treats Women as Patients and Professionals.* New York: William Morrow.

Coser, Lewis, 1975. "Presidential Address: Two Methods in Search of a Substance." *American Sociological Review* 40 (December).

———. 1977a. "George Simmel's Neglected Contribution to the Sociology of Women." *Signs: Journal of Women, Culture and Society* 2:869–76.

———. 1977b. *Masters of Sociological Thought: Ideas in Historical and Social Context,* 2nd ed. New York: Harcourt Brace Jovanovich.

Cott, Nancy. 1986. "Feminist Theory and Feminist Movements: The Past Before Us." In *What is Feminism?,* eds., Juliet Mitchell and Ann Oakley. New York: Pantheon, pp. 49–62.

Coyner, Sandra. 1983. "Women's Studies as an Academic Discipline: Why and How to Do It." In *Theories of Women's Studies,* eds., Gloria Bowles and Renate Duelli Klein. Boston: Routledge and Kegan Paul, 1983, pp. 46–71.

Cox, Ronald R. 1978. *Schutz's Theory of Relevance: A Phenomenological Critique.* Boston: Martinus Nijhoff.

Cuff, E. C. and G. E. F. Payne, eds. 1984. *Perspectives in Sociology,* 2nd ed. London: Allen and Unwin.

Dallmayr, Fred R. 1981. *Beyond Dogma and Despair: Toward a Critical Phenomenology of Politics.* Indiana: University of Notre Dame Press.

Daly, Mary. 1970. "Women and the Catholic Church." In *Sisterhood is Powerful: An Anthology of Writings From the Women's Liberation Movement,* ed., Robin Morgan. New York: Vintage, 1970, pp. 124–138.

———. 1973. *Beyond God the Father: Toward a Philosophy of Woman's Liberation.* Boston: Beacon Press.

Daniels, Arlene Kaplan. 1975. "Feminist Perspectives in Sociological Research." In *Another Voice: Feminist Perspectives on Social Life and Social Sciences,* eds. Marcia Millman and Rosabeth Moss Kanter. New York: Anchor, 1975, pp. 340–80.

deBeauvoir, Simone. 1952. *The Second Sex.* Translated and edited by H. M. Parshley. New York: Vintage.

Delmar, Rosaline. 1986. "What is Feminism?" in *What is Feminism?*, eds. Juliet Mitchell and Ann Oakley. New York: Pantheon, pp. 8–33.

Demetrakopoulos, Stephanie. 1983. *Listening to Our Bodies: The Rebirth of Feminine Wisdom.* Boston: Beacon Press.

Depner, Charlene. 1981. "Toward the Further Development of Feminist Psychology." Paper presented at the mid-winter conference of the Association of Women in Psychology. Boston.

Derber, Charles. 1979. Review of *Phenomenology and Sociology,* ed., Thomas Luckman. New York: Penguin Books, 1978 in *Contemporary Sociology* 8:4 (July).

Descartes, René. 1960. *Discourse on Method and Meditations.* Translated with an Introduction by Laurence J. Lafleur. New York: Liberal Arts Press.

Dewey, John. 1922. *Human Nature and Conduct.* New York: Modern Library.

Dick-Read, Grantly, M.D. 1959. *Childbirth Without Fear.* New York: Harper and Row.

Dinnerstein, Dorothy. 1977. *The Mermaid and the Minotaur: Sexual Arrangements and Human Malaise.* New York: Harper and Row.

DiOrio, Judith. 1980. "Toward a Phenomenological Feminism: A Critique of Gender Role Research." Paper presented at the Second Annual Women's Studies Association Conference, Bloomington, Ind., May 18.

Douglas, Jack D. 1970. "Understanding Everyday Life." In *Understanding Everyday Life: Toward the Reconstruction of Sociological Knowledge,* Jack D. Douglas, ed. Chicago: Aldine, pp. 3–44.

Douglas, Jack D., Patricia A. Adler, Andrea Fontana, C. Robert Freeman, and Joseph A. Kotarba. 1980. *Introduction to the Sociologies of Everyday Life.* Boston: Allyn and Bacon.

DuBois, Barbara. 1983. "Passionate Scholarship." in *Theories of Women's Studies,* Gloria Bowles and Renate Dueli Klein, eds. Boston: Routledge and Kegan Paul, pp. 105–116.

DuBois, Ellen Carol, Gail Kelly Paradise, Elizabeth Lapovsky Kennedy, Carolyn W. Korsmeyer, and Lillian S. Robinson. 1985. *Feminist Scholarship: Kindling in the Groves of Academe.* Chicago: University of Illinois Press.

Durkheim, Emile. 1951. *Suicide,* translated by J. A. Spaulding and G. Simpson. New York: Free Press.

———. 1964. *The Division of Labor in Society.* New York: Free Press.

Eichler, Margaret. 1979. *The Double Standard: A Feminist Critique of Feminist Social Science.* New York: St. Martins Press.

Eisenstein, Hester. 1983. *Contemporary Feminist Thought.* Boston: G. K. Hall.

Elshtain, Jean B., ed. 1982. *The Family in Political Thought.* Amherst, Mass.: University of Massachusetts Press.

Epstein, Cynthia Fuchs. 1970. *Woman's Place: Options and Limits in Professional Courses.* Berkeley, Calif.: University of California Press.

Evans, Mary. 1983. "In Praise of Theory: The Case for Women's Studies." In *Theories of Women's Studies,* Gloria Bowles and Renate Duelli Klein, eds. Boston: Routledge and Kegan Paul, pp. 219–28.

Farber, Marvin. 1966. *The Aims of Phenomenology: The Motives, Methods, and Impact of Husserl's Thought.* New York: Harper Torchbooks.

Fee, Elizabeth. 1983. "Women's Nature and Scientific Objectivity." In *Woman's Nature: Rationalizations in Equality,* Marian Lowe and Ruth Hubbard, eds. New York: Pergamon Press, pp. 9–27.

Ferguson, Kathy E. 1980. *Self, Society, and Womankind: The Dialectic of Liberation.* Westport, Conn.: Greenwood Press.

Firestone, Shulamith. 1970. *The Dialectic of Sex*. New York: Bantam.

Fishman, Pamela M. 1978. "Interaction: The Work Women Do." *Social Problems* 25 (April): 397–406.

Fowlkes, Diane L., and Charlotte S. McClure. 1984. *Feminist Visions: Toward a Transformation of the Liberal Arts Curriculum*. Alabama: University of Alabama Press.

Freeman, C. Robert. 1980. "Phenomenological Sociology and Ethnomethodology." In *Introduction to the Sociologies of Everyday Life*, Jack D. Douglas *et al*. Boston: Allyn and Bacon, pp. 113–154.

Freidson, Eliot. 1961. *Patients' Views of Medical Practice*. New York: Russell Sage Foundation.

———. 1970b. *Profession of Medicine*. New York: Harper and Row.

———. 1970a. *Professional Dominance: The Social Structure of Medical Care*. New York: Atherton Press.

———. 1971. *The Professions and Their Prospects*. Beverly Hills: Sage.

Freidson, Eliot and Judith Lorber, eds. 1972. *Medical Men and Their Work*. New York: Atherton.

Friday, Nancy. 1977. *My Mother/Myself: The Daughter's Search for Identity*. New York: Dell.

Friedlander, Judith, Blanche Wiesen Cook, Alice Kessler-Harris, and Carroll Smith-Rosenberg, eds. 1986. *Women in Culture and Politics: A Century of Change*. Bloomington, Ind.: Indiana University Press.

Fuchs, Estelle. 1978. *The Second Season: Life, Love and Sex for Women in the Middle Years*. New York: Anchor.

Garfinkel, Harold. 1967. *Studies in Ethnomethodology*. Englewood Cliffs, N.J.: Prentice-Hall.

Giddens, Anthony. 1976a. *New Rules of Sociological Method: A Positive Critique of Interpretive Sociologies*. New York: Basic Books.

———. 1976b. "Classical Social Theory and the Origins of Modern Sociology." *American Journal of Sociology* 81 (January).

Gill, Harrell J. 1981. Review of *Beyond Dogma and Despair: Toward a Critical Phenomenology of Politics*, Fred R. Dallmayr. (Notre Dame: University of Notre Dame Press). *Contemporary Sociology*, November 1982, p. 770.

Gilligan, Carol. 1977. "In a Different Voice: Women's Conceptions of Self and of Morality." *Harvard Educational Review* 47: 481–511.

———. 1979. "Woman's Place in Man's Life Cycle." *Harvard Educational Review* 49: 431–66.

———. 1982. *In a Different Voice: Psychological Theory and Women's Development*. Cambridge, Mass.: Harvard University Press.

Glazer, Nona, and Helen Youngelson Waihrer, eds. 1977. *Woman in a Man-Made World: A Socioeconomic Handbook*, 2nd ed. Chicago: Rand McNally College Publishing.

Goffman, Erving. 1963. *Stigma*. Englewood Cliffs, N.J.: Prentice-Hall.

Goreau, Angeline. 1975. "Aphra Behn: A Scandal to Modesty." In *Voices of the New Feminism*, Mary Lou Thompson, ed. Boston: Beacon Press.

Gorman, Robert A. 1977. *The Dual Vision: Alfred Schutz and the Myth of Phenomenological Social Science*. Boston: Routledge and Kegan Paul.

Gornick, Vivian. 1971. "Women as Outsiders." In *Woman in Sexist Society: Studies in Power and Powerlessness*, Vivian Gornick and Barbara K. Moran, eds. New American Library, pp. 126–44.

Gould, Meredith. 1980. "The New Sociology." *Signs: Journal of Women in Culture and Society* 5 (3): 459–67.

Gouldner, Alvin W. 1962. "Anti-Minotaur: The Myth of Value-Free Sociology." *Social Problems* (Winter): 199–213.

————. 1970. *The Coming Crisis of Western Sociology.* New York: Equinox Books.

Grathoff, Richard, ed. 1978. *The Theory of Social Action: The Correspondence of Alfred Schutz and Talcott Parsons.* Bloomington: Indiana University Press.

Greer, Germaine. 1984. *Sex and Destiny: The Politics of Human Fertility.* New York: Harper and Row.

Griffin, Susan. 1975. *Voices.* New York: Feminist Press.

————. 1978. *Woman and Nature: The Roaring Inside Her.* New York: Harper & Row.

Gurwitsh, Aron. 1966. *Studies in Phenomenology and Psychology.* Evanston, Ill.: Northwestern University Press.

Hamilton, Roberta. 1978. *The Liberation of Women: A Study of Patriarchy and Capitalism.* Boston: George Allen and Unwin.

Harding, Sandra, and Merrill B. Hintikka, eds. 1983. *Discovering Reality: Feminist Perspectives on Epistemology, Metaphysics, Methodology, and Philosophy of Science.* Boston: D. Reidel Publishing.

Harper, Anne L. 1984. "Human Sexuality, New Insights from Women's History." In *Feminist Visions: Toward a Transformation of the Liberal Arts Curriculum,* Diane L. Fowlkes and Charlotte S. McClure. Alabama: University of Alabama Press, pp. 170–83.

Hartsock, Nancy C. M. 1983. "The Feminist Standpoint: Developing the Ground for a Specifically Feminist Historical Materialism." Sandra Harding and Merrill B. Hintikka, eds. In *Discovering Reality: Feminist Perspectives on Epistemology, Methodology, and Philosophy of Science,* Sandra Harding and Merrill B. Hintikka, eds. Boston: D. Reidel Publishing, pp. 283–310.

————. 1984. "Exchange Theory: Critique from a Feminist Standpoint." Paper prepared for delivery at the 1984 meetings of the ASA, San Antonio, Texas, August 26–29, 1984.

Hays, Hoffman R. 1967. *The Dangerous Sex.* New York: Pocket Books.

Heap, James L., and Phillip A. Roth. 1973. "On Phenomenological Sociology." *American Sociological Review* 38 (June): 354–67.

Herman, Debra. 1984. "Does Equality Mean Sameness." In *Feminist Visions: Toward a Transformation of the Liberal Arts Curriculum,* Diane L. Fowlkes and Charlotte S. McClure. Alabama: University of Alabama Press, pp. 149–57.

Hochschild, Arlie Russell. 1975. "The Sociology of Feeling and Emotion: Selected Possibilities." In *Another Voice: Feminist Perspectives on Social Life and Social Sciences,* Marcia Millman and Rosabeth Moss Kanter, eds. New York: Anchor, pp. 280–307.

Housman, Judy. 1982. "Mothering, the Unconscious, and Feminism." *Radical America* 16 (6):47–61.

Hubbard, Ruth. 1983. "Social Effects of Some Contemporary Myths About Women." In *Woman's Nature: Rationalizations in Equality,* Marian Lowe and Ruth Hubbard, eds. New York: Pergamon, pp. 1–18.

Hubbard, Ruth, Mary Sue Henfin, and Barbara Fried. 1982. *Biological Woman.* Cambridge: Mass.: Schenkman.

Hunter College Women's Studies Collective. 1983. *Women's Realities, Women's Choices: An Introduction to Women's Studies.* New York: Oxford University Press.

Husserl, Edmund. 1962. *Ideas: General Introduction to Pure Phenomenology.* New York: Collier Books.

————. 1964. *The Phenomenology of Internal Time-Consciousness.* Bloomington, Ind.: Indiana University Press.

————. 1969. *Cartesian Meditations: An Introduction to Phenomenology,* translated by Dorion Cairns. The Hague: Martinus Nijhoff.

——. 1980. *Phenomenology and the Foundations of the Sciences,* translated by Ted Klein and William Pohl. The Hague: Martinus Nijhoff.

Illsley, R. 1967. "The Sociological Study of Reproduction and Its Outcome." In *Childbearing: Its Social and Psychological Aspects,* S. A. Richardson and A. F. Guttmacher, eds. Baltimore: Williams and Wilkins.

Inch, Salley. 1985. *Birthright: What Every Parent Should Know About Childbirth in Hospitals.* New York: Pantheon.

Jaggar, Slidon, M. and Paula S. Rothenberg. 1984. *Feminist Frameworks: Alternative Theoretical Accounts of the Relations Between Women and Men,* 2nd ed., New York: McGraw-Hill.

Janeway, Elizabeth. 1971. *Man's World, Woman's Place: A Study of Social Mythology.* New York: Del Publishing.

——. 1974. *Between Myth and Morning: Women Awakening.* New York: William Morrow.

——. 1980. *Powers of the Weak.* New York: Aflred A. Knopf.

Janssen-Jurreit, Marielouise. 1982. *Sexism: The Male Monopoly of History and Thought.* New York: Farrar Strauss Giroux.

Jayaratne, Toby Epstein. 1983. "The Value of Quantitative Methodology for Feminist Research." In *Theories of Women's Studies,* Gloria Bowles and Renate Duelli Klein, eds. Boston: Routledge and Kegan Paul, pp. 140–61.

Kanter, Rosabeth. 1975. "Women and the Structure of Organizations." In *Another Voice: Feminist Perspectives on Social Life and Social Sciences,* Marcia Millman and Rosabeth Kanter, eds. New York: Anchor, pp. 415–30.

Keller, Evelyn Fox. 1980. "Feminist Critique of Science: A Forward or Backward Move?" *Fundamenta Scientiae* 1.

——. 1983. "Gender and Science." In *Discovering Reality: Feminist Perspectives on Epistemology, Metaphysics, Methodology, and Philosophy of Science,* Sandra Harding and Merrill B. Hintikka, eds. Boston: D. Reidel Publishing, pp. 187–205.

——. 1985. *Reflections on Gender and Science.* New Haven, Conn.: Yale University Press.

Keller, Evelyn Fox and Christine R. Grontowski. 1983. "The Mind's Eye." In *Discovering Reality: Feminist Perspectives on Epistemology, Metaphysics, Methodology, and Philosophy of Science,* Sandra Harding and Merrill B. Hintikka, eds. Boston: D. Reidel Publishing, pp. 207–224.

Keohane, Nanerl O., Michelle Z. Rosaldo, and Barbara C. Gelpi. 1983. *Feminist Theory: A Critique of Ideology.* Chicago: University of Chicago Press.

Kessler, Suzanne J. and Wendy McKenna. 1978. *Gender: An Ethnomethodological Approach.* Chicago: University of Chicago Press.

Kitzinger, Sheila. 1972. *The Experience of Childbirth,* 3rd ed. Maryland: Penguin.

——. 1978. *Women as Mothers.* New York: Vintage.

Klein, Renate Duelli. 1983. "How to Do What We Want to Do: Thoughts About Feminist Methodology." In *Theories of Women's Studies,* Gloria Bowles and Renate Duelli Klein, eds. Boston: Routledge and Kegan Paul, pp. 88–104.

Kockelmans, Joseph J. 1967. "What is Phenomenology? Some Fundamental Themes of Husserl's Phenomenology." In *Phenomenology: The Philosophy of Edmund Husserl,* Joseph H. Kockelmans, ed. New York: Anchor, pp. 24–36.

——. 1967. *Phenomenology: The Philosophy of Edmund Husserl.* New York: Anchor.

Kuhn, Thomas. 1970. *The Structure of Scientific Revolution,* 2nd ed., enlarged. Chicago: University of Chicago Press.

Lamaze, Fernand. 1970. *Painless Childbirth,* translated by L. R. Celestin. Chicago: Henry Regnery.

Lang, Raven. 1972. *Birth Book*. Cupertino, Calif.: Genesis Press.

Langer, Sandra L. 1984. "Against the Grain: A Working Feminist Art Criticism." In *Feminist Visions: Toward a Transformation of the Liberal Arts Curriculum*, Diane Fowlkes and Charlotte S. McClure, eds. Alabama: University of Alabama Press, pp. 84–96.

Langland, E. and W. Gove, eds. 1981. *A Feminist Perspective in the Academy*. Chicago: University of Chicago Press.

Lengerman, Patricia Madoo and Ruth A. Wallace. 1985. *Gender in America: Social Control and Social Change*. Englewood Cliffs, N.J.: Prentice-Hall.

Lennon, Mary Clare. 1982. "The Psychological Consequences of Menopause: The Importance of Timing of a Life Stage Event." *Journal of Health and Social Behavior* 23 (December): 353–66.

Lerner, Gerda. 1977. *The Female Experience: An American Documentary*. Indianapolis: Bobbs-Merril Educational Publishing.

Levesque, Louise T. 1976. "There's More to Childbirth Than Having a Baby." Dissertation, Department of Sociology, Brandeis University, February.

––––––. 1981. *Being Pregnant: There is More to Childbirth Than Having a Baby*. Ontario, Canada: Diliton.

Levesque-Lopman, Louise. 1983. "Decision and Experience: A Phenomenological Analysis of Pregnancy and Childbirth." *Human Studies* 6:244–77.

Levine, Donald N., ed. 1977. *Georg Simmel: On Individuality and Social Forms*. Chicago: University of Chicago Press.

Lewis, A. 1950. *An Interesting Condition*. New York: Doubleday.

Locke, Mamie. 1984. "Sexism and Racism: Obstacles to the Development of Black Women in South Africa." In *Feminist Visions: Toward a Transformation of the Liberal Arts Curriculum*, Diane L. Fowlkes and Charlotte S. McClure. Alabama: University of Alabama Press, pp. 119–29.

Lofland, L. 1975. " 'Thereness' of Women: A Selective Review of Urban Sociology." In *Another Voice: Feminist Perspectives on Social Life and Social Sciences*, Marcia Millman and Rosabeth Kanter, eds. New York: Anchor, pp. 144–70.

Lowe, Marian, and Ruth Hubbard, eds. 1983. *Woman's Nature: Rationalizations in Equality*. New York: Pergamon.

Luckmann, Thomas, ed. 1978. *Phenomenology and Sociology: Selected Readings*. New York: Penguin.

Lyons, Nona. 1983. "Two Perspectives on Self, Relationships and Morality." *Harvard Educational Review* 53: 125–45.

McCall, Raymond J. 1983. *Phenomenological Psychology*. Madison: University of Wisconsin Press.

McClure, Charlotte S., and Diane L. Fowlkes. 1984. "Women Knowing: Feminist Theory and Perspectives in Pedagogy." In *Feminist Visions: Toward a Transformation of the Liberal Arts Curriculum*, Diane L. Fowlkes and Charlotte S. McClure. Alabama: University of Alabama Press, pp. 27–30.

McCormack, Thelma. 1975. "Toward a Nonsexist Perspective on Social and Political Change." In *Another Voice: Feminist Perspectives on Social Life and Social Sciences*, Marcia Millman and Rosabeth Moss Kanter, eds. New York: Anchor, pp. 1–33.

McCrea, Frances B. 1983. "The Politics of Menopause: The 'Discovery' of a Deficiency Disease." *Social Problems* 31(1):111–23 (October).

McKinlay, John B. 1972. "The Sick Role: Illness and Pregnancy." *Social Science and Medicine* 6:561–62.

McNall, Scott and C. M. James Johnson. 1975. "The New Conservatives: Ethnomethodologists, Phenomenologists, and Symbolic Interactionists." *The Insurgent Sociologist* 5(4): 49–65.

Mandell, Nancy. 1984. "Where are the Women? The Tradition of G. H.

Mead." Paper presented at the American Sociological Association Meetings, August, San Antonio, Texas.

Maraini, Dacia. 1979. "On Of Woman Born." Translated by Mary Jane Ciccarello. *Signs: Journal of Women in Culture and Society* 4(4) (Summer): 687–94.

Martindale, Don. 1960. *The Nature and Types of Sociological Theory*, 1st ed. Boston: Houghton Mifflin.

Martindale, Don. 1980. *The Nature and Types of Sociological Theory*, 2nd ed. Boston: Houghton Mifflin.

Marx, Karl and Frederick Engels. 1947. *The German Ideology*. New York: International Publications.

May, Rollo. 1969. *Love and Will*. New York: Dell.

Mead, George Herbert. 1934. *Mind, Self and Society*. Chicago: University of Chicago Press.

————. 1934. "Thought as Internalized Conversation." In *Mind, Self and Society*, George Herbert Mead. Chicago: University of Chicago Press.

Mead, Margaret. 1949. *Male and Female: A Study of Sexes in a Changing World*. New York: Dell.

Mednick, Martha Shuch and Sandra Schwartz Tangri. 1972. "New Perspectives on Women." *Journal of Social Issues* 28(2):1–16.

Midgley, Mary, and Judith Hughes. 1983. *Women's Choices: Philosophical Problems Facing Feminism*. New York: St. Martin's Press.

Mies, Maria. 1983. "Towards a Methodology for Feminist Research." In *Theories of Women's Studies*, Gloria Bowles and Renate Duelli Klein, eds. Boston: Routledge and Kegan Paul, pp. 117–39.

Mill, John Stuart. 1970. *The Subjection of Women*. Introduction by Wendell Robert Carr. Cambridge, Mass.: M.I.T. Press.

Miller, Jean Baker. 1977. *Toward a New Psychology of Women*. Boston: Beacon.

Miller, John Seldon. 1963. *Childbirth*. New York: Atheneum.

Millet, Kate. 1969. *Sexual Politics*. New York: Avon.

Millman, Marcia and Rosabeth Moss Kanter, eds. 1975. *Another Voice: Feminist Perspectives on Social Life and Social Sciences*. New York: Anchor, 1975.

Mills, C. Wright. 1959. *The Sociological Imagination*. New York: Oxford University Press.

Mitchell, Juliet. 1973. *Woman's Estate*. New York: Vintage.

Mitchell J., and Ann Oakley. 1986. *What is Feminism?* New York: Pantheon.

Moffat, Mary Jane, and Charlotte Painter, eds. 1974. *Revelations: Diaries of Women*. New York: Vintage.

Morgan, David. 1981. "Men, Masculinity and the Process of Sociological Inquiry." In *Doing Feminist Research*, Helen Roberts, ed. Boston: Routledge and Kegan Paul, pp. 83–113.

Morgan, Elaine. 1972. *The Descent of Women*. London: Souvenir Press.

Morgan, Robin, ed. 1970. *Sisterhood is Powerful: An Anthology of Writings From the Women's Liberation Movement*. New York: Vintage.

————. 1978. *Going Too Far: The Personal Chronicle of a Feminist*. New York: Vintage.

————, ed., 1984. *Sisterhood is Global: The International Women's Movement Anthology*. New York: Anchor.

Moulton, Janice. 1976. "Philosophy." *Signs: Journal of Women in Culture and Society* 2(2):422–33. (Winter).

Natanson, Maurice. 1962. "Editor's Introduction." In *Collected Papers*, vol. 1: *The Problem of Social Reality*, Alfred Schutz. The Hague: Martinus Nijhoff, pp. xxv–xlvii.

————, ed. 1963. *Philosophy of the Social Sciences: A Reader*. New York: Random House.

———. 1968a. "Alfred Schutz on Social Reality and Social Science." *Social Research* 35 (Summer): 218–44.

———. 1968b. "Philosophy and Science." In *Literature, Philosophy and Social Science*. The Hague: Martinus Nijhoff.

———. 1970. *Phenomenology and Social Reality*. The Hague: Martinus Nijhoff.

———, ed. 1973. *Phenomenology and the Social Sciences*, vols. I and II. Evanston, Ill.: Northwestern University Press.

———. 1974. *Phenomenology, Role, and Reason*. Springfield, Ill.: Charles C. Thomas.

Neisser, Hans. 1959. "The Phenomenological Approach in the Social Sciences." *Philosophy and Phenomenological Research* 20 (December): 198–212.

Nelson, Margaret K. 1983. "Working-Class Women, Middle-Class Women, and Models of Childbirth." *Social Problems* 30 (3):284–97.

Oakley, Ann. 1974a. *The Sociology of Housework*. New York: Pantheon.

———. 1974b. *Woman's Work: The Housewife, Past and Present*. New York: Vintage.

———. 1979. "A Case of Maternity: Paradigms of Women as Maternity Cases." *Signs: Journal of Women in Culture and Society* 4 (4) (Summer):607–31.

———. 1980. *Women Confined: Towards a Sociology of Childbirth*. New York: Schocken.

———. 1984. *Taking It Like a Woman*. New York: Random House.

———. 1986. "Feminism, Motherhood and Medicine: Who Cares: In *What is Feminism?* Juliet Mitchell and Ann Oakley, eds. New York: Pantheon, pp. 127–150.

O'Brien, Mary. 1981. *The Politics of Reproduction*. Boston: Routledge & Kegan Paul.

O'Neill, John, ed. 1974. *Phenomenology, Language and Sociology: Selected Essays of Maurice Merleau-Ponty*. London: Heinemann.

Panuthos, Caludia. 1984. *Transformation through Birth: A Women's Guide*. So. Hadley, Mass.: Bergin and Garvey Publishers.

Parsons, Talcott. 1951. *The Social System*. New York: Free Press.

Pearsall, Marilyn. 1986. *Women and Values: Readings in Recent Feminist Philosophy*. California: Wadsworth.

Pearson, Juxy Cornelia. 1985. *Gender and Communication*. Dubuque, Iowa: William C. Brown Publishers.

Petchesky, Rosalind Pollack. 1983. "Reproductive Freedom: Beyond a Woman's Right to Choose." In *Women and the Politics of Culture: Studies in the Sexual Economy*, Michele Wender Zak and Patricia A. Moots. New York: Longman, pp. 283–94.

Peterson, Gayle H. 1981. *Birthing Normally: A Personal Growth Approach to Childbirth*, 2nd ed. Berkeley, Calif.: Mindbody Press.

Petit, Philip. 1975. "The Life-World and Role-Theory." In *Phenomenology and Philosophical Understanding*, Edo Pivcecic, ed. New York: Cambridge University Press, pp. 251–70.

Pettigrew, Joyce. 1981. "Reminiscences of Fieldwork Among the Sikhs." In *Doing Feminist Research*, Helen Roberts, ed. Boston: Routledge and Kegan Paul, pp. 62–82.

Pierce, C. 1975. "Review Essay—Philosophy." *Signs: Journal of Women in Culture and Society* 2:487–503.

Psathas, George, ed. 1972. *Phenomenological Sociology: Issues and Applications*. New York: John Wiley and Sons.

———. 1986. "Ethnomethods and Phenomenology." *Social Research* xxxv:500–520.

Reinharz, Shulamit. 1979. *On Becoming a Social Scientist*. San Francisco: Jessey-Bass.

———. 1983. "Experiential Analysis: A Contribution to Feminist Research." In *Theories of Women's Studies*, Gloria Bowles and Renate Duelli Klein, eds. Boston: Routledge and Kegan Paul, pp. 162–91.

Reitz, Rosetta. 1977. *Menopause: A Positive Approach*. New York: Penguin.

Rich, Adrienne. 1977. *Of Woman Born: Motherhood as Experience and Institution*. New York: Bantam.

———. 1979. *On Lies, Secrets and Silence: Selected Prose 1966–1978*. New York: W. W. Norton & Co.

Richardson, Laurel and Verta Taylor. 1983. *Feminist Frontiers: Rethinking Sex, Gender, and Society*. Reading, Mass.: Addison-Wesley Publishing Co.

Ritzer, George. 1983a. *Contemporary Sociological Theory*. New York: Alfred A. Knopf.

———. 1983b. "Phenomenological Sociology and Ethnomethodology." In *Sociological Theory*. New York: Alfred A. Knopf, pp. 326–57.

Roberts, Helen, ed. 1981a. *Doing Feminist Research*. Boston: Routledge & Kegan Paul.

———. 1981b. "Women and Their Doctors: Power and Powerlessness and the Research Process." In *Doing Feminist Research*, Helen Roberts, ed. Boston: Routledge and Kegan Paul, pp. 7–27.

Roberts, Joan I. 1980. "Beyond Intellectual Sexism." In *Issues in Feminism: A First Course in Women's Studies*, Sheila Ruth. Boston: Houghton Mifflin.

Rogers, Carol. 1978. "Woman's Place: A Critical Review of Anthropological Theory." *Comparative Studies in Society and History* 20:123–62.

Rogers, Mary F. 1983. *Sociology, Ethnomethodology and Experience*. New York: Cambridge University Press.

Romalis, Chelly, ed. 1981. *Childbirth: Alternatives to Medical Control*. Austin, Texas: University of Texas Press.

Rosaldo, Michelle Zimbalist and Louise Lamphere, eds. 1974. *Woman, Culture, and Society*. California: Stanford University Press.

Rosengren, W. R. 1961. "Social Sources of Pregnancy as Illness or Normality." *Social Forces* 39:260–67.

Rosser, Sue V. and Charlotte A. Hogsette. 1984. "Darwin and Sexism: Victorian Causes, Contemporary Effects." In *Feminist Visions: Toward a Transformation of the Liberal Arts Curriculum*, Diane L. Fowlkes and Charlotte S. McClure. Alabama: University of Alabama Press, pp. 42–52.

Rossi, Alice. 1968. "Transition to Parenthood." *Journal of Marriage and The Family* 30:26–39.

———. 1973. "Maternity Sexuality and the New Feminism." In *Contemporary Sexual Behavior: Critical Issues in the 1970s*, J. Zubin and J. Money, eds. Baltimore: John Hopkins University Press.

Rossi, Alice. 1977. "A Biosocial Perspective on Parenting." *Dedaelus* 106:1–31.

———. 1983. "A Biosocial Perspective on Parenting." In *Feminist Frontiers: Rethinking Sex, Gender, and Society*, Laura Richardson and Verta Taylor. Reading, Mass.: Addison-Wesley, pp. 118–28.

Rothman, Barbara Katz. 1979. "Women, Health and Medicine." In *Women: A Feminist Perspective*, Jo Freeman, ed. Palo Alto, Calif.: Mayfield Publishing Company, pp. 27–40.

———. 1982. *In Labor: Women and Power in the Birthplace*. New York: W. W. Norton.

———. 1984. *Giving Birth: Alternatives in Childbirth*. New York: Penguin.

Rothschild, Joan, ed. 1983. *Machina Ex Dea: Feminist Perspective on Technology*. New York: Pergamon.

Rousseau, Jean Jacques. 1983. "Women Observes, Man Reasons." In *Women and the Politics of Culture: Studies in the Sexual Economy*, Michele Widner Zak and Patricia A. Moots. New York: Longman.

Rowbotham, Sheila. 1972. *Women, Resistance and Revolution: A History of Women and Revolution in the Modern World.* New York: Vintage.
———. 1973a. *Hidden From History: Rediscovering Women in History From the 17th Century to the Present.* New York: Vintage.
———. 1973b. "Woman's Consciousness, Man's World." Baltimore, Md.: Penguin.
Russell, Dora. 1982. *Woman and Knowledge.* Folcroft, Pa.: Folcroft Library.
Ruth, Sheila. 1980. *Issues in Feminism: A First Course in Women's Studies.* Boston: Houghton Mifflin.
Safilio-Rothschild, Constantina. 1972. *Toward a Sociology of Women.* Lexington, Mass.: Xerox College Publishing.
Sallach, David. 1973. "Class Consciousness and the Everyday World in the Work of Marx and Schutz." *Insurgent Sociologist* 3 (Summer): 27–37.
Sayers, Janet. 1986. *Sexual Contradictions: Psychology, Psychoanalysis, and Feminism.* New York: Travistock.
Schmitt, Richard. 1967. "Husserl's Transcendental-Phenomenological Reduction." *Phenomenology.* New York: Anchor, pp. 58–68.
Schneir, Miriam, ed. 1972. *Feminism: The Essential Historical Writings.* New York: Vintage.
Schur, Edwin. 1980. *The Politics of Deviance.* Englewood Cliffs, N.J.: Prentice-Hall.
Schutz, Alfred. 1966. *Collected Papers, Vol. III.* The Hague: Martinus Nijhoff.
———. 1967. *The Phenomenology of the Social World.* Translated by George Walsh and Frederick Lehnert, with an introduction by George Walsh. Illinois: Northwestern University Press.
———. 1971. *Collected Papers, Vol. II, Studies in Social Theory.* Edited and introduced by Arvid Brodersen. The Hague: Martinus Nijhoff.
———. 1973. *Collected Papers, Vol. 1, The Problem of Social Reality.* Edited and with an introduction by Maurice Natanson. The Hague: Nijhoff.
———. 1978. "Parsons' Theory of Social Action: A Critical Review." In *The Theory of Social Action: The Correspondence of Alfred Schutz and Talcott Parsons,* Richard Grathoff, ed. Bloomington: Indiana University Press.
Schutz, Alfred and Thomas Luckmann. 1973. *The Structure of the Life World.* Illinois: Northwestern University Press.
Schwarzer, Alice. 1984. *After the Second Sex: Conversations with Simone de-Beauvoir.* Translated from the French by Mariane Howarth. New York: Pantheon.
Seifer, Nancy. 1976. *Nobody Speaks for Me: Self Portraits of American Working Class Women.* New York: Touchstone.
Sharrock, Wes, and Bob Anderson. 1986. *The Ethnomethodologists.* New York: Travistock.
Shaw, Nancy Stoller. 1974. *Forced Labor: Maternity Care in the United States.* New York: Pergamon.
Sheets-Johnstone, Maxine. 1980. *Phenomenology of Dance.* Salem, N.H.: Ayer Publishers.
Sherman, Julia, and Evelyn Torton Beck, eds. 1977. *The Prism of Sex: Essays in Sociology of Knowledge.* Wisconsin: University of Wisconsin Press.
Shostak, Arthur B., ed. 1977. *Our Sociological Eye: Personal Essays on Society and Culture.* New York: Alfred Publishing.
Showalter, Elaine, ed. 1985. *Feminist Criticism: Essays on Women, Literature, and Theory.* New York: Pantheon.
Shulman, Alix Kates. 1975. "Emma Goldman: 'Anarchist Queen'." In *Voices of the New Feminism,* Mary Lou Thompson, ed. Boston: Beacon Press.
Simmel, George. 1911. *Philosophische Kultar.* Leipzig: Klinkardt.

———. 1984. *Georg Simmel: On Women, Sexuality, and Love.* Translated and with an introduction by Guy Oakes. New Haven: Yale University Press.

Skinner, Quentin, ed. 1985. *The Return of Grand Theory in The Human Sciences.* New York: Cambridge University Press.

Smith, Dorothy E. 1973. "Women, the Family and Corporate Capitalism." In *Women in Canada*, M. L. Stephenson, ed. Toronto: Newpress.

———. 1974. "Women's Perspective as a Radical Critique of Sociology." In *Sociological Inquiry* 44:7–13.

———. 1977. "A Sociology for Women." In *The Prism of Sex: Essays in the Sociology of Knowledge*, Julia A. Sherman and Evelyn Torton Beck, eds. Wisconsin: University of Wisconsin Press, pp. 135–87.

———. 1978. "A Peculiar Eclipsing: Women's Exclusion from Man's Culture." *Women's Studies International Quarterly* 1(4):281–96.

Smith, F. J., ed. 1970. *Phenomenology in Perspective.* The Hague: Martinus Nijhoff.

Smith-Rosenberg, Carroll. 1975. "The Female World of Love and Ritual: Relations between Women in Nineteenth-Century America." *Signs: Journal of Women in Culture and Society* 1(1):1–29.

Snyder, Eloise C., ed. 1979. *The Study of Women: Enlarging Perspectives of Social Reality.* New York: Harper & Row.

Spender, Dale. 1981. "The Gatekeepers: A Feminist Critique of Academic Publishing." In *Doing Feminist Research*, Helen Roberts, ed. Boston: Routledge & Kegan Paul, pp. 186–202.

———, ed. 1982. *Men's Studies Modified: The Impact of Feminism on the Academic Disciplines.* Oxford and New York: The Athene Series, Pergamon Press.

———, ed. 1983a. *Feminist Theorists: Three Centuries of Key Women Thinkers.* New York: Pantheon.

———. 1983b. "Modern Feminist Theorists: Reinventing Rebellion," In *Feminist Theorists: Three Centuries of Key Women Thinkers*, Dale Spender, ed. New York: Pantheon, pp. 366–80.

———. 1983c. "Theorising About Theorising." In *Theories of Women's Studies*, Gloria Bowles and Renate Duelli Klein, eds. Boston: Routledge & Kegan Paul, pp. 27–31.

Spielgelberg, Herbert. 1970. "On Some Human Uses of Phenomenology." In *Phenomenology in Perspective*, F. J. Smith, ed. The Hague: Martinus Nijhoff, pp. 16–31.

Stacey, Judith and Barrie Thorne. 1985. "The Missing Feminist Revolution in Sociology." *Social Problems* 32 (4) (April):301–16.

Stanley, Liz, and Sue Wise. 1979. "Feminist Research, Feminist Consciousness and Experience of Sexism." *Women's Study International Quarterly* 1(3).

———. 1983a. " 'Back to the Personal' or: Our Attempt to Construct Feminist Research." In *Theories of Women's Studies*, Gloria Bowles and Renate Duelli Klein, eds. Boston: Routledge & Kegan Paul, pp. 192–209.

———. 1983b. *Breaking Out: Feminist Consciousness and Feminist Research.* Boston: Routledge & Kegan Paul.

Stanton, Elizabeth Cady. 1972. "Womanliness." In *Feminism: The Essential Historical Writings*, Miriam Schneir, ed. New York: Vintage, pp. 155–56.

Steiner, Shari. 1977. *The Female Factor: Women in Western Europe.* Chicago: Intercultural Press, Inc.

Steward, George Lee. 1977. "On First Being a John." In *Our Sociological Eye: Personal Essays on Society and Culture*, Arthur B. Shostak, ed. New York: Alfred Publishing, pp. 39–53.

Stewart, David and Algis Mickunas. 1974. *Exploring Phenomenology.* American Library Association.

Stimpson, Catharine R. 1984. "Women as Knowers." In *Feminist Visions:*

Toward a Transformation of the Liberal Arts Curriculum, Diane L. Fowlkes and Charlotte S. McClure. Alabama: University of Alabama Press, pp. 15–24.

Strauss, Anselm. 1959. *Mirrors and Masks: The Search for Identity*. Glencoe, Ill.: The Free Press.

Strauss, E. 1963. *The Primary World of the Senses*. London: Free Press.

Szymanski, Albert. 1973. "Marxism or Liberalism: A Response to Pozzuyo." *Insurgent Sociologist* 3 (Summer):56–62.

Thio, Alex. 1974. "The Phenomenological Perspective of Deviance: Another Case of Class Bias." *The American Sociologist* 9 (August):146–49.

Thomason, Burke C. 1982. *Making Sense of Reification: Alfred Schutz and Constructionist Theory*. With a Foreword by Tom Bottomore. Atlantic Highlands, New York: Humanities Press.

Thompson, Mary Lou, ed. 1975. *Voices of the New Feminism*. Boston: Beacon Press.

Timasheff, Nicholas S., and George A. Theodorson. 1976. *Sociological Theory: Its Nature and Growth*, 4th ed. New York: Random House.

Tiryakian, Edward A. 1973. "Sociology and Existential Phenomenology." In *Phenomenology and the Social Sciences*. vol. 1, Maurice Natanson, ed. Evanston, Ill.: Northwestern University Press, pp. 187–222.

Turner, Johnathan H. 1986. *The Structure of Sociological Theory*, 4th ed. Chicago: Dorsey Press.

Turner, Roy, ed. 1974. *Ethnomethodology: Selected Readings*. Baltimore: Penguin.

Vetterling-Braggin, Mary, Frederick A. Williston, and Jane English, eds. 1977. *Feminism and Philosophy*. Totowa, N.J.: Rowman and Littlefield.

Volkart, Edmund, ed. 1951. *Social Behavior and Personality: Contributions of W. I. Thomas to Theory and Social Research*. New York: Social Science Research Council.

Wagner, Helmut R. 1975. "Sociologists of Phenomenological Orientations: Their Place in American Sociology." *The American Sociologist* 10 (August):179–86.

———, ed. 1976. "Alfred Schutz: Subjective Action and Objective Interpretation." *Annals of Phenomenological Sociology* 1:31–44.

———. 1983. *Alfred Schutz: An Intellectual Biography*. Chicago: University of Chicago Press.

Wallace, Ruth A., and Alison Wolf. 1980. *Contemporary Sociological Theory*. Englewood Cliffs, N.J.: Prentice-Hall.

———. 1986. *Contemporary Sociological Theory: Continuing the Classical Tradition*, 2nd ed. Englewood Cliffs, N.J.: Prentice-Hall.

Ward, Charlotte, and Fred Ward. 1976. *The Home Birth Book*. With an Introduction by Ashley Montagu. Washington, D.C.: Inscape Publishers.

Weber, Max. 1947. *Theory of Social and Economic Organization*. Translated by Talcott Parsons. New York: Oxford University Press.

———. 1968. *Economy and Society*. New York: Bedminster Press.

Weideger, Paula. 1977. *Menstruation and Menopause*. New York: Delta.

Weisstein, Naomi. 1978. "Psychology Constructs the Female." In *Woman in Sexist Society: Studies in Power and Powerlessness*, Vivian Gornick and Barbara K. Moran, eds. New York: New American Library, pp. 207–24.

Wertz, Richard, and Dorothy C. Wertz. 1979. *Lying-In: A History of Childbirth in America*. New York: Shocken.

Westkott, Marcia. 1979. "Feminist Criticism of the Social Sciences." *Harvard Educational Review* 49(4) (November):422–30.

———. 1983. "Women's Studies as a Strategy for Change: Between Criticism and Change." In *Theories of Women's Studies*, Gloria Bowles and Renate Duelli Klein, eds. Boston: Routledge & Kegan Paul, pp. 210–18.

Wild, John. 1965. "Authentic Existence: A New Approach to Value Theory." In *An Invitation to Phenomenology*, James M. Edie, ed. New York: Quadrangle.

Willmuth, L. R. 1975. "Prepared Childbirth and the Concept of Control." *Journal of Obstetrical and Gynecological Nursing* 4 (Fall):38.

Wolff, Kurt H. 1950. *The Sociology of Georg Simmel*. Translated, edited, and with an Introduction by Kurt H. Wolff. New York: Free Press.

———. 1974. "Surrender and the Body." *Cultural Hermaneutics* 2.

———. 1976. *Surrender and Catch: Experience and Inquiry Today*. Boston: D. Reidel.

———. 1978. "Phenomenology and Sociology." In *History of Sociological Analysis*, Tom Bottomore and Robert Nisbet, eds. New York: Basic Books.

Young, Iris Marion. 1984. "Pregnant Embodiment: Subjectivity and Alienation." *Journal of Medicine and Philosophy* 9:45–62.

Zak, Michele Wender, and Patricia A. Moots. 1983. *Women and the Politics of Culture: Studies in the Sexual Economy*. New York: Longman.

Zaner, Richard M. 1961. "Theory of Intersubjectivity: Alfred Schutz." *Social Research* 28:71–93.

———. 1970. "Awakening: Towards a Phenomenology of the Self." In *Phenomenology in Perspective*, F. J. Smith, ed. The Hague: Martinus Nijhoff, pp. 171–86.

Zeitlin, Irving M. 1973. *Rethinking Sociology: A Critique of Contemporary Theory*. New York: Appelton-Century-Crofts.

Zimmerman, Mary K. 1977. *Passage Through Abortion: The Personal and Social Reality of Women's Experiences*. New York: Praeger Publishers.

Zola, Irving Kenneth. 1972. "Medicine as an Institution of Social Control." *Sociological Review* 20(4)(November):487–504.

INDEX

Act, as projected, 107; understanding of, 24
Action, as conduct, 27; conscious and unconscious, 106; covert and overt, 105; meaning of, 104–6; as working, 108
Actor, meaning attached to, 23, 25–27
Arms, S., 54, 101, 119
Attention à la vie, 125, 132

Because-motive, 28–29, 72–73, 105
Belenky, M. E., xviii, 92
Berger, P., 14, 70, 95, 134, 157–158
Bergson, H., 28, 70, 129, 134, 161
Bernard, J., 3, 11
Bernikow, L., 48
Biographically determined situation, 40; bracketing of, 19; as description, 86–87
Birth. *See* Childbirth
Bowles, G., 4, 161
Bracketing, 17–19
Brentano, F., 13

Childbirth, 27–29, 40, 42, 48–49, 92–93, 155, 164; as alienation, 115; as central to woman's life, 132; as creative experience, 65–55, 99; doctor-patient relationship, 115–20; in hospital environment, 142; labor, 124–128; meaning for women, 54; medical management of, 80, 102–3, 115–17, 158; as self-transforming, 98–99, 137; sociological research of, 139–41; as subjective experience 3, 42, 97–98, 103, 120–124

Chodorow, N., xvii, 4, 11, 50, 164
Classical scholarship, 35
Common-sense attitude, 23
Common-sense world, 44–45
Comte, A., 6, 10, 161, 163
Consciousness, acts of, 16–17; individual, 20; objects of, 33; reproductive, 96; streams of, 26–27, structures of, 16, 33–34; transformation of, xviii–xix; woman-centered, 52, 59–60. *See also Durée*
Cooley, C. H., 13
Coyner, S., 58, 96

Dallmayr, F., 39
Daly, M., 10–12
Deliberation, 105; of pregnancy, 104–7
Demetrakopoulis, S., 13, 20, 121
Dewey, J., 105
Dimensions in time, during birthing, 129–32, 136
Dinnerstein, D., 4, 50
DuBois, B., 4
Durée, 32, 72–73, 155; as dimension in time, 32, 129–32, 136
Durkheim, E., 6–7

Eisenstein, H., 47, 49, 56
Emotion, study of, 64
Empirical world, 17, 37
Epoché of the natural attitude, 16–21, 29, 31, 34, 41, 71, 154–55
Ethnomethodology, 14, 161
Everyday world. *See* Common-sense world
Experience, meaning of, 25–28

185